图书在版编目（ＣＩＰ）数据

中国陶瓷茶具珍赏 / 李文年编著． −− 北京 ：文物
出版社，2016.3
　　ISBN 978−7−5010−4530−3

　　Ⅰ．①中… Ⅱ．①李… Ⅲ．①陶瓷茶具－鉴赏－中国
Ⅳ．①K876.3

中国版本图书馆CIP数据核字(2016)第025036号

中国陶瓷茶具珍赏

编　　著：李文年

责任编辑：贾东营

责任印制：梁秋卉

策　　划：李　楠

摄　　影：黄　鹏

英文翻译：李　楠

出版发行：文物出版社

社　　址：北京市东直门内北小街2号楼

网　　址：http://www.wenwu.com

邮　　箱：web@wenwu.com

经　　销：新华书店

制版印刷：北京图文天地制版印刷有限公司

开　　本：635×965　　1/8

印　　张：22.5

版　　次：2016年3月第1版

印　　次：2016年3月第1次印刷

书　　号：ISBN 978−7−5010−4530−3

定　　价：390.00元

中国陶瓷茶具珍赏

Chinese Pottery & Ceramic Tea Vessels

李文年　编著

Edited by Li wennian

文物出版社

Cultural Relics Press

序 言

中国在世界上有"瓷器之国"的美誉，瓷器的发明、发展及灿烂辉煌的陶瓷文化，是中国对人类文明所作出的杰出贡献。

陶瓷是水、火、土的完美结合，是巧妙利用和驾驭自然力的杰出技术成就。自问世以来，她已有近万年历史，品种繁多，造型典雅，制作精美，内涵广博。既是物质文化，又是精神财富，充分体现了中华民族独有的艺术风格和博大精深的文化内涵。

我国饮茶历史悠久，相传始于炎帝神农氏，但当时系作为药饮。随着社会的进步和生活的需要，商周时期已出现了原始青瓷，人们开始在器物的用途、造型、工艺等方面不断改进创新。唐代是我国制瓷业的高峰，唐代盛行饮茶、饮酒，这种习俗增长了对茶具的需求，逐渐形成了以浙江越窑为代表的青瓷和以河北邢窑为代表的白瓷，两大瓷窑系统称之为"南青北白"。宋代是我国制瓷业的又一高峰，在民窑生产的基础上，逐步建立了专为皇室制作御用瓷器的瓷窑，这些官窑瓷器技术精湛，器形隽美，釉色莹润，代表了宋代制瓷的最高水平，被后世称为宋代"五大名窑"。

元代为满足外销瓷为朝廷带来的巨大收入，在景德镇设立了"浮梁瓷局"，生产大量的元青花和龙泉窑茶具远销至阿拉伯国家。

明清两代是我国陶瓷史上最为辉煌的时期，茶具器形丰富多彩，一些精美瓷器除了专供宫廷使用、作陈设外，还赠与来中国朝贡的外国使臣，成就空前。这些瓷器极具魅力，将柔软的泥土变成了造型优美、绚丽多姿的陶瓷艺术品，名扬中外，长盛不衰。

在众多的收藏者中，李文年先生的收藏之路值得收藏爱好者借鉴。对中国古陶瓷的热爱及刻苦钻研精神使他博学多能。李先生从 20 世纪 80 年代开始从事收藏，当时他在政府部门从事外事工作，经常有机会到欧美国家访问或常驻，接触到大量的中国古代艺术品，并不断丰富了个人古陶瓷茶具的收藏。李先生每钻研一件器物，都虚心向师长请教，为人的真诚和虚心使他结识了许多良师益友，得益甚多，博采众家之长，使他的鉴赏能力和水平很快得到了全面的提高。

几年前，李先生发起成立了"大都会馆"等公益机构，并出任中国古陶瓷壶具研究会会长。他亲自筹划在北京举办了"磁州窑"、"建窑"、"龙泉窑"、"明清瓷器"、"元青花"、"宋代瓷器"等特展，得到了业内人士及专家的认可及好评。为支持四川汶川地震后博物馆

的恢复工程，他与朋友合作，为"三星堆博物馆"义务修复了一批文物。李先生曾对我说，他的一生似乎与慈善和公益事业有缘。不久前，他与我商定在他多年潜心收藏的300余件古陶瓷茶具藏品中精选出130余件茶具作一展览，并出版《中国陶瓷茶具珍赏》一书，以回报社会各界。

这本书介绍了从新石器时代至今中国历代陶瓷茶具的多样化风格、面貌及其背后承载的历史文化。当然有些学术问题至今仍未有定论，如在历史上，用以盛载或倾注不同液体的水注、酒具与茶具相继成形，在研究这些器物的演变及用途时，必须着眼于它们的实用性和社会功能。

相信此书的出版，对收藏爱好者来说，都是一本难得的教科书，既可研究历史，也可以赏心悦目，修身养性，使更多的收藏爱好者关注中国陶瓷的发展历史，丰富国人的精神生活。

国家文物鉴定委员会委员
中国古陶瓷学会副会长　　张浦生
南京博物院研究员

2015年10月书于沪上片瓷山房

PREFACE

Known as the "Kingdom of Porcelain" around the world, China has created splendid oriental porcelain culture as the invention and development of porcelain in ancient history of China, which is an outstanding contribution to the mankind.

With the skillful use and control of natural force, porcelain is an excellent technological achievement integrating water, fire and clay. It has a history of nearly ten thousand years and features great varieties, elegant shape, exquisite craft and profound connotation. As both material culture and spiritual wealth, it fully reflects unique artistic style, broad and profound cultural connotation of Chinese nation.

According to legend, the long history of tea can date back to Yan Emperor-Shen Nung, but tea was regarded as medicinal drink at that time. With the development of society and growing living needs, celadon wares appeared during the Shang and Zhou dynasties, and people started to improve and change the purpose, shape and technology of ware. During Tang Dynasty, porcelain industry reached the peak. Since tea and wine were popular in Tang Dynasty, the demands for tea sets went up due to such custom; therefore, two major kilns gradually took form, i.e. celadon wares from Yue Kiln of Zhejiang and white porcelains from Xin Kiln of Hebei, which were called as "celadon wares in southern China and white porcelains in northern China". The porcelain industry reached another peak in Song Dynasty. On the basis of folk kilns, there were other kind of kilns used to produce porcelains for imperial family. Featuring remarkable skills, exquisite shapes, smooth glazing color and greenish glaze, the porcelains produced by royal kilns stood for the highest porcelain making level in Song Dynasty, so these kilns were later known as "the Five Great kilns" of Song Dynasty.

In Yuan Dynasty, for the purpose of generating revenue by exporting porcelains, Fuliang Porcelain Bureau was set up in Jingdezhen, producing a great deal of blue and white porcelains of Yuan Dynasty and tea sets of Longquan Kiln to export to Islam and Arab countries.

Ming and Qing Dynasties were the most splendid period in Chinese porcelain history, and unprecedented success was made in porcelain industry. During this period, tea sets had a great variety of shapes, while some exquisite porcelains were not only dedicated for royal family and decoration, but also presented as gifts to foreign envoys paying tribute to China. Made from soft clay, these fascinating porcelains were regarded as gorgeous and colorful artworks with appealing design, enjoying eternal fame all over the world.

For many collectors, the collection experience of Mr. Li Wennian is worth of learning. With the passion for Chinese ancient porcelains and hard-working spirit, Mr. Li went into collection in 1980s, thus obtaining extensive knowledge and great capacity. He worked on foreign affairs

in government sector at that time, so he often had opportunities to visit and maintain permanent presence in European and American countries, see lots of Chinese ancient artworks and enrich his personal collections of ancient porcelain tea sets. Every time Mr. Li studied an artifact, he would take advice from teachers with an open mind, thus he has get acquainted with many good teachers and friends and benefited a lot. By learning others' virtues, he has fully improved his ability and level appreciation.

A few years ago, Mr Li launched Dadu Guild Hall and other public interest organizations and served as the chairman of the Chinese Ancient Porcelain and Tea Ware Research Association. He has held such special exhibitions as "Cizhou Kiln", "Jian Kiln", "longquan Kiln", "Porcelains of Ming and Qing Dynasties", "Blue and White Porcelains of Yuan Dynasty" and "Porcelains of Song Dynasty", etc., which were recognized and praised by insiders and experts. After Wenchuan earthquake in Sichuan, he was engaged in museum restoration project with his friends, volunteering for the restoration of historical relics in Sanxingdui Museum. Mr Li once told me that all his lifetime is associated with charity and public welfare undertakings. Recently, he discussed with me to select about 130 tea sets from over 300 well-collected ancient porcelain tea sets for an exhibition and publish a book named Chinese pottery & Ceramic Tea vessels, thus to repay the society.

This book introduces the diverse styles, features and historical and cultural background of porcelain tea sets from the Neolithic Age to the contemporary age. Since some academic problems are still up in the air, for example, in history, water jet, wine set and tea set used for carrying or pouring liquid came into being in succession, we must focus on practicability and social function when studying the evolution and application of these artifacts.

I believe this book will be a valuable textbook for collectors, because they can not only study history, but also appreciate artifacts and cultivate their mind from this book. This book is designed to make more collectors know about the history of Chinese porcelains and enrich people's spiritual life.

Zhang Pusheng
Member of National Committee of Cultural Relics
Vice-chairman of Chinese Ancient Porcelain Society
Researcher of Nanjing Museum
Written in Pianci Study Room, Shanghai
October, 2015

壶中乾坤

从古至今，饮茶品茗，一直与人们生活息息相关。从历代君主、文人雅士到平常百姓，都能领略到品茶的情趣。

我国饮茶历史悠久，相传始于炎帝神农氏，但当时系作为药饮。神农崇拜起源于原始的农耕文明，我们的祖先在神农时代就开始了茶叶利用。在商周时期出现原始青瓷，壶具用来盛酒、祭神。秦汉至魏晋南北朝时期，茶具用来混煮羹饮和祭礼。随着饮茶方式的改变，制茶方法的变化，茶具亦随之变化和更新。

壶能拥天地，容纳百川，又有不吝供人欣赏的包容。一把壶有独立的型制，构成了自己的小宇宙，这个小宇宙是圆满自足的。壶体自成一个世界，冰清玉洁、脱尽尘泽。在人类几千年的文明发展史中，壶一直与人们的日常生活息息相关，人们对自然及宗教文化崇拜的图腾也自然利用壶具作为载体而反映和发展起来。

孔子是公元前 6 世纪到公元前 5 世纪中国春秋时期伟大的哲学家、政治家和教育家。孔子的美学思想核心为"美"和"善"的统一，对后世的文艺理论影响巨大。儒家的学说和思想观念一直是我国古代社会的精神支柱，根深蒂固地扎根于我们的生活之中。儒家思想主张崇尚礼乐和饮食礼仪，在人们的日常品茗中挖掘出了"修身，齐家与治国"之道，悟出了处世的进退之道。儒家文化的精神集中体现一个"正"字；道家文化精神集中体现一个"清"字；佛家文化精神集中体现一个"和"字；茶文化精神体现一个"雅"字。正、清、和、雅四个字分别体现了儒、释、道和茶文化精神。茶具的出现，迎合了人类的这一需求。

我国自唐朝以来，佛教兴盛，宫廷中的重要活动，都有一定规模的大典，都有一定的茶、酒文化大礼相伴，礼仪之严，可见一斑。唐代宫廷盛行饮茶，皇帝以茶赐近臣，以茶祭祖，以茶礼佛。陕西扶风法门寺唐代地宫出土的宫廷越窑秘色瓷，就是唐僖宗供奉佛祖释迦牟尼指骨舍利的茶具。唐代的茶道与禅道有着密不可分的关系，佛教中人认为饮茶有助静思入定。寺庙中住持请斋，请茶，乃是禅寺中常有的礼仪。当时的寺院茶文化是一个很大的群体，以僧侣为主，官员和文人往往参与其中。僧人利用茶布道弘法，陶冶性情，在饮茶中追求"恬淡闲寂"。因此对壶、茶具的型制，功能及观赏性有一定的标准。当时的禅僧在禅寺中饮茶，是一种礼仪繁复而又严格的事情，茶禅结缘，茶禅一味，异曲同工。参禅的妙语是"空"，饮茶也能领悟到空。唐玄宗时，有一名叫封神的进士，在《封氏见闻记》中说："玄宗开元中，泰山灵严寺之降魔大师普及禅教，

当他坐禅时，只喝点茶，于是一般人争相效仿，都把茶当做饮料用，遂成风俗。"盛唐时的茶具受波斯金银器影响颇显华贵。晚唐时，一种新的末茶饮用方式即点茶法开始流行，注壶不仅用来盛水而且煮水，茶具便派上了大用场。在这种情形下，尤其是奉茶仪式，对应有茶具等设计及其功能各方面，自然十分讲究。唐代陆羽在公元八世纪中叶所著的《茶经》中，陈述了各种备茶方法，他指出饮茶可分为"觕茶、散茶、末茶、饼茶"四大类，大致可归纳为以下几种以末茶为主的饮用方法。其中一种先把梼制好的茶末，置于风炉上的热水器中；另一种把预先焙炙，春制好的茶末，放置热水器中煮饮；第三种方法，即是利用注壶把沸水注入盛有茶末的茶盏内饮用。陆羽的风炉设计亦反映出茶道中茶具配合务求和谐，环境亦务求清静雅致。儒家还认为饮茶可以使人清醒，更可以使人自省，可养廉，可修身，亦可修德。而道教是我国固有的宗教，认为道是化生宇宙万物的本源，在中国有悠久的历史，立于北魏而盛于隋唐，道教宣称经过辟谷修行，人可以得道成仙，长生不死，并将这种得道后能超脱生死，变幻莫测的人称之为神仙。如出现了"八仙人物"的故事等图案。道教有自然崇拜，讲究天人合一，有图腾崇拜，如崇拜龙、凤、玄鸟、花、槐等，这些崇拜及图腾都在当时及以后的茶具型制和纹饰上有所表现。

宋代是末茶点饮盛行的时代，儒家思想更加深入到宫廷乃至百姓的日常生活之中。在皇室贵族与文人雅士的推崇下，备茶礼仪显得十分严格和成熟，茶艺发展一日千里，我国陶瓷茶具的发展也达到历史上的高峰。宋徽宗绘有一幅《文会图》，图下方有一个点茶，备茶的场景：在炉中和桌子上各置两把汤瓶，壶流末端细圆峻削，壶体瘦长丰满，易于点茶注汤。到了南宋，煎水壶和注水壶分工明确，从刘松年的《撵茶图》中可以看出，煎水用的壶置于炉上，注水用壶专作点茶之用，桌上所有托盏的制作亦十分考究。宋代在所谓的家礼之中，无不举行茶礼，甚至有"无茶不成礼"的说法。所用茶具与"礼"亦必须和谐统一，人品与茶具的高度统一，无意中达到了心灵与自然的契合，这正是儒家所提倡的"天人合一"的最高境界。这些数千年前在瓦内中焠练的泥料所制成注壶，其釉色、其造型、其由"流"到"柄"展现的美感，是宋人高度精致文明的体现。在本人的收藏中，就有一些具有特色的宋代注壶，如北方的定窑、耀州窑、磁州窑、河南青瓷、南方的越窑、龙泉窑、景德镇的青白瓷等等。比较与壶配套使用的众多茶盏的品种和型制后，应该说圆锥、斗笠形最宜作奉茶之用。

元代虽存在不足百年，但制瓷业也有进一步发展。当时，一般文人不愿在异族统治下作官，寄情于山水，追求闲适，以写意山水画为消遣，怡情养性。王重阳是一位全真道道士，以诗歌传道布道，在其《解佩令·茶肆茶无绝品至真》词中提"茶无绝品，至真为上"。青花瓷上的山水画"初始"于元代中晚期。元代后期道家与大自然相契的思想占主要地位，茶艺方面用"散茶"，崇尚绿茶的口味由此而生。注壶逐渐演变出一种崭新的茶具，茶盏也转变为使用茶杯。我国瓷都景德镇由烧制釉下青花"元青花"而名声大噪。元代青花瓷上的人物画多为历史故事如"鬼谷子下山"和杂剧等。绘制多用进口钴料，发色纯正艳丽，绘画技艺高超，线条流畅自然。以茶具为例，就有元青花凤首扁壶、僧帽壶、竹菊纹执壶、葫芦型壶等。这种茶具与杯、盏吸收西亚的钴蓝做原料，发色艳丽，造型优美，莹体玉质，深受海内外统治者和上流社会的追捧。元代虽然是少数民族执政，但其为稳固政权而宣扬的则是"儒、释、道"精神。

明代在我国历史上疆域辽阔，文化繁荣，也是汉族统治者的最后一个王朝。明太祖朱元璋建立明代政权后，认为饮用固形茶是奢侈浪费，已经失去茶的真味。同时要人民节省劳力，于是废止末茶，而是鼓励人民喝一种连茶叶的煎茶。明、清两朝的"儒、释、道"思想更为普及，景德镇的瓷绘大师创作的青花瓷画，尤为技艺超群。他们将儒、释、道的精髓与自身的艺术修养、天赋悟性、哲思人格、心灵理念等巧妙地融合在一起，在茶具的型制和茶具上的纹饰，绘画中更多的体现了文人社会的影子，如文徵明的《试茶图》、《松下品茶图》等，明初皇室的需求拉动了瓷制茶壶的发展。茶具中纹饰的发展由花鸟、山水到人物触笔多样，用以感染人们的思想和品茗氛围。"读书做官"和"高官厚禄"是明清时期儒家思想和科举制度对社会的深刻影响，这种影响在明代瓷器的纹饰上有充分反映，如"状元及第"，"五子登科"等图案。至于宫廷所用茶具上的龙纹图腾则非常凶猛，寓意天子之权势至高无上。青花瓷上的宗教画面，也反映了历代皇帝的信仰和喜欢。如明代正德皇帝崇尚伊斯兰教，那时候的青花瓷器上出现了阿拉伯文。嘉靖皇帝信奉道教，那个朝代的青花瓷器常有老子和八仙人物。茶具上的高士人物是一种真实的想象，文人自身，若仙飘逸，也蕴含着壶如其人的会意情趣。在封建社会中，出现一个被称之为"隐士"、"高士"的人群，这些人见到社会黑暗，官场腐败而不满现实，或躲进深山过着隐居生活；或躬耕于田园，自食其力；或陶冶与琴棋书画之中，不科考，不入仕，崇尚自由和自然，如"携琴访友"、"竹林七贤"图等等。茶具上的单色釉，隐含着空灵，含蓄与平淡，趣味高雅，这种寓意如陶渊明的"采菊东篱下，悠然见南山，此中有真味，欲辨已忘言。"反映出文人面对茶具品茗而表达的深层内省，感悟此时的人生观。

清代，经顺治时期的过渡，到康熙时期社会经济逐步发展。清代皇帝多信佛陀，特别是顺治皇帝曾多次出家，所以该朝青花器物上大量出现佛教人物。康熙年的"渔樵耕读"，虽描绘农耕的场面，但总会出现一个读书人，暗示"万般皆下品，唯有读书高。"步入清代盛世的雍正、乾隆时期，制瓷工业发展到了历史上的鼎盛时期。此时期的壶、茶具瓷器上，出现了许多有关神话故事传说及对道士人物崇拜的图案。反映道教题材的有"老子炼丹"、"老子骑牛"、"八仙人物"、"群仙祝寿"以及"刘海戏蟾"、"和合二仙"等。道教将得道后能"超脱生死"变幻莫测的人称之为神仙，他们神通广大，不图富贵、劝人向善、摒弃邪恶，是人们心中的偶像和寄托。反映佛教题材的有"达摩面壁"、"苇叶渡江"等。据说达摩曾在嵩山少林寺面壁九年，达到"舍伪归真"、"无自无他"的境界，是中国佛教禅宗的初祖。

清代，瓷器上表现的画面，题材丰富多彩，既有着强烈的皇权意志的体现：如在一定时期只有皇家方可使用的官窑图案，以及"读书做官"和"高官厚禄"等反映科举制度的图案；也有民意民心的反映：如青花缠枝莲纹，寓意"清廉"；飞龙寓意风调雨顺；雄狮寓意武兆喜庆；麒麟寓意太平；三阳开泰寓意吉祥；蝙蝠寓意五福临门等。茶具的盖钮，或用龙型、或成莲花型装饰等；凝聚着社会的心态，积淀着儒释道思想的历史和文化，以博大精深的内涵，深刻的艺术感染力，令人陶醉。

新中国成立后，由于党和政府对恢复和发展传统产品的重视，我国的陶瓷工业得到了迅速地发展，特别是在 20 世纪 80 年代，随着中国改革开放的实施，许多陶瓷研究所和学校都将我国五千多年的文明史和传统作为学习继承的主要内容。纵观历史，陶瓷仿品首次大量地出现是在宋代。明代仿古之风丝毫不减宋朝，追求的是宋代瓷器的如冰似玉"天人合一"的感觉。清代特别是康、雍、乾三朝的帝王多好古，以此来显示本朝制瓷业之技艺水平。20 世纪五十年代，出于特殊的时代背景，壶、茶具的纹饰上，曾涌现出一批反映"大丰收"、"农林牧副渔"以及构图生动的山水画面。此后，为恢复传统工艺产品，中央相关部门也曾指示一些地方的陶瓷研究所仿制宋代五大名窑、元青花以及用于博物馆陈列的明、清官窑产品。由于高科技的介入，许多仿品具有相当的艺术水准，可与过去的真品相媲美，技艺已达到了炉火纯青的程度，这些是古代艺术的再现和升华，而且价值可观。

前几年，笔者前往英国访问时，曾有幸前往位于伦敦的维多利亚阿尔伯特博物馆参观，令我感到震惊的是，在其"远东中国馆"中陈列的堆积如山的明清瓷器之中，有数十件中国的"文革"时期的瓷器陈列展出，其中不乏彩绘茶具，及描绘精致的粉彩瓷板，极为引人注目，精细的制作与绘画工艺令人拍案称绝。应该说它们是时代的产物，是现当代中国陶艺工人智慧的结晶。

瓷器是中国在世界上最负盛名的代表，中国瓷器的发展伴随着中国工艺美术史的发展和演变，不仅关联着，常常还取决于政治、经济、思想、民族和宗教等诸多因素。在人的因素中，出自统治集团的，特别是其代表帝王的意志、好尚及宗教信仰等尤为重要。中国茶具和茶文化中所承载的文明和传统，是中国儒、释、道三教合一的文化精神，它们在茶具的造型，装饰及其材料中得到融合，传达给人类的是一种意境深远的视觉语言，平静、平和、自在、自然。佛与道的智慧，博大精深，包罗万象，不仅只是一些精神的禅理，也有诸多关于人生的通俗哲理。壶之称为壶，是一种文化，壶中自有乾坤。

中国古陶瓷研究会常务副会长　李文年

2015 年 10 月撰于缘珍山房

UNIVERSE IN THE TEA WARE

In all ages, Tea is closely linked with people's life. Whether emperors and refined scholars in history or ordinary people, they all can enjoy the fun of tea-tasting.

According to legend, the long history of tea can date back to Yan Emperor-Shen Nung, but tea was regarded as medicinal drink at that time. Shen Nung worship began from agriculture civilization, and our ancestors started to make use of tea in Shen Nung Era. Celadon wares appeared during the Shang and Zhou dynasties, while tea ware was used for wine vessel or worship. During the period of Qin, Han, Wei, Jin, Southern and Northern Dynasties, tea set is used for boiling soup and drink and sacrificial rites. As the way of tea drinking and tea making changes, tea set changes and updates as well.

With inclusive spirit for people to admire, tea pot is as grand and magnificent as the universe. Every uniquely-shaped tea pot constitutes a small universe, complete and self-contained, while the pot body forms a pure and refined world. In the history of civilization for thousands of years, tea pot is closely linked with people's life, and it is also regarded as carrier and totem to show people's worship to the nature, religion and culture.

As a great philosopher, politician and educator in Spring and Autumn period (6th century BC-5th century BC), Confucius advocated aesthetic ideology centering on the integration of "virtue" and "goodness", which has huge impact on theory of literature and art of later ages. In ancient China, Confucian doctrines and ideas were spiritual support embedded in people's life. Since Confucianism advocates rites, music and eating etiquette, the doctrine of "self–cultivation, family regulation and statecraft" and philosophy of life are revealed from daily tea-drinking. Generally speaking, spirit of Confucian culture centers on "uprightness"; spirit of Taoist culture centers on "peace"; spirit of Buddhist culture centers on "harmony", and spirit of tea culture centers on "elegance". Therefore, the emergence of tea set caters to people's demands.

Since Buddhism thrived from Tang Dynasty, major events in palace would be accompanied with grand ceremony and rigorous rite reflecting tea and wine culture. During Tang Dynasty, tea prevailed in palace, and emperors used to serve tea to courtier, worship ancestors with tea and pay respect for Buddha with tea. The secret color porcelains of Yue Kiln, which were unearthed from the underground palace of Famen Temple in Fufeng County, Shannxi, are tea sets used to worship the phalanx relics of Sakyamuni by Emperor Xizong of Tang Dynasty. There is close relation between tea ceremony and Zen Tao, because Buddhists think drinking tea is helpful for meditation. It's the common rite for abbot of Zen temple to invite others to taste Buddhist diet and drink tea. As a large group in that time, tea culture of temple was involved with monks, officials and scholars. Monks

carried out preaching and sermon with tea, to cultivate their temperament and pursue tranquilness and solitude. Consequently, they set certain standards on the shapes, function and ornamental characteristics of tea ware and sets. At that time, it was a complicated and rigorous rite for monks to drink tea, to realize mutual integration of tea and Zen Tao. The core of Zen Tao is "emptiness", while one also can perceive emptiness by drinking tea. According to the Feng's Information Handbook written by a scholar named Fengshen during the reign of Emperor Xuanzong of Tang Dynasty: In Kaiyuan period of Emperor Xuanzong, when master of Lingyan Temple of Taishan Mountain popularized Zen Tao and sat in meditation, he only drank tea, which was soon followed by common people, thus drinking tea became a custom. During the flourishing period of Tang Dynasty, under the influence of Persian gold and silver wares, tea sets were extremely luxury. In late Tang Dynasty, a new method by infusing tea with hot water started to prevail, and pouring ware was used for boiling, so tea sets were put to good use. Under such circumstance as tea serving ceremony, particular care is devoted to the design and function of tea sets. According to the Classic of Tea written by Lu Yu of Tang Dynasty (middle of 8th Century AD), various methods for preparation of tea have been stated. He indicated that there were such four categories as coarse tea, loose tea, dust tea and cake tea, and methods for drinking dust tea can be reduced to the following: One is to put pounded dust tea into water heater on wind furnace; another method is to put baked and pounded dust tea into water heater for boiling, while the third method is to use pouring ware to infuse hot water into tea ware filled with dust tea. The wind furnace designed by Lu Yu also reflects that tea sets must be correlated with each other in the tea ceremony, and surroundings must be quite and elegant. The Confucianists believed that one might get soberness, carry out self-communion and cultivate honesty, mind and morality by drinking tea. As an inherent religion with a long history in China, Taoism is considered as the origin of cosmic inventory. Established in the Northern Wei Dynasty and prevailing in Sui and Tang Dynasties, Taoism asserts that people can become immortal after refraining practice, and people who can live forever and never die are called as supernatural beings, therefore, stories and patterns about the Eight Immortals come into being. There are nature worship and totemism in Taoism. Nature worship is particular about unity of heaven and man, while totemism stresses on the worship of dragon, phoenix, sunbird, flowers and Chinese scholar tree, etc.. These worships and totem are reflected in the shapes and patterns of tea sets in later ages.

Infusion method of dust tea prevailed in Song Dynasty, and Confucianism went deep into the daily life of palace and common people. Due to the advocation of royal family, nobles and refined scholars, tea preparation rite was extremely rigorous and well-developed. With the rapid development of tea art, porcelain tea sets in China also boomed to a peak. As shown in the Picture of Refined Scholars Gathering in Tea Party by Emperor Huizong of Song Dynasty, a scene described preparation and infusion of tea: there are two bottles on furnace and table, with slender and round spout and plump body, which is convenient for infusing and pouring. During the Southern Song Dynasty, water boiler and pouring ware were distinct from each other: the pouring ware was used for infusion, while all saucers and cups on table were particularly manufactured. Among all family rites in Song Dynasty, tea rite was absolutely necessary, and there was even proverb that rite cannot be accomplished without tea. All tea sets must be in harmony with rite, and moral quality must be consolidated with tea sets, thus to realize the highest state of "unity of heaven and man" advocated by confucianist- mutual integration of spirit and nature. Made from fired clay thousands of years ago, these pouring wares feature exquisite glazing color, exquisite shape, spout and handle, revealing high level of civilization. I have collected some unique pouring wares of Song Dynasty, such as wares made in Ding Kiln, Yaozhou Kiln and Cizhou Kiln, celadon of Henan, wares made in Yue Kiln and Longquan Kiln, greenish white porcelain of Jingdezhen and so on. After comparing types and shapes of various tea cups supporting the use of wares, I think tea cups of cone and bamboo hat shape are most suitable for serving tea.

Although Yuan Dynasty only has a history of less than one hundred years, porcelain industry also further developed. Since many scholars were unwilling to be officials under the rule of different races, they devoted themselves to landscaping and pursuing leisure, amusing themselves and building character by painting landscapes. As a Taoist of Chhuan Chen Tao, Wang Chongyang preached with poetry, and his poetry said that: nonsuch exists in tea, but genuineness comes first. The landscape pattern on blue and white porcelains can date from the middle and late Yuan Dynasty. In the late Yuan Dynasty, the ideology integrating Taoism and nature dominated, and loose tea and green tea gradually came into being. As new tea sets were evolved from pouring pot, tea ware was replaced by tea ware. Due to the manufacture of underglazed blue and white porcelains of Yuan Dynasty, Jingdezhen, the hometown of porcelains, gains considerable fame. Most figure paintings on blue and white porcelains of Yuan Dynasty describe historical stories, such as Guiguzi going downhill and other poetic drama. With the use of imported cobalt and superb painting skills, these paintings featured gorgeous colors and smooth lines. For example, tea sets can be divided into Blue and White Flat Pot of Phoenix Head Shape of Yuan Dynasty, Mitral Pot, Ewer with Bamboo and Chrysanthemum Pattern, Gourd-Shaped Pot, etc., such tea sets and cups were made from blue cobalt, featuring gorgeous colors, appealing designs and jade-like body, so they were greatly favored by rulers and high society at home and abroad. Under the rule of minority, Confucianism, Buddhism and Taoism were still advocated in Yuan Dynasty, so as to stable regimes.

As the last dynasty governed by rulers of Han nationality, Ming Dynasty featured vast territory and culture prosperity. After establishing the regime of Ming Dynasty, Emperor Zhu Yuanzhang thought that it was extravagance and waste to drink solid-form tea, and the original taste of tea lost. What's more, it was labor consuming to make such kind of tea. Therefore, dust tea was abolished; instead, people were encouraged to decoct tea with primitive tea leaves. During Ming and Qing Dynasties, as Confucianism, Buddhism and Taoism became more popular, skilled painters of

Jingdezhen painted blue and white porcelains by integrating the essence of Confucianism, Buddhism and Taoism with their own artistic culture, gift and comprehension, philosophical personality and spirit. The patterns and designs on tea sets reflected scholar society, such as Painting of Tea Tasting and Painting of Tea Tasting under Pine by Wen Weiming, etc. In order to produce impact on people's thoughts and tea-tasting atmosphere, the patterns and designs on tea wares developed from flowers, birds and landscapes to figures and other brushworks. "Studying to become officials" and "high post with matched salary" were the profound influence of Confucianism and imperial examination system on the society during Ming and Qing Dynasties, and such influence were fully reflected by the patterns and designs on porcelains of Ming Dynasty, such as pattern of "Scholar Coming Out First in the Palace Examination" and "Five Young Men Passing Civil Examinations". The dragon totems on royal tea sets are extremely fierce, which represents supreme power and influence of the emperor. The royal demands of early Ming Dynasty facilitated the development of porcelain teapot. The religious patterns on blue and white porcelains also reflect the belief and favor of emperors. For example, Emperor Zhengde of Ming Dynasty upheld Islam, so Arabic appeared on blue and white porcelains of that time, while Emperor Jiajing of Ming Dynasty believed in Taoism, so there were patterns of Lao Zi and the Eight Immortals on blue and white porcelains. Since pot mirrors the person, the patterns of profound scholars on tea pots were real imagination, to indicate that the scholars were as noble as the pot. In feudal society, a group of people named as "hermit" or "profound scholar" emerged. Discontent with the reality, dark side of the society and official corruption, they escaped to remote mountains for reclusion, or earned their own living by tilling in countryside or indulged in lyre-playing, chess, calligraphy, and painting and pursued freedom and nature instead of participating imperial examination and engaging in politics., such as the patterns of "Visit Friends by Carrying Lyre" and "Seven Sages of the Bamboo Grove". Featuring ethereality, connotation, plainness and elegant taste, the monochrome glaze of tea sets indicated the same meaning as what indicated in verses written by Tao Yuanming: I pick chrysanthemums under the eastern hedge, and far away to the south I can see the mountains. In all these things there lies a profound meaning. I is going to explain…but now I forget what it is, which reflects scholars' deep introspection and insights on life when they tasted tea with tea sets.

During Qing Dynasty, the social economy gradually developed in the reign of Emperor Kangxi after transition from the reign of Emperor Shunzhi. Most emperors of Qing Dynasty believed in the Buddhism, especially Emperor Shunzhi who became a monk for several times, so there were a lot of patterns of Buddhist figures on blue and white porcelains. As for the pattern of "fisherman, woodcutter, farmer and scholar", although this pattern describes farming scene, there is a scholar, which indicates that "To be a scholar is to be the top of society". During the reign of Emperor Yongzheng and Qianlong of Qing Dynasty, porcelain industry was in thriving period of history. At that time, there were many patterns in relation to mythological tales and worship to Taoists and Buddhists, such patterns about Taoism as "Lao Zi practicing alchemy", "Lao Zi riding a bull", "the Eight Immortals", "the Eight Immortals offering birthday congratulations", "Liu Hai playing toad" and "Gods of He-He". Taoism asserts that people who can live forever and never die are called as supernatural beings. As the idol and spiritual support of people, these almighty immortals have no desire for wealth and persuade people to do goodness instead of evils. Patterns of "Dharma facing the wall for meditation" and "Dharma crossing river by standing on a reed leaf" reflect Buddhism theme. It is said that Dharma used to face the wall and meditate for nine years in Songshan Shaolin Temple and reached the realm of "giving up hypocrisy and return to innocence" and "no self and no others", therefore, Dharma was the forerunner of Zen Buddhism in China.

During Qing Dynasty, the patterns and designs of porcelains are very wide, some of which reflect strong royal sovereign, such as patterns of Royal Kiln that can only be used by imperial family during certain period, patterns of "study to become officials" and "high post with matched salary" that reflect imperial examination system and so on; while some other patterns and designs also reflect popular wishes, such as design of blue and white entangled branches and lotus that implies incorruptness, flying dragon pattern that implies favorable weather, lion pattern that implies celebration, Kylin pattern that implies peace, patterns of three sheep that implies auspiciousness and bat pattern that implies blessings, etc.; the buttons of covers feature dragon shape and lotus shape, etc.. With profound connotation and deep artistic appeal, these patterns and designs reflect social attitude and the history and culture of Confucianism, Buddhism and Taoism.

After new China was founded , the Party and state government attached importance to the restoration and development of traditional products, so porcelain industry in China grew rapidly. Especially in 1980s, due to the reform and opening-up policy, many porcelain research institutes and schools considered civilization and tradition of more than 5000 years as the major contents to learn and carry forward. Throughout history, it was in Song Dynasty that porcelain imitation sprang up in large number. Comparable to the imitation in Song Dynasty, the imitation trend in Ming Dynasty attached great importance to ice and jade-like texture and quality of "Unity of heaven and man". During Qing Dynasty, especially emperors Kangxi, Yongzheng and Qianlong, they were keen about ancient porcelains, to highlight the skills of porcelain industry. Under the special background in 1950s, there were a lot of patterns indicating "Abundant harvest" and "Farming, forestry, animal husbandry, by-product and fishery" and other vivid landscape patterns appearing on pots and tea sets. After that, with the aim to restore traditional craft products, relevant central departments used to require some porcelain research institutes to imitate porcelains of the Five Great kilns, blue and white porcelains of Yuan Dynasty and products of Royal Kiln of Ming and Qing Dynasties that are used for museum display. Thanks to high technology, many imitations feature high artistic standards and skills and can be comparable with the genuine one. With considerable commercial value, these imitations reveal and sublimate the ancient art.

When I visited the United Kingdom a few years ago, I got the chance to visit Victoria and Albert Museum in London. To my surprise, among various porcelains of Ming and Qing Dynasties in "Far East China Exhibition Pavilion", there were dozens of porcelains made in the Cultural Revolution period (1966-1976). With elaborate processing and painting technology, some color-painted tea sets and exquisite pastel porcelain plate catch people's eyes. They are products of the times, revealing the wisdom of craftsmen of contemporary China.

Porcelain is the synonym of China across the world. With the development and evolvement of Chinese history of arts and craft, porcelains in China also develop. However, there are also many other factors affecting its development, including politics, economy, ideology, nationality and religion, etc.. As for the factors of human beings, dominance hierarchies are particularly prominent-the will, inclinations and religious faith of emperors are extremely important. Embodied in the shape, decoration and materials of tea sets, the civilization and tradition of tea sets and tea culture reflect the spiritual integration of Confucianism, Buddhism and Taoism, to deliver visual language to people and show profound connotation-tranquilness, peace, freedom and nature. Being extensive and profound, the wisdom of Buddhism and Taoism is not only about spiritual Buddhist principles, but also about philosophy of life. It's a culture origin to call a pot as "pot", because it can hold the universe.

Li Wennian
Standing Vice - Chairman of the Chinese Ancient Porcelain Research Association
Written in Yuanzhen Collection Room
October, 2015

目 录

CONTENTS

图版目录
CATALOGUE

《竹林七贤图》局部　唐　孙位

一　唐代以前的陶器（～618年）

　　唐代以前几个世纪，在中国不少地区饮茶已成一种习惯。红山文化时代的陶壶是用黏土烧制而成，是人们最常用的盛贮器，随着人类审美思想的进步，人们还烧制出一些异形壶，如彩陶人头器口壶（图1），除使用功能外，反映出人类对早期图腾的崇拜。

　　商周时期出现了原始青瓷，瓷器比陶器坚固而耐用，易于清洗，而且比当时的青铜器制作容易，因而很快代替了陶器和青铜器。春秋战国时期，很多茶具在器型上仍仿青铜器，如本书中青釉夔龙三足提梁壶（图5），其造型与战国青铜提梁盉十分相似。此壶直口，覆盖，其间满饰"虺龙"纹，丰肩，圆腹，三兽首足，腹部置有出戟龙提梁，设计精妙，纹饰精美，令人赞叹！

　　汉代是原始瓷向瓷器进化的成熟期，东汉烧瓷温度已能达到1200摄氏度以上，出现了真正意义上的瓷器（图8）。到了东、西晋时，茶具的样式有了进一步的发展和改进。为了美观，制作瓷器的胎、釉有了较大提高，壶具设计在肩部仍保留桥形系外，还增加了一些实心的动物如鸡头作装饰（图10），这些装饰除了美观以外，还有祈福和辟邪的作用，也是人类崇拜的图腾。

　　佛教自西汉末年传入我国后，受到历代统治者的崇奉，在社会生活中也一直占据着重要的地位。南北朝时期佛教极为盛行，随之佛教文化、思想及其艺术对瓷器的装饰艺术产生了巨大的影响。佛教题材中盛行的莲花图案和卷草纹样也成为当时的时尚纹饰，迅速在南、北各地的瓷器纹样上流行开来，如南北朝青瓷鸡首壶（图13）就是具有那个时代特征的制品，壶通体施青绿釉，肩部刻有一周莲瓣纹作为装饰。

　　佛教在隋朝时很流行。隋朝制瓷技术的重要成就之一，就是在隋朝末年烧制出了白瓷，白瓷的出现是我国瓷器史上一项重要的创新，没有白瓷就没有以后的青花、五彩、粉彩等各种精细瓷器。用白瓷烧制的执壶，器形仍沿袭传统式样，但胎釉洁白，釉面莹润，淡雅如玉，不仅显示出隋朝制瓷艺术的崭新水平，而且反映出当时朝廷及统治阶层除日用需要外，用于佛教文化相关的祭祀、供奉等活动的需求很大。

　　进入唐代以后，茶具与中国茶文化息息相关，参禅以茶、慎独以茶、书画以茶、琴香以茶、待客以茶、待酒以茶、清赏以茶……

I. PRE-TANG WARES (~ 618 AD)

A couple of centuries before Tang Dynasty, drinking tea became a habit in many areas of China. The clay pots of the Hongshan Culture were the most commonly used containers of the time. With the advancement of human aesthetics, people began to make pots of various shapes, such as Painted Pot with Head-Shaped Spout. (fig.1) In addition to its practical functions, such design reflects human worship of early totems.

Celadon wares appeared during the Shang and Zhou dynasties. As they were more solid and durable than potteries, and easier to wash and produce compared with bronze wares, celadon soon replaced potteries and bronze wares. During the Warring States period, a great deal of tea sets still imitated bronze wares in terms of shape and pattern, such as the Handled Tripod Celadon Pot Carved with Dragons from the Yue kiln during the Warring States referred to in this book. (fig.5) Its shape largely resembles that of the handled bronze wine vessels of the time. Decorated with dragon patterns, the pot has a straight spout, a cover, broad shoulders, three beast-head-shaped legs, and a round body part with a handle in the shape of a horned-dragon. Its design is sophisticated and the ornamentation is exquisite.

Han Dynasty is the maturation phase for the proto-porcelain beginning to evolve into porcelain, and firing temperature could reach over 1200°C during the Eastern Han Dynasty, thus the real porcelain emerged. (fig.8) With the further development and improvement on the shapes of tea sets during the Eastern and Western Jin Dynasties, porcelain body and glaze were greatly improved and beautified. In addition to bridge-shaped handle on shoulder, there are additional solid animal-shaped decorations, such as chicken head-shaped decoration. (fig.10) As the totem worshiped by people, such decorations not only serve for aesthetics, but also function as blessing and protection against evil.

After being introduced in China during the last years of the Western Han Dynasty, Buddhism was worshiped by all emperors and played an important role in social activities. Since Buddhism highly prevailed in the Northern and Southern Dynasties, Buddhist culture, ideology and art had great impact on the decorative art of porcelain. As popular Buddhism themes, lotus pattern and curly grass design became fashion ornamentation of the time, widely used on porcelains around the country. With dark green-glazed body and lotus petal decorated around the shoulder, Chicken Head-Shaped Celadon Pot of the Northern and Southern Dynasties is representative product of that time. (fig.13)

One of the major achievements of the Sui Dynasty porcelain technology is the production of white porcelain, an important innovation in Chinese history. It is based on such techniques that

the refined blue-and-white, colorful and pastel porcelains come into being. The shape of this white porcelain ewer still follows that of the traditional ones, yet its white glaze is shiny and as elegant as jade, which represents not only a new level of porcelain production in the Sui Dynasty, but also the great demands of ceremonial use by the prevailing Buddhism of the time, in addition to daily household use by the ruling class.

Since Tang Dynasty, tea sets were closely linked with Chinese tea culture, and tea could be involved into meditation, inner concentration, painting and calligraphy, music enjoyment, entertainment of guests, wine tasting and appreciation, etc..

1 彩陶人头器口壶

新石器时代马家窑文化（约公元前3300～公元前2050年）

高 28 厘米

"Man-head" painted pottery ewer

Majia Yao culture Neolithic , 3300 BC ～ 2050 BC

H. 28cm

壶呈人形，泥质红陶，口部塑成人头形，粗颈，腹部呈椭圆形，平底。五官比例准确，面部神态怡然。壶体施红色陶衣，并施黑彩。此壶用雕塑和彩绘相结合的技法塑造，在新石器早期彩陶中较为罕见。

甘肃省博物馆藏有一件彩陶人头器口瓶（高 31.8 厘米）与之类似。

人类进入新石器时代，开始了定居的氏族生活，审美意识日趋强烈，加快了走向文明的步伐。

2　红陶豆

红山文化（约公元前 4500～公元前 3000 年）

高 8.8 厘米

口径 6.5 厘米

Red-Pottery Cup

Hongshan Culture Neolithic, 4500 BC ～ 3000 BC

H. 8.8cm

D. 6.5cm

　　泥质红陶，圆唇，器壁较薄，椭圆型腹，撇足。腹部下方四个称钮作为装饰，为饮食器。该器表面呈光滑和发暗光泽，显然用竹、石等坚硬而光滑的工具轧磨过，表现当时工艺修饰艺术上的提高。

　　豆是新石器时代的食器和礼器，山东泰安大汶口文化遗址已有陶豆出土。豆流行于春秋战国时期，用于盛放黍、稷等谷物，并作为礼器常与鼎、壶配套使用，构成原始礼器的组合。

　　此器以细泥红陶制成，表面呈红色，表里磨光。腹部下方以称钮装饰，似抽象的花瓣纹。韵律明显，勾连回旋。

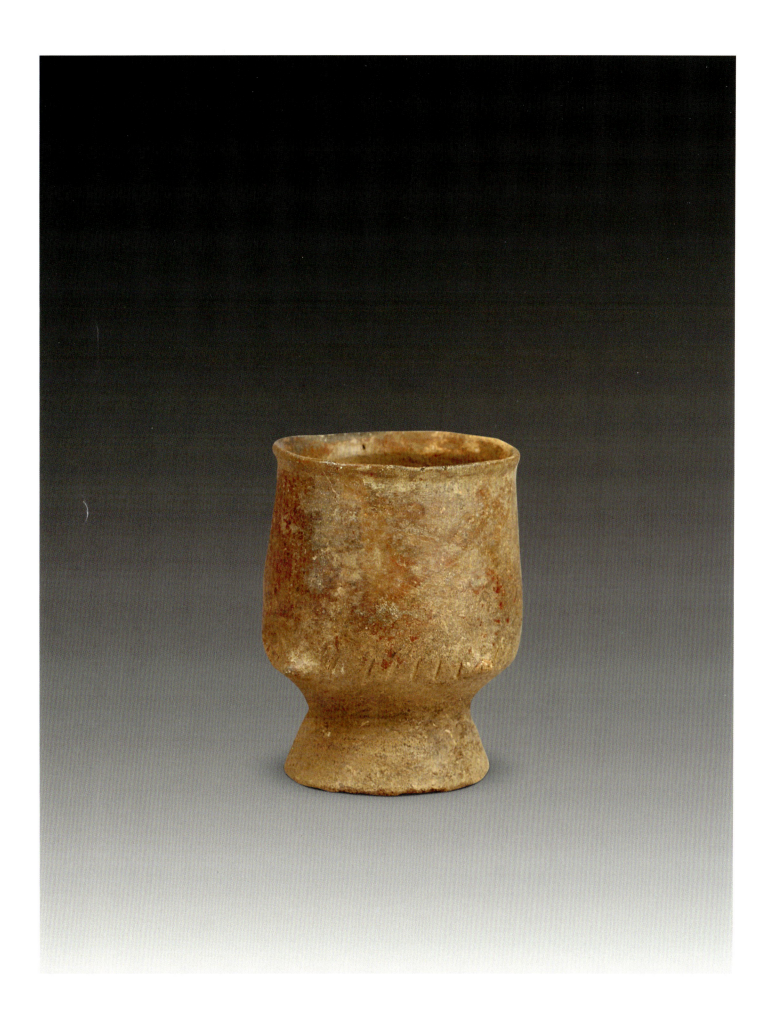

3 菱形纹彩陶壶

新石器时代马家窑文化（约公元前3300～公元前2050年）

高 14.8 厘米

Painted Pottery Ewer With Diamond Pattern

MaJiaYao Culture Neolithic, 3300 BC ～ 2050 BC

H. 14.8cm

壶质泥陶。直口、长颈、鼓腹、平底、单宽柄。施黑红彩。口部绘网格纹，颈下饰黑锯齿纹用红线勾圈，其间留出三角形和圆形图饰，此壶造型与纹饰协调一致。给人以高雅与神秘之感。

马家窑文化是黄河上游新石器时代中晚期文化遗存，从距今5000年开始到距今4000年结束，持续时间长达1000多年。有专家认为这是西部炎帝带领的氏族部落，在黄河上游兴起的空前繁荣的马家窑类型彩陶，彩绘使用矿物材料，花纹精美，主要纹样均是几何图形。这些图形至今受到许多人赞美，认为是人类早期最佳的装饰艺术，是中国史前彩陶艺术的顶峰。

此壶为甘肃马家窑文化半山型彩陶。

彩陶纹饰除了装饰目的外，还反映了史前人类与大自然接触中体现出的物质生活状况和心灵世界。

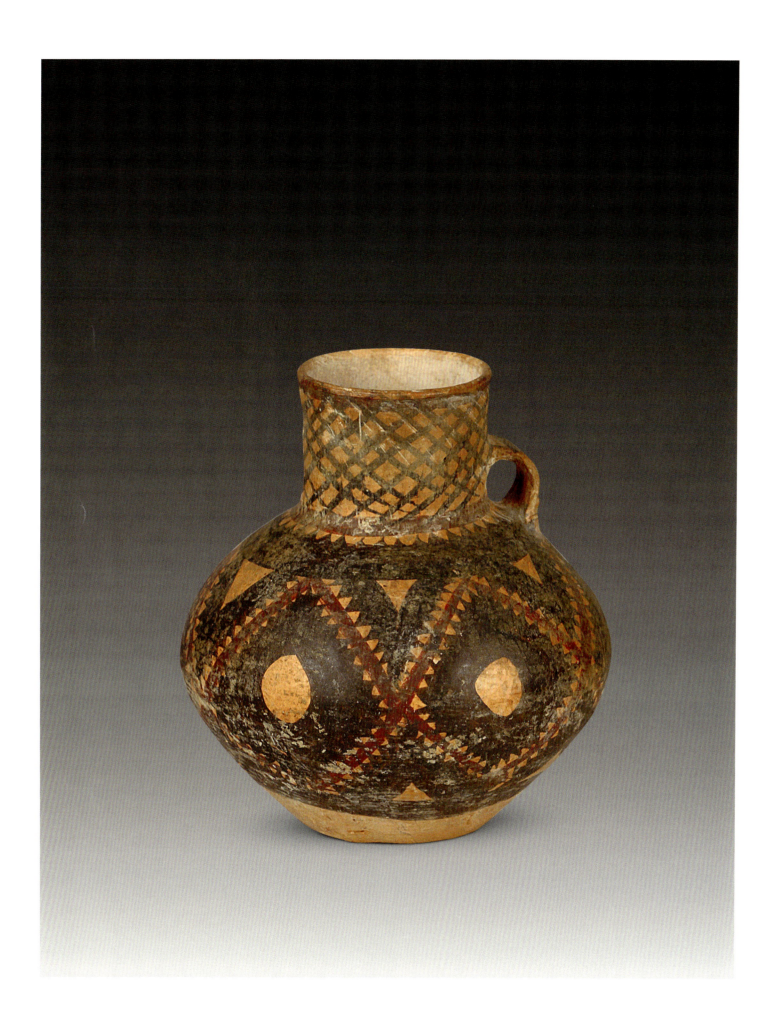

4　三角网纹彩陶杯

新石器时代齐家文化（约公元前 2000 年前后）

高 5.6 厘米

口径 8.4 厘米

Painted Pottery Cup with Net Pattern

Qijia Culture Neolithic, 2000 BC

H. 5.6cm

D. 8.4cm

泥质黄陶，直口，腹壁较直呈圆筒形，圈足。腹部绘对顶三角纹，以梯形纹相隔，内填规则圆点纹。纹饰新颖，色彩浓艳，造型别致。

齐家文化的陶器以素陶为主，彩陶数量很少，陶质较细腻，器型挺拔。花纹多以褐红单色彩绘，并辅以直线造型，多见菱格网纹和网线带纹，给人以整齐刚健的感觉。

齐家文化遗址，主要分布在甘肃、青海两省。

此件彩陶的几何纹饰都有一定的规律，在图形和色彩的组织与描绘中，反映和承载着先民的观念、信仰及行为方式。

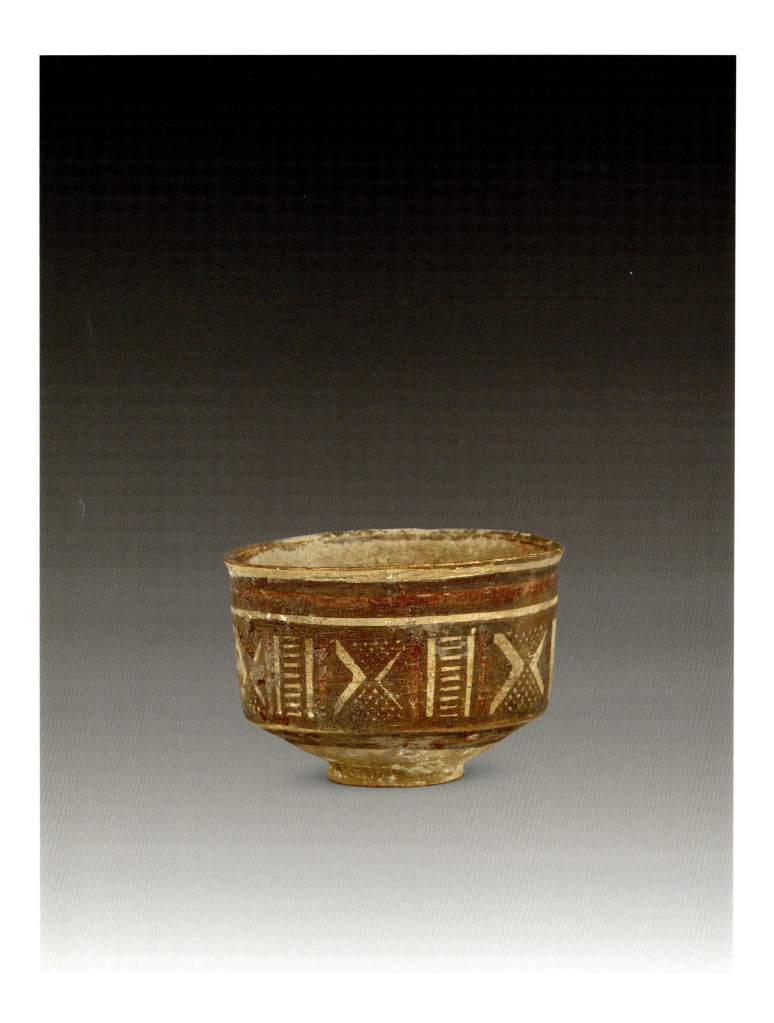

战国（公元前 475 ～公元前 221 年）

Warring state period, 475 BC ～ 221 BC

高 23 厘米

H. 23cm

阔 19 厘米

L. 19cm

　　三足壶附提梁，丰肩，圆腹，胎质灰白坚硬。直口，覆盖，盖面扁平。器身施橄榄绿青釉，饰三圈仿青铜器漩涡印纹，器盖饰漩涡型等五道印纹，中心置一圆钮。肩部一侧置一龙头流，另一侧置出戟龙尾，提梁置一出戟夔龙身，仿青铜盉造型，器形丰满，栩栩如生。窑址为浙江绍兴地区。

　　早期原始青瓷出现于商代前期。春秋战国时期，青瓷制作精良，纹饰细密，还有很多仿生造型，他们有的源于宗教信仰，师法自然，达到同期艺术审美的最高水准。

　　龙的概念反映了一种宗教概念。此器以龙身为提梁，表现出静中有动，寓动于静的艺术魅力。"龙纹是陶瓷器装饰的传统纹样之一。……因此，装饰在远古时代陶瓷器上的龙纹图案大都与氏族图腾崇拜有关。"

　　（引自冯先铭主编《中国古陶瓷图典》，文物出版社，1998年）

6　布纹陶盌

战国（公元前 475 ～公元前 221 年）

口径 8.5 厘米

高 6.2 厘米

Pottery Bowl with Fabric Pattern

Warring state period, 475 BC ～ 221 BC

D. 8.5cm

H. 6.2cm

此盌敞口平底，粗灰胎，外部饰以精细方格印纹。由于高温焙烧，敲击器身所发出声音清脆，器表面似曾施以原始釉色。

这种早期精致带釉器物，应是中国东部地区产品。

印纹陶，有的是在做好的陶坯上，趁未干前用麻布织物作印模将所需花纹拍印上去后进行烧制，其纹饰多与器形相协调。此件陶盌饰纹细密，结构严谨，富有较高的审美和韵律感。

"一般认为我国最早饮茶的器具，是与酒具、食具共用的，这种器具是陶制的缶，一种小口大肚可作汲水器用的容器。"（引自胡小军、姚国坤编著《中国古代茶具》，上海文化出版社，1998 年）

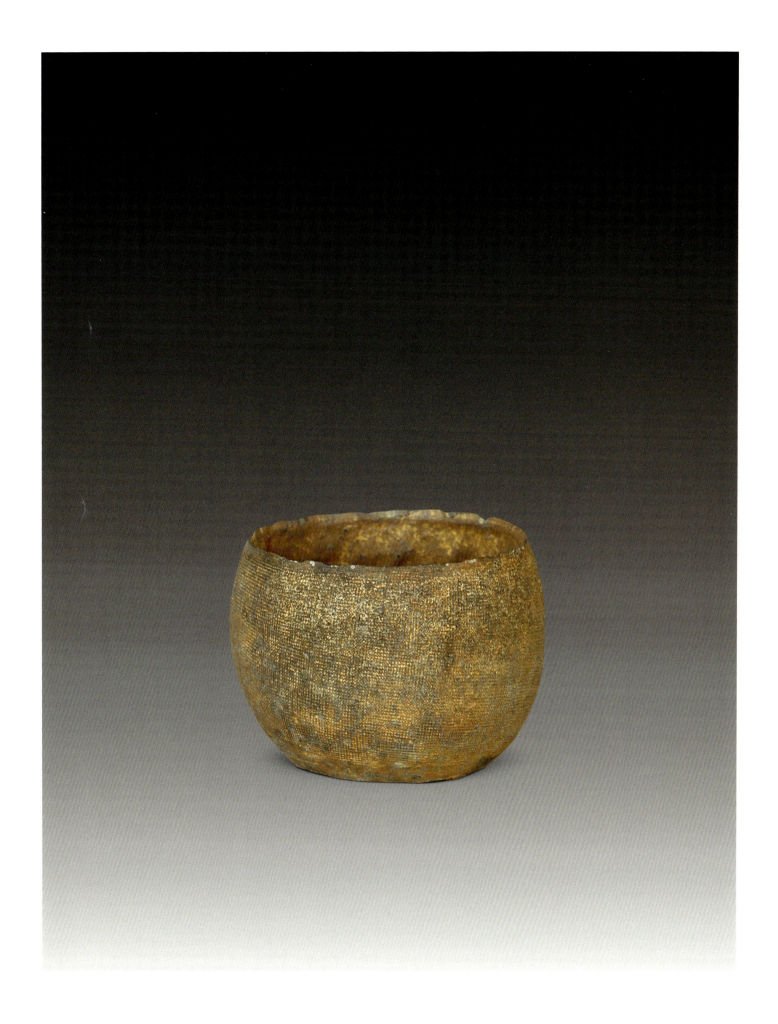

西汉（公元前 206 ～公元 9 年）

Western Han Dynasty（206 BC ～ 9 AD）

宽 11.8 厘米

L. 11.8cm

高 4.6 厘米

H. 4.6cm

泥质灰陶，器呈椭圆型，两侧宽柄呈耳状，故称耳杯。胎质坚实、轻薄，口沿及两耳施以黑色涂料，内壁施以红色涂料，仿汉代漆器工艺，凝重、朴实、秀美。

耳杯，又称羽觞，是三国至汉代常见的酒具。一般为漆器、青瓷较多见，彩绘者较稀少。

此器外形椭圆，两侧有半月形双耳，似鸟羽状。道家思想发展到两汉时，自然之道的概念逐渐普及。此时道教以清静无为，自然而然的态度追求着神仙世界，并与茶意兼解能使人轻身换骨，羽化成仙。此器构思巧妙，古朴自然。

8　灰陶把杯

汉（公元前 206 ~ 220 年）

口径 8.2 厘米

高 8.2 厘米

Grey-Pottery Cup

Han Dynasty（206 BC ~ 220 AD）

L. 8.2cm

H. 8.2cm

泥质灰陶，器身呈圆柱筒型，近口及近底处各修旋纹两道，器身一侧置桥形柄，型制古朴，釉面泛铅，质地坚硬，为汉代饮用器。

这种外形简洁的把杯制作精细，具北方色彩，出自河南荥阳。

汉代陶器用泥土为坯胎，烧制各种饮食器、贮藏器，大体可分灰陶、硬陶、釉陶和青瓷四大类。两汉前后延续了近 500 年，这件硬陶把杯的形制直

至今天的演绎依然。

唐代陆羽《茶经》："引述西晋八王之乱时，晋惠帝司马衷（209 ~ 306 年）蒙难，从河南许昌回洛阳，待从'持瓦盂承茶'敬奉之事。说明当时茶具、酒具在内的饮具之间，区分并不严格，在很长一段时间内，两者是共用的。"（引自胡小军，姚国坤编著《中国古代茶具》，上海文化出版社，1998 年）

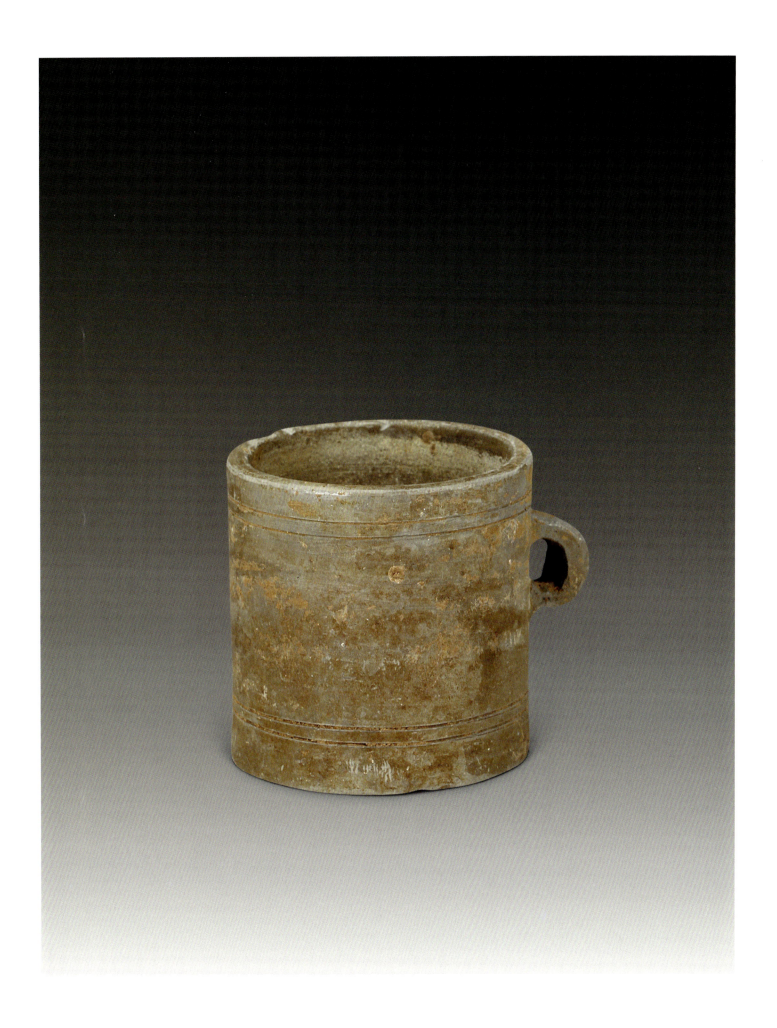

9 青瓷鸡首壶

西晋（265～317年）

高 9.3 厘米

"Chicken-head" Ewer with Celadon Glaze

Western Jin（265～317）

H. 9.3cm

茶绿色釉，浅灰胎，盘口短颈，圆肩，鼓腹，平底。肩部正面贴塑鸡头，后面雕塑鸡尾，两侧环耳各一。肩腹间饰联珠纹，装饰手法有虚有实，动静相宜，装饰效果极佳。釉面呈细开片。

三国两晋时期，江浙平原土地肥沃，经济发达，青瓷制瓷业亦随之兴旺。

此器为西晋时期余姚地区烧制。

魏晋的名士在对人世的一切失望之后，转而关注于美的事业，造就了一次中国艺术史上空前的"唯美时期"。两晋时期鸡的造型常在青瓷中出现，汉代将鸡视为阳性的象征，汉人应邵的《风俗通义》云，鸡可以"御死辟恶"。由于鸡能报时，人们认为它有驱鬼、祛百病、辟邪的功能。

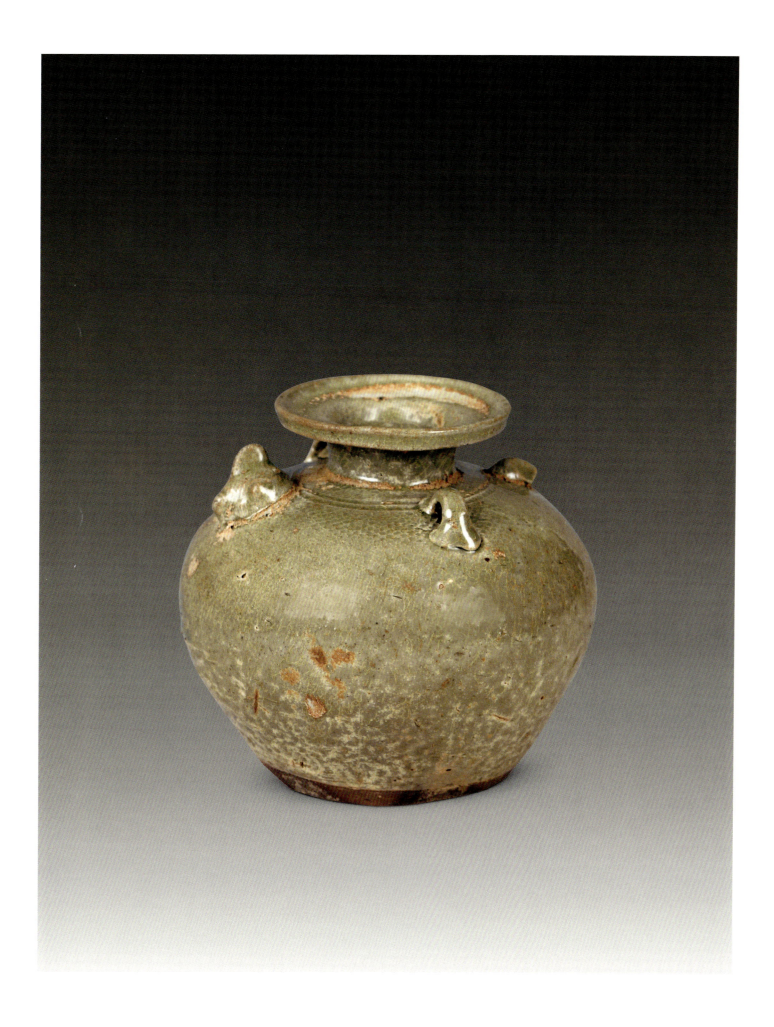

10 青釉鸡首双系盘口壶

西晋（265 ～ 317 年）

直径 16 厘米

高 19 厘米

"Chiken-head" Ewer with Twin Handl

Western Jin（265 ～ 317）

L. 16cm

H. 19cm

　　盘口，短颈，深腹，平底，底部见支烧痕。肩部两侧贴双桥形系，既为装饰又可系绳提携，肩部一周以双线勾画并饰斜方格纹。一侧饰一凸起鸡首假流，另一侧饰一凸起鸡尾。通体施橄榄绿釉，釉面肥腴。

　　此器为西晋时期东南部越窑产品。

　　三国两晋时期越窑制瓷业的成就，主要表现为青瓷质量的提高和造型。窑工们经过长期实践经验，已能较好地掌握烧成气氛，釉呈现出青中微泛绿的优雅色调。

　　西晋创烧的鸡首壶，鸡首短而无颈，无流孔，还塑有鸡尾，这些仅是一种装饰。

11　青釉褐彩鸡首壶

东晋（317 ~ 420 年）

直径 18 厘米

高 22 厘米

"Chicken-head" Ewer with Brown Spot

Eastern Jin（317 ~ 420）

L. 18cm

H. 22cm

橄榄绿釉，胎质灰白，壶口浅小，扁圆形腹，盘口，平底。对称桥形系斜附肩部。一侧塑鸡首，细颈高昂，为流。另一端为环耳形柄。盘口，系及鸡首装饰深褐色点彩，疏密得当，不仅典雅，庄重，而且给人以极大的美感和想象力。

两晋至南北朝时期，越窑鸡首壶式样在中国东南地区有着流行和发展。

鸡能报时，故名"报时鸡"、"五时鸡"、"司夜鸡"。东晋以后，鸡首壶的鸡首变得高而有颈，且翘首远眺，形态生动。此件壶的鸡首塑有高高的鸡冠，鸡颈前挺，目视前方，恰似引吭报鸣的雄鸡。

12　青瓷小盌

东晋（317 ～ 420 年）

口径 6 厘米

高 2.5 厘米

Celadon-Glazed Bowl

Eastern Jin（317 ～ 420）

D. 6cm

H. 2.5cm

盌口内敛，腹上部微向外鼓，下部斜收，平底
略大而稳重，盌内外壁施青绿色釉，口沿点有四处
酱斑。盌是六朝时期的饮用器之一。

东晋时期浙江越窑早期产品。

东晋时越窑器物多以褐色点彩和莲瓣纹为主要
装饰。此器褐色点彩疏密得体，富于装饰美感。

13　青瓷鸡首壶

南北朝（420 ~ 589 年）

高 23.3 厘米

"Chicken-head" Ewer with Celadon Glaze

Southern–Northern dynasties,（420 ~ 589）

H. 23.3cm

　　壶体青色，深盘口，细颈，弧腹，平底，通体细小开片。盘口处以点褐彩装饰。鸡首昂立，做流。肩部有两个桥形耳，曲形壶柄粗壮有力。器身上腹部以纤细的线条刻画出莲瓣纹，腹部丰满，底部微内凹，有明显的支烧痕。

　　此青釉褐彩壶是东晋晚期出现的品种，以后逐渐流行。东晋南北朝时期，刻划花在青瓷生产中得到广泛应用，它的主要题材是佛教艺术中的莲花。

　　南北朝时期长期分裂局面，战祸连绵，现实充斥苦难。于是佛教走进了人们的心灵，人们在宗教中得到安慰，得以遁避现实世界。瓷器的造型和纹饰是它精神魂魄所在。这件青釉褐彩盘口壶，带给人当年战祸离乱，士人遁世避难隐逸的无奈。

14 青釉刻莲瓣托盏

南朝（420 ~ 589 年）

盏径 11 厘米

托径 16.8 厘米

Celadon-Glazed Cup and Stand with Carved Lotus Petal

Southern dynasty,（420 ~ 589）

D.（cup）11cm

D.（saucer）16.8cm

托，浅式，直沿，平底，托心刻二层复线水波纹一周。内外施釉。盏呈墩式，敞口，外壁刻复线莲瓣纹，施釉到近足处，里外施釉，底足及盏心有四个垫烧痕。

汉代至南朝时期，人们好饮粥茶，即将茶叶放入炊具中煮，有时还加入葱、姜、枣、桂皮等。茶煮好后盛入盏中，茶盏置于托盘上，不致烫手。

用刻划的曲线构成图案来美化器物，早在新石器时代就已是一种普遍现象了。东晋南北朝时期，佛教盛极一时，莲花纹装饰在瓷器上多有表现。越窑、洪洲窑等青瓷上的莲瓣纹通常用刻刀饰成浮雕状。此器丰满深厚，瓷盘内划一周莲瓣纹，中央用圆管戳成莲蓬纹，整个图案既形象又别致，是佛教文化艺术与陶瓷艺术的完美结合。

15　黑釉鸡首执壶

东晋（317～420年）

高 15.8 厘米

"Chicken-head" Ewer with Black Glaze

Eastern Jin,（317～420）

H. 15.8cm

　　壶盘口、细颈、腹鼓圆，壶身肥大，呈球状，平底，腹底部近足处露胎，胎呈浅褐色，器身施黑釉，开细纹片，釉质温润如漆，龙形柄，上端连于口沿，下端连于腹上部，流呈鸡首型，长颈高冠，圆腹上部两侧有对称的桥型钮。此壶造型生动俊美，灵气毕现，神采奕奕，令人叫绝，属当时上乘之作。

　　德清窑，位于浙江省德清县，是以黑瓷闻名的古窑场。专家们认为，德清地区是商周时期的制瓷中心，是中国瓷器的发源地。德清窑瓷胎中含铁、钛较高，普遍呈紫色、砖红或浅褐色，胎体外普遍施有化妆土。黑瓷釉精者色黑如漆，釉层较厚。

　　据说，黑色器物的起源跟宗教的传播有很大的渊源，代表了"玄"学思想的诞生。这件黑釉鸡首壶是东晋德清窑生产的主要器型。它通常作饮器用。多用来盛茶贮酒，在1500多年前的东晋时代，能烧造出如此高水平的黑釉壶具，充分反映了我国先民的聪明智慧与高超技艺。

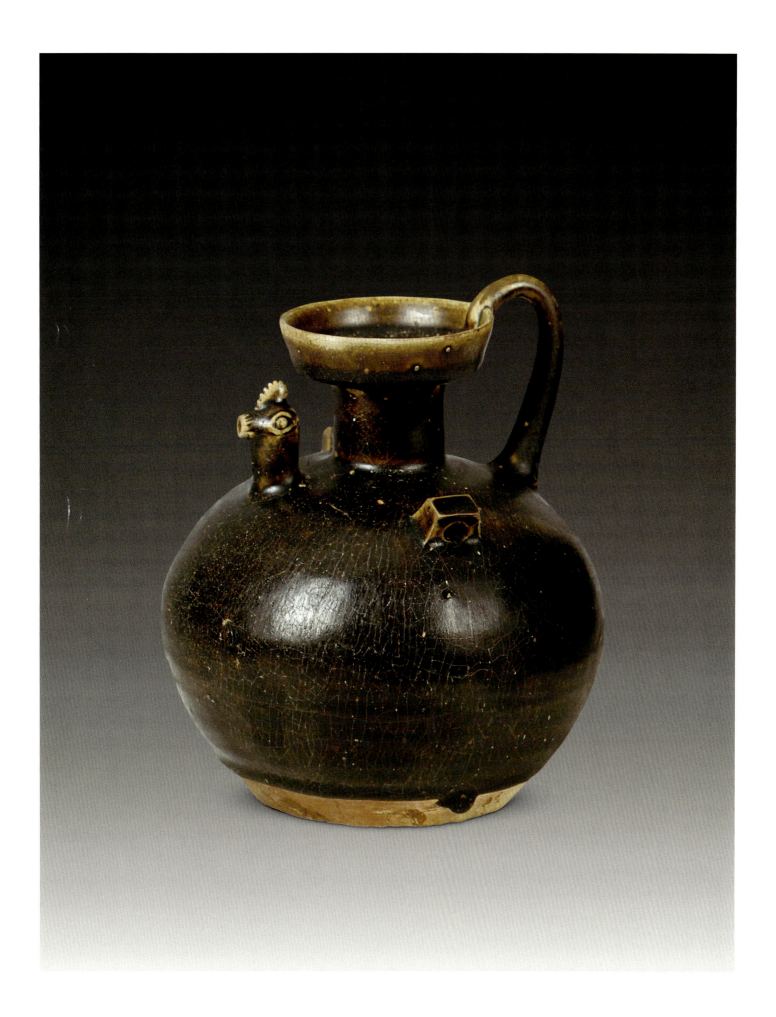

16 褐釉盘口鸡首壶

南朝（420 ~ 589 年）

高 13.3 厘米

"Chicken-head" Ewer with Brown Glaze

Southern Dynasty,（420 ~ 589）

H. 13.3cm

壶作盘口，短颈，自肩部以下腹部内收。平底，施釉，支钉烧。肩部向前伸出一鸡首，张口作啼鸣状，肩部向后伸出一把手，把柄呈螭首，张口衔壶之盘口，肩部左右各有一小系。全器施褐色釉，开细小纹片。器型挺拔，秀丽。

此器底部为满釉支钉烧。查早期支钉烧造，常见于三国、两晋、南北朝时期的南方窑口。

汉代《韩诗外传》中将鸡称为具有"文、武、勇、仁、信"五德的"德禽"。此器造型简朴，鸡首造型富有活力而极具装饰特点。

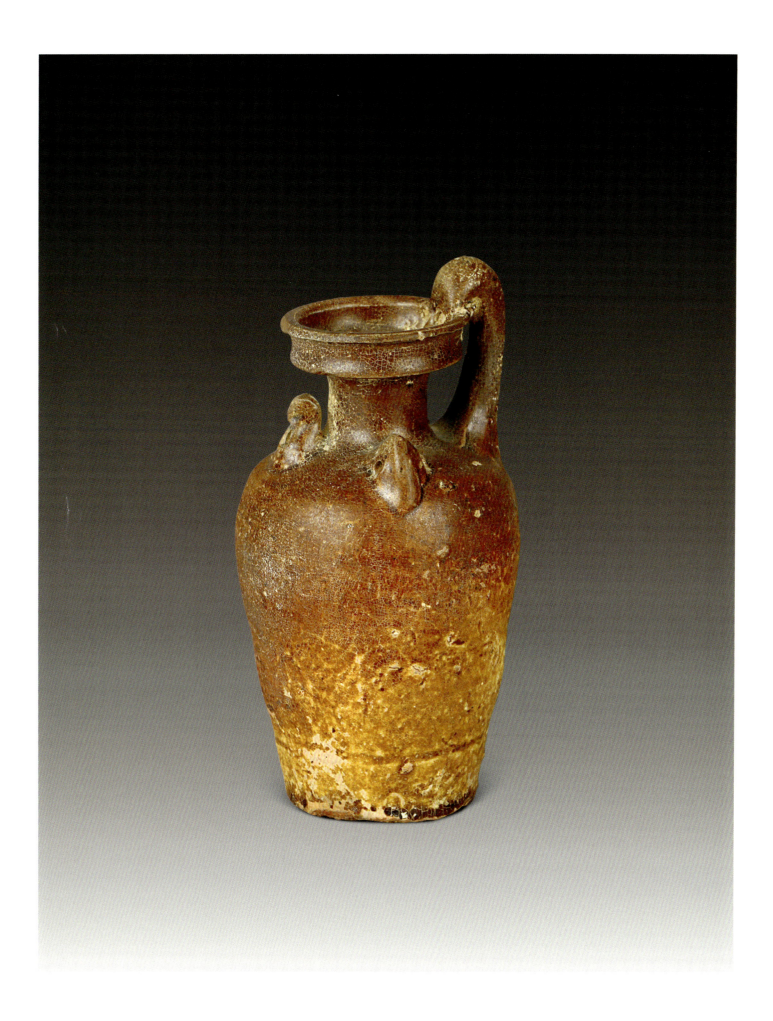

17 青釉杯

隋代（581～618年）

口径9.3厘米

Celadon-Glazed Cup

Sui Dynasty,（581～618）

D. 9.3cm

圆唇，直口，深弧腹，饼足微削一周。沿下修一周凹弦纹，内底粘接有三足支烧。胎色灰白。青白釉，器内满釉，器表釉不及底。

巩义窑发现了北方最早的青釉窑炉，北魏时期以来巩义窑选用含铁量较低的原料制作瓷坯，提高了胎色的白度，但真正烧制成熟期则在隋代，此时期釉质细腻，釉色白度较高，工艺较为成熟。

此器造型古朴，线条流畅，优美大方。工艺融铸南北，既有北方的刚劲风格，又有南方的清秀之美，极富艺术美感。

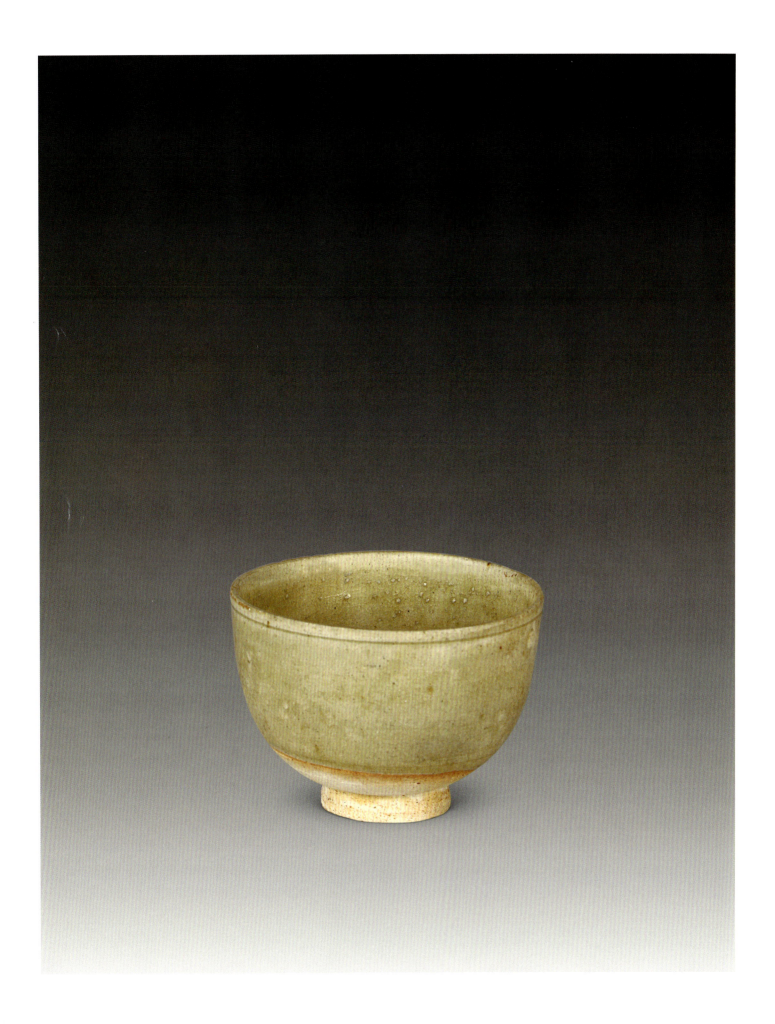

《宫乐图》 唐 佚名

《萧翼赚兰亭图》 唐 阎立本

二　唐代时期的茶具（618～907年）

　　唐代盛行佛教文化，佛教中人认为饮茶有助静思入定。在唐代，饮茶之风流行各地，873年，唐懿宗捐献了一套华贵的茶具给陕西扶风法门寺，作为供养舍利的奉献。1987年，法门寺地宫出土了14件越窑青瓷，多为茶具，称其为秘色瓷。唐代越窑壶（水注）的出现，是唐人高度精致文明的证明，完美的造型和越窑青瓷釉光，闭着眼睛体会的千峰翠色，使人冥思。如唐越窑执壶（图40）。莲花、莲瓣纹是佛教装饰图案，深深影响着茶具的装饰，这也是茶具与禅佛修为的互动。壶器上的仰、覆莲出现在壶肩与腹底部，仿佛是一株不染的莲花。陆羽在8世纪中叶所著的《茶经》提供了饮茶资料，陈述了各种备茶方法及应用器具的设计，当时的奉茶仪规，十分讲究。

　　唐代的瓷窑遍及中国南北，随着品茗之风盛行，这种习俗使茶具的需求量不断增加。制瓷业在技术、规模、造型、纹饰等方面都发展迅速，逐渐形成了以浙江越窑为代表的青瓷和以河北为代表的白瓷两大瓷窑，被称之为"南青北白"。唐代注壶器物多为喇叭口、短颈、椭圆形腹、平底、短流，有的壶身还制成瓜棱形，如湖南长沙窑青釉褐斑贴花执壶（图20），亦有色彩鲜明亮丽，绘画简洁而富有诗意。1998年印尼海域打捞的"黑石号"沉船中，在六万件外销瓷器中，长沙窑瓷器占绝大多数，船上的青釉碗更说明了当时长沙窑是以烧制与茶器相关的器物为主（图21）。又如本书中唐代长沙窑青釉四系穿带壶，壶身正面釉下绿彩勾绘七层宝塔，各层翼角挑起，塔两侧绘蠹天大树，塔静树动相映成趣，有较强的艺术感染力，将禅与壶文化巧妙地融合在一起，是长沙窑釉下彩绘的典型代表（图22）。唐三彩以造型生动，色泽艳丽，生活气息浓厚，别具风格而著称中外。唐代生产的类似胡瓶、凤首壶等酒具，其型制是仿造波斯萨珊朝的金银器器型。如唐绿釉璎珞纹贴花执壶（图41），通体绿釉上用堆贴和模印技法，在器腹部饰宝相花，火珠葡萄纹，此壶受波斯文化影响，造型优美，装饰富丽，是唐三彩的代表作。唐代褐釉白斑执壶亦是唐代花瓷中的代表作，此壶器形高大，壶身以黑釉为底色，黑釉上再饰有特意涂绘的灰蓝色釉，入窑焙烧后，灰蓝色釉熔融流动后，出现片片云雾状彩斑，映衬在黑釉上奇现"日、月、山"三字草书，令人叹为观止，它似在告诉后世之人，壶中自可以容下山河日月，可容纳百川。（图26）

II. TEA SETS OF TANG DYNASTY (618 AD ~ 907 AD)

Due to the prevalence of Buddhist culture in Tang Dynasty, drinking tea was popular across the country, because Buddhists thought tea was helpful for meditation. In 973 A.D., for the purpose of enshrining and worshiping Buddhist relics, Emperor Yizong of Tang Dynasty donated a sumptuous tea set to Famen Temple in Fufeng County, Shaanxi. In 1987, 14 celadon wares of Yue Kiln were unearthed in the underground palace of Famen Temple, most of which are tea sets called as secret colour ware. The water-jet pot of Yue Kiln of Tang Dynasty shows high civilization of people of that time. (fig.40) With perfect design and celadon glaze of Yue Kiln, ewer of Yue Kiln of Tang Dynasty features green colour with well-distributed glaze layers, as if thousand peaks in emerald colour leading people into meditation. Designs of lotus and lotus petal are Buddhist decorative patterns and have great impact on the decoration of tea set, so tea set is interrelated with Zen Buddhism. Facing upwards or downwards, lotus design appears on the shoulder or bottom of pot, as if it were pure and unsoiled lotus. In the Classic of Tea written by Lu Yu in the middle of the 8th Century A.D., information about drinking tea, various preparation methods of tea and design of application tools are described. From this book, we can see that tea serving ceremony of that period is fastidious.

Kilns spread all over the country during Tang Dynasty, and the demands for tea wares constantly increased due to the prevalence of tea drinking. As porcelain industry rapidly developed in terms of the technology, scale, shapes and designs, two major kilns gradually took form, i.e. celadon wares from Yue Kiln of Zhejiang and white porcelains from Xin Kiln of Hebei, which were called as "celadon wares in southern China and white porcelains in northern China". Most pouring artifacts of Tang Dynasty feature horn-shaped mouth, short neck, oval belly, flat base and short spout, while some spots were shaped with melon ridges. For example, Celadon-Glazed Ewer with Brown Clay Applique of Changsha Kiln has bright colors, concise painting and poetic quality. (fig.20) In the "Batu Hitam" sunken ship salvaged in 1998 in Indonesian waters, the vast majority of sixty thousand exported porcelains are porcelains of Changsha Kiln, and from celadon-glazed bowls on the ship we can see that Changsha Kiln was mainly involved in manufacturing artifacts related to tea set at that time. (fig.21) For the Celadon-Glazed Pot with Four Handles of Changsha Kiln of Tang Dynasty as referenced in this book, there is green- colored underglazed seven-story pagoda on the pot body, with upturned roof-ridge of each story upward and upright trees on both sides of pagoda, to form a delightful contrast. By integrating Zen and pot culture, underglazed painting of Changsha Kiln has strong artistic appeal. Tri-colored glazed pottery of the Tang Dynasty is well known for its lifelike shape, bright colors, strong vitality and unique style. The shape and structure of Hu ewer, phoenix head-shaped pot and other wares produced in Tang Dynasty are reproduced

from that of gold and silver wares made by Persian Sassanid Dynasty. For example, under the impact of Persian culture, Green-Glazed Pouring Pot with Clay Applique of Tang Dynasty features appealing design and splendid decoration by using clay applique and stamping techniques, with Baoxiang flower decoration and grape design on pot belly, thus it is the master work of tri-colored glazed pottery of the Tang Dynasty. (fig.41) As the masterpiece of fancy-glazed porcelains of Tang Dynasty, Fancy-Glazed Pouring Pot with Double Handles of Lushan Kiln features tall and big shape as well as ground color of black glaze. Painted on black glaze, grey and blue glaze will fuse and flow after the pot is fired in kiln, and then colorful cloud-like strips come into being, silhouetted against three Chinese characters " 日 , 月 , 山 " (sun, moon and mountain) on black glaze. This amazing masterpiece seems to tell us that the pot can contain mountain, river, sun, and moon. (fig.26)

18　三彩注子

唐代（618 ~ 907 年）

高 7.3 厘米

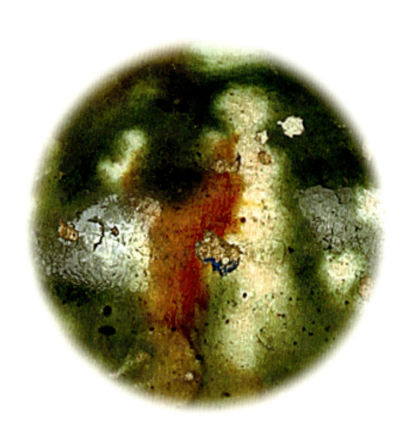

器身呈椭圆形，口部呈喇叭状，短流，双股把柄连接口沿和肩部。实心圈足，陶胎上敷白泥釉，施绿釉琥珀斑，釉面伴有细小开片纹，釉色变换多样，绚丽多姿，绮丽无比。此器身矮腹丰，凸显浑厚庄重。

巩县窑历史悠久，始于汉，发展于北魏，成熟于隋，鼎盛于唐。

唐三彩是唐代生产的一种低温釉陶器，釉彩有黄、绿、白、褐、蓝、黑等色，而以黄、绿、白三色为主，所以人们习惯称之为"唐三彩"。河南洛阳、巩县均有烧制。此器为唐代河南巩县窑烧制。

唐代国力空前繁盛，中外文化交流频繁。此器在色彩的相互辉映中，尽显富丽堂皇的艺术魅力。

19 唐三彩执壶

唐代（618 ~ 907 年）

高 16.5 厘米

Tang Ewer with SanCai Glaze

Tang Dynasty，（618 ~ 907）

H. 16.5cm

　　器身呈椭圆型，口部呈盘口喇叭状，肩部有双系并饰以鸡头，实心矮圈足。陶胎上敷白泥釉，器身加施泛褐、黄、绿彩琥珀色斑。胎质坚实细腻，白中泛粉，应是河南巩县窑产品。

　　唐三彩是唐代低温彩釉陶器的总称。它是以细腻的白色黏土作胎料，用含铜、铁、钴等元素的矿物质作着色剂，在同一器物上，釉色呈黄、绿、蓝、白、紫、褐等多种色彩，形成绚丽多彩的艺术效果。

　　这件唐三彩执壶手柄缺失，但器型浑厚丰满，线条流畅。壶身各种颜色浸润，形成了斑驳灿烂的颜色，宛如太空云彩，虚幻缥缈。说明此时的人们试图通过对欢乐和幸福的幻想表达心灵的满足。贞观之治以后的唐代经济，达到了空前繁荣。社会安定，物质生活极为丰富，呈现出举世闻名的大唐盛世。唐三彩最能体现大唐的盛世风采和大唐文化雄浑博大的气度。

唐代（618～907 年）

高 16.5 厘米

Tang Dynasty,（618～907）

H. 16.5cm

椭圆形器型，圆平足，撇口小颈，把柄作三股状，八棱形短流，肩饰双系。器身腹部两侧饰以三个模印贴花纹饰，饰小鸟在棕榈叶上对峙，贴花上敷以褐斑。器身开有均匀细小的纹片，胎色米黄。

这种褐斑贴花壶系长沙窑器物中代表性作品，出土数量较多，但绝大部分有破损，特别是在口沿和把柄部分。同时，粗颈大口的贴花壶居多。本品釉色光洁、明亮，造型隽美、饱满，完整无损，非常珍贵。

唐代的长沙窑将中国陶瓷带进了彩瓷时代，受外来宗教文化和儒家学说的影响，长沙窑陶瓷装饰艺术和纹饰也深深打入这些宗教信仰和文化的烙印。此器在长沙窑题记中称之为瓶，是唐代盛汤点茶的器具。器身上褐斑贴印棕榈叶纹，刻画生动。棕榈树象征智慧和潜能，相传佛祖释迦牟尼诞生于无忧树下，而得道顿悟于菩提树下。古代印度僧人为了弘扬佛法，常以棕榈叶为介书写经文，习称贝叶经。

21 长沙窑釉下彩花盏

唐代（618～907 年）

直径 15.2 厘米

ChangSha Bowl with Under-Glaze Flower

Tang Dynasty,（618～907）

D. 15.2cm

盏浅壁，口沿微敛，圈足，浅黄色胎。器身遍施小开片，米黄色釉，盏口沿处以四块褐斑作底色，盏心以铜绿彩绘画兰草纹。受西亚风格影响，笔触娴熟，彩绘生动。

长沙窑即铜官窑，位于长沙市望城区铜官镇一带，是唐代彩瓷的发源地。8 世纪，世间只有青、白单色瓷器，而长沙窑的技工在瓷器上创立了釉下多种色调，尤其是红色。1998 年，在印尼海域打捞的唐代沉船"黑石号"中，发现了大量的长沙窑器物，其中有同样的釉下彩花盏。

此器盏心部分以兰草纹为主要装饰图案。兰花亦称为禅花，为佛教的六供奉之一，代表着佛教中因果的因。据说，修行者见花当思"修今世好的因，来世才有好的果"之因果福报。

22 长沙窑宝塔纹四系穿带壶

唐代（618 ~ 907 年）

高 17.5 厘米

ChangSha Ewer with Green Pagoda Pattern

Tang Dynasty, （618 ~ 907）

H. 17.5cm

　　此壶筒形小口，八边形短流，曲柄，瓜形深腹，平底。两肩与腹部上下各有穿带式系。流下用青花绘七层宝塔纹饰，上部有宝塔顶。宝塔两侧亦以青花绘娑罗树各一棵。器身开有细小纹片。

　　唐代青花极为少见，仅在湖南长沙窑及河南巩县窑窑址中发现。此壶造型新颖，品相完整，并绘有青花宝塔纹，应是湖南长沙窑制品中之稀品。

　　由于当时佛教在长沙的迅猛发展，佛教文化为长沙窑的发展提供了装饰素材，长沙窑广泛吸取佛教文化，也为佛教的传播起到了间接的作用。

　　这件穿带壶正面绘有宝塔一座，两侧各绘一棵"娑罗树"。娑罗树又称七叶树，原生于印度，相传佛祖释迦牟尼弘扬佛法和涅槃均与此树有关，佛祖释迦牟尼就涅槃于娑罗双树间，被称为"佛门圣树"。

唐代（618 ~ 907 年）

Tang Dynasty,（618 ~ 907）

高 18.2 厘米

H. 18.2cm

喇叭形口，粗短颈，蛋圆形深腹，平底，肩部前置八棱短流，两侧置两系，颈至腹部配龙形曲柄。系流处饰褐色斑状釉，釉彩晶莹。外罩青釉，腹下部至底部露胎，平底外撇，胎呈灰白色。胎体厚重。器身开有细小纹片。

这件青釉龙柄褐斑壶用小印模直接在壶的流下两侧用氧化铁作呈色剂模印图案作为装饰，然后在纹饰外面罩一层透明的青釉，在 1200 度的高温下烧制出褐彩装饰。此器点有褐彩装饰的龙柄尤其生动、可爱。

长沙窑器物中以龙柄少见。龙是数千年来中华民族的标志和精神象征，它以特殊的神灵含义和图腾形象渗透到唐代各个文化领域，甚至成为古代政治崇拜的核心。

24 长沙窑褐绿彩执壶

唐代（618 ~ 907 年）

高 16 厘米

ChangSha Ewer Painted in Brown and Green

Tang Dynasty,（618 ~ 907）

H. 16cm

壶口微侈，细颈，溜肩，平底，肩部一面有短流，一面为曲柄，浅黄胎身釉下饰以褐绿相间的漩涡状纹饰，造型优美而稳重。釉面有不规则细小开片。

此器以釉下泼墨式的彩绘，经 1200 ~ 1270 度高温烧制，釉汁相互渗透变化而形成的漩涡状。

漩涡纹体现了古人对水的一种崇拜。古人认为，

水是生命的源泉，生活的需要，最后乃至死亡以后的归宿。认为万物都是从这个漩涡里出来，万物最后又要归聚到这个漩涡中去。唐代是道教发展的鼎盛时期，长沙窑瓷器中的道教文化因素以多种形式表现出来。此器通过娴熟的绘画，呈现道教文化对民间艺术的影响是极其深远而广泛的。

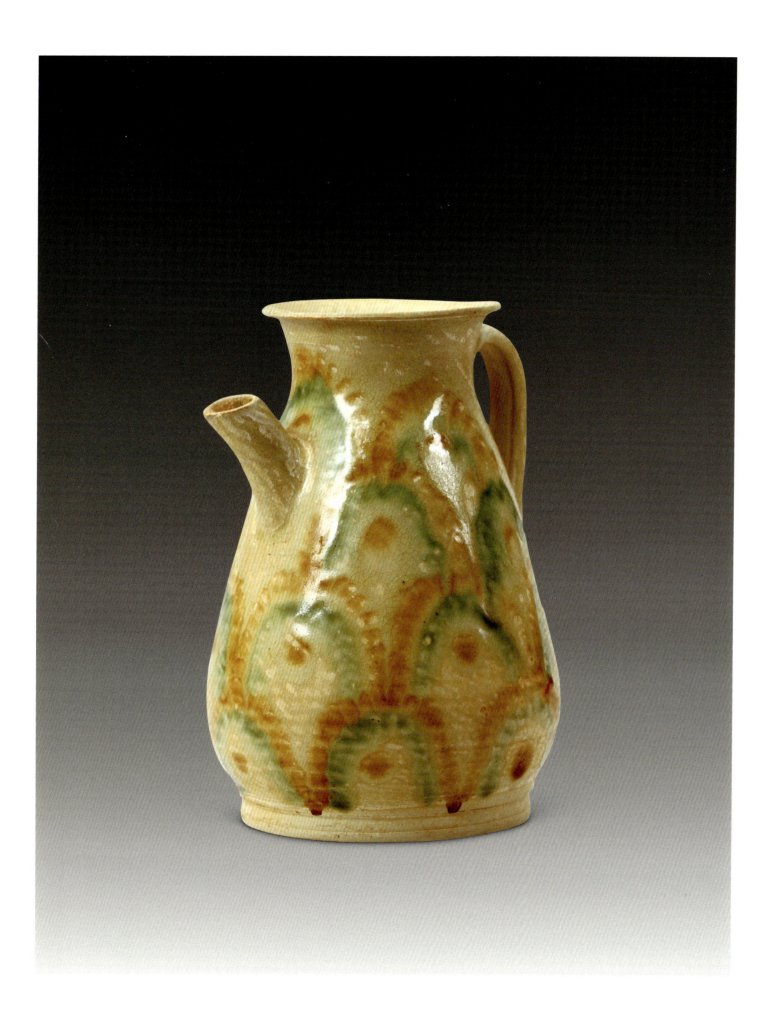

25 黑釉彩斑执壶

唐代（618 ～ 907 年）

高 17 厘米

Black-glazed Ewer with Pained Spot

Tang Dynasty,（618 ～ 907）

H. 17cm

　　执壶撇口，短颈，长腹，腹上部丰满，平底，胎质灰白细腻，壶肩部一侧有短流，流口削平，一侧有双带形曲柄，曲柄连于口与肩之间。壶里外均施釉，外部施釉不及底，釉呈黑褐色，口、柄及器身上布满乳白间蓝色斑纹，色斑纹无一雷同，流淌自然，富有飘洒动感，天然成趣。

　　花釉瓷器又称"花瓷"，自唐代初期创烧，鼎盛于唐代中期，是我国迄今发现最早的窑变釉瓷。鲁山花瓷创造了二液分相釉的技术，经 1250 ~1300 度高温烧制，使黑釉瓷器出现了绚丽斑斓的窑变效果，形成了空间美和色彩美，是唐代鲁山段店窑的精美之物。

　　唐人南卓在《羯鼓录》中，已有"鲁山花瓷"的记载。此器经高温烧制，釉彩熔融，彩斑呈现，变幻莫测。如云霞，似岩浆，纵情泼洒，天极超逸，奇妙无比，全凭观者想象，果真是无人造化，鬼斧神工。表现出大唐盛世的豪迈气魄。

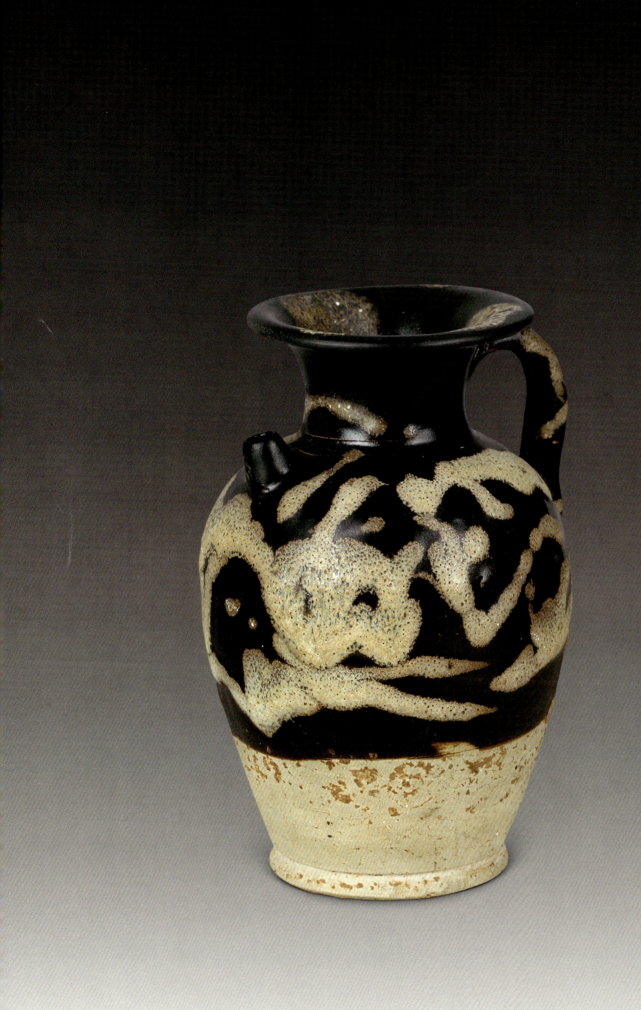

26　褐釉白斑执壶

唐代（618～907年）

高 21.5 厘米

Brown-glazed Ewer with White Spot

Tang Dynasty,（618～907）

H. 21.5cm

胎体厚重，直颈，口略外翻，腹鼓圆，平底，胎质白色，两侧置短流和曲柄，肩置双系，壶体饱满。腹底部露胎，其他部分先施褐釉，再施乳白彩料，经高温烧制，釉汁相互渗透而变化，泛出"日月山"三字彩斑。

此器再现了先人"壶中日月"的理念，以及精湛的艺术表现力。壶体厚实，张弛有度，使人领略到大唐雄风。

唐代时期，黑釉器物的发展跟此时"禅宗"的发展有很大的关系。以鲁山窑为代表的花釉系列，引入了多元化思想和文化，在黑釉器物上以白色彩料泼彩，这种处理方式体现了对宇宙奥秘的崇拜，符合禅宗"顿悟"的理念。中国宗法性传统宗教以天神崇拜和祖先崇拜为核心，以社稷"日、月、山、川"等自然崇拜为翼羽，形成了相对稳固的郊社制度，宗庙制度以及其他祭祀制度，成为维系社会秩序和家族体系的精神力量，也是慰藉人们心灵的精神源泉。

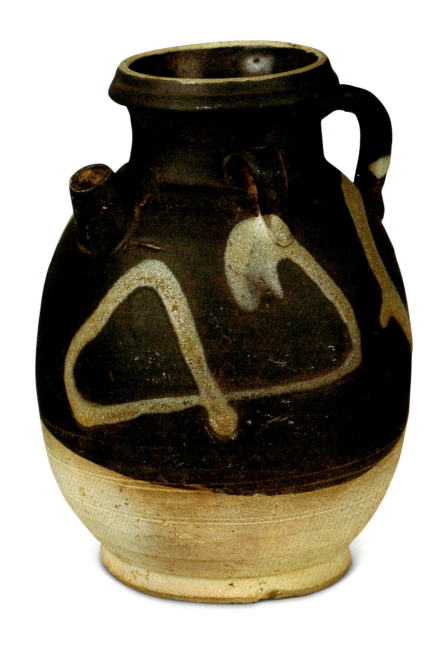

27　褐釉盘口执壶

唐代（618 ~ 907 年）

高 19.8 厘米

Brown-glazed Ewer

Tang Dynasty,（618 ~ 907）

H. 19.8cm

壶长颈，盘口，橄榄形长腹，平底，曲柄，短流。胎质灰白色，器身施褐色釉，釉光温润，近颈部饰弦纹两道，装饰效果极佳。

本器线条柔和饱满，端庄，系唐代巩义黄冶窑烧制。

唐代的壶，与唐代人们饮茶的方式有关。当时沏茶的方式最普遍的是用煎茶法，即用镀将水煮沸，尔后将茶投入其中，调成汤料饮用。只有少数地区（或人）采用点茶法沏茶。壶代替镀来煎水注汤。

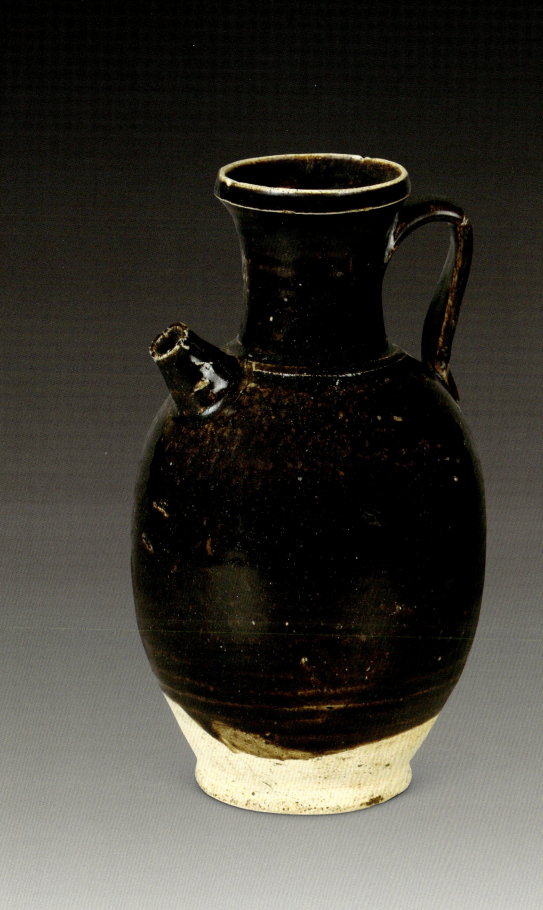

28 酱釉执壶

唐代（618 ~ 907 年）

高 11.3 厘米

Reddish Brown Glazed Ewer

Tang Dynasty, （618 ~ 907）

H.11.3cm

壶喇叭口，短颈，椭圆形，短流，双股龙形柄连接于口沿及肩部，平底，圈足外撇，胎质灰白，坚实，外部褐釉不到底，褐釉呈琥珀窑变状，晶莹润泽，绚丽多姿，给人以梦幻般的色彩。

唐时执壶多壶嘴短小，口似喇叭。此器器型浑圆饱满，小型大器，精巧而有气魄，单纯而有变化。双股龙形柄以捏塑手法表现，信手浑成，反映了人神沟通的宗教思想。

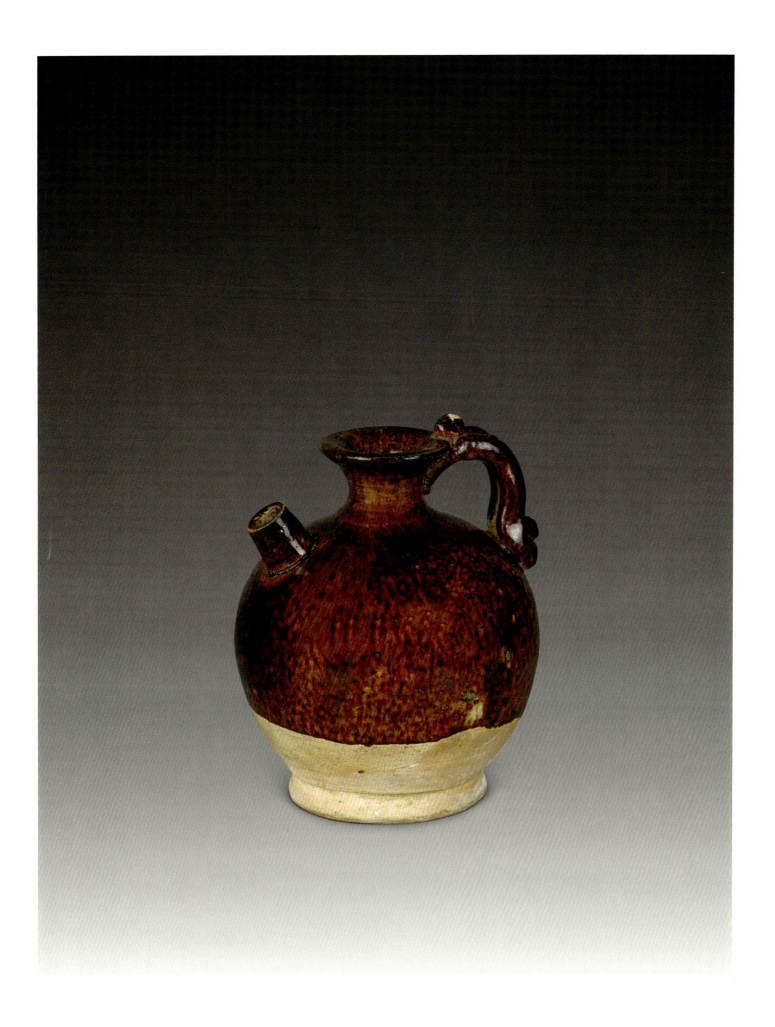

29 茶叶末釉执壶

唐代（618～907 年）

高 21.5 厘米

Teadust-Glazed Ewer

Tang Dynasty,（618～907）

H. 21.5cm

壶唇外翻平口，短颈，腹上部丰满，下部渐收，灰白胎，平底，外撇。壶身一侧肩上凸起短流，一侧曲柄连接于口、肩之间，壶身外部施茶叶末色釉，施釉不到底。釉光温润，器型优美工整，秀丽。

耀州窑，始于唐代，其窑址位于陕西省铜川市黄堡镇。唐代时茶叶末釉器物釉色青黄，釉层较厚，胎釉交接处呈姜黄色。青釉釉面上有的出现小的露胎褐斑，为其他青釉瓷器所不见。

此器艳于茶，美如花，黄杂绿色，妖娆而不俗。器型浑厚古朴，气质高雅，是一件素质为美的茶器。

30 黄釉蓆纹执壶

唐代（618 ~ 907 年）

高 18.5 厘米

Yellow-Glazed Ewer with Mat Pattern

Tang Dynasty,（618 ~ 907）

H. 18.5cm

壶直唇口，粗颈，短流，曲柄。流柄之间置双系，釉下施白色化妆土，施半截黄釉，平底坯胎上拍印席纹，釉透明度高，有碎开片。釉下席纹的运用，使光素的器物产生出一种错落有致的节奏感，是唐代一种装饰方法。

寿州窑窑址在安徽淮南，是唐代七大瓷窑之一。

繁盛期器物釉色有蜡黄、鳝鱼黄等，釉层呈玻璃状，光润透明。

唐代陶工所烧制席纹执壶，多见黄釉器。此器纹饰与天然草席交映天成，别无二致，表现了自然之美。饰而不显，故而不兴。

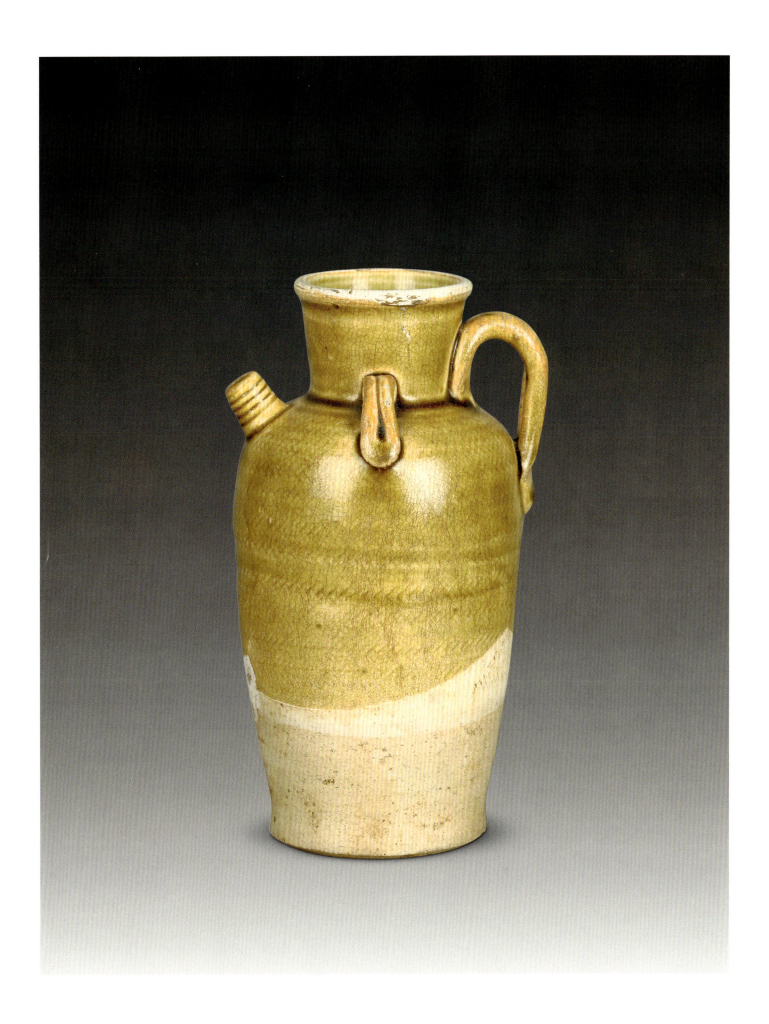

唐代（618～907 年）

Tang Dynasty,（618～907）

高 12.8 厘米

H. 12.8cm

壶形椭圆，圆形口，有短流，壁形底，近足处外撇，提梁柄为弓形蒲牢形，蒲牢双脚连肩上部，尾盘于柄上，头衔壶口，似水从兽口中流出，造型小巧，生动别致，极具艺术魅力。壶身上半部施褐色釉，下腹露胎，釉光莹润，有细小开片。

蒲牢为古代传说中生活在海边的兽，为龙的九子之一，平生好音好吼，多充作洪钟提梁的兽钮，助其鸣声远扬。此器为唐代长沙窑壶中罕见之品种。

32 耀州窑红釉执壶

唐代（618 ~ 907 年）

高 20.8 厘米

YaoZhou Red-Glazed Ewer

Tang Dynasty,（618 ~ 907）

H. 20.8cm

　　椭圆形，下部向内敛。粗颈，唇口，平底，圈足外撇，底足内凹。肩部一侧置一短流，另一侧置两股把柄。灰黄色胎，施以褐红色釉，釉面光洁均匀，附有小冰裂纹开片。

　　中国人的红色崇拜，起源于对太阳与火的崇拜以及血液崇拜，具有崇高、尊贵又神秘的色彩。至今人们将红色作为最吉祥、最喜庆的符号。红色崇拜深入人心。

　　耀州窑是中国陶瓷烧制的著名产地，唐代开始烧黑釉、青釉、茶叶末釉、此器能在焙烧温度和氧化还原气氛中烧成褐红色釉，实属难得，十分罕见。

　　耀州窑传世执壶出现不断的惊奇，也体现在纹饰和釉色的创新。遥想先人品茗茶叙，触目所及红色美器加上芳香的茶汤等待用品的期待心情。

33　邢窑褐红釉执壶

唐代（618 ~ 907 年）

高 18.3 厘米

Xing Yao Ewer with Deep Red Glaze

Tang Dynasty,（618 ~ 907）

H. 18.3cm

唇口，粗颈，深腹，圈足。肩部一侧短流，另一侧置双股形柄连接颈与肩之间。胎体厚重，胎质坚致，细白，施肥厚的褐红色釉，壶身呈橄榄型，更显唐代以肥而美，雍容华贵之气。

邢窑的黑釉瓷目前已知始于隋代，到唐代生产量已经很大。这一时期的黑釉瓷器釉面肥厚，部分产品黑亮如漆。（北京艺术博物馆编《中国邢窑·中国古瓷窑大系》，中国华侨出版社，2012 年）

唐代佛教几度兴盛，直接反映在邢窑瓷器的器型和釉色上。此器敦厚端庄，简洁优美，釉色褐红。虽经千年时光的侵蚀，釉光仍可照人，凝聚着古代陶瓷工匠的智慧和创造精神，颇具时代感，具有较高的艺术审美价值。

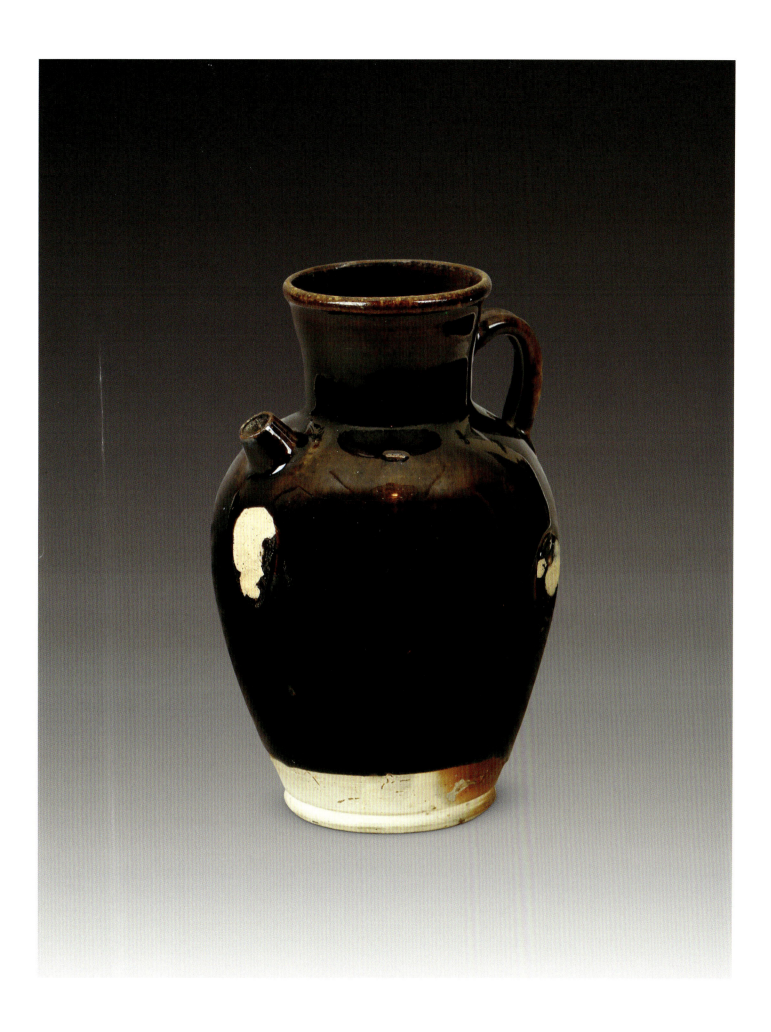

34 邢窑褐釉龙柄壶

唐代（618 ~ 907 年）

高 18 厘米

Xing Yao Brown-Glazed Ewer with Dragon Handle

Tang Dynasty，（618 ~ 907）

H. 18cm

花瓣形口，细颈溜肩，鼓腹，实心短圈足。细颈上有花瓣状流，双股高身把柄作龙衔口状，肩部双线弦纹。白瓷胎上施褐色釉，釉质莹润。为邢窑黑釉器物。

唐代的金银器对当时瓷器的影响很大。这件褐釉龙柄壶是按照波斯萨珊王朝金银器的形式制作，以其优美的造型，动人的釉色，迎合了贵族阶层喜爱浮华奢靡的追求。

35　邢窑白釉执壶

唐代（618 ～ 907 年）

高 12 厘米

执壶圆口，短颈，圆肩，长圆腹深，腹壁向下收，圈足。肩部前方出一短流，后部为一扁带把手。器身施白色釉，釉色均匀润泽，胎白细腻，白中泛青。质地较硬。该器形由两晋时期的执壶演变而来，呈唐代常见器形。

唐代邢窑白瓷，负有盛名，素有"南青北白"誉称。窑址在河北邢台内丘，它在工艺上取得的成就，在中国陶瓷史上占有极其重要的地位。此器与河北省邢窑博物馆收馆藏一件"白釉执壶"相仿。

此器釉面光滑，色泽雪白莹润。陆羽《茶经》中所赞"邢瓷类银"、"类雪"便是指其釉色而言。不同颜色在佛教中表示圆满的觉悟和佛法。据说白色代表佛法的清静和其所带来的解脱。

36　邢窑白釉玉璧底托盏

唐代（618 ～ 907 年）

盏口径 13.6 厘米

托口径 14.9 厘米

Xing Yao White-Glazed Cup and Stand

Tang Dynasty,（618 ～ 907）

D.（cup）13.6cm

D.（sauce）14.9cm

　　盏，敞口，斜壁，浅腹，玉璧底。内壁四条出筋，施白釉。托盘平出，中空内凹，用以托盏，宽口沿出筋四条用以装饰。盏，托白釉莹润，聚釉处泛青，有泪痕，胎质细腻坚致，为唐代中晚期典型茶盏形制，源于金银器造型。唐邢窑及越窑青瓷玉璧足茶盏皆为陆羽《茶经》所载。唐代盏的托口一般较矮，口沿作花瓣状，颇为精美。

　　唐代邢窑在西安寺院及宅邸等遗址有发现，唐人举茶多见茶托为金属器（台北故宫有一套北宋定窑牙白莲花纹盏托）。此器盏、托均为唐代白釉瓷器者少见。

　　唐代瓷业"南青北白"的局面史有定论。白瓷向青瓷的传统优势地位提出了挑战。唐代大诗人杜甫写过一首脍炙人口的诗："大邑烧瓷轻且坚，扣如哀玉锦城传，君家白碗胜霜雪，急送茅斋也可怜。"（见《又于韦处乞大邑瓷碗》）

37　唐白釉执壶

唐代（618 ～ 907 年）

高 19.2 厘米

White Ewer of Tang Dynasty

Tang Dynasty,（618 ～ 907）

H. 19.2cm

壶长颈，唇口，腹身椭圆形，平底，近足处外撇，灰白胎。器身施青白釉，不到底，釉光莹润，有细小开片。壶身肩部饰弦纹，两侧置曲柄，短流。器身修长是唐代中期向五代过渡之器型特征。

唐代中期，巩义窑的白瓷制作达到高峰，其产品不仅为民间使用，而且其精细制品还作为地方贡瓷进献给当时的宫廷官府。

唐代，经济繁荣，制瓷业发达。壶具为适应时代的发展产生了相应的造型，此器即为代表。唐代中期以后，出现了俗称"短嘴注壶"。

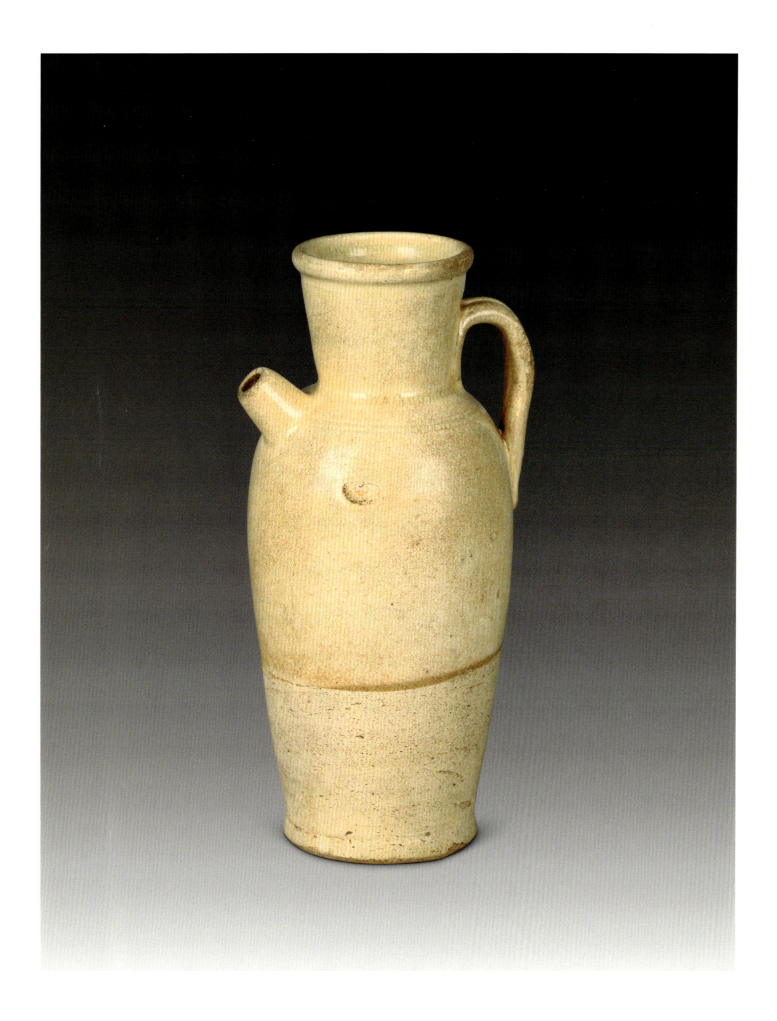

38 邢窑白釉执壶

唐代（618 ~ 907 年）

高 18.2 厘米

Xing Yao White-Glazed Ewer

Tang Dynasty,（618 ~ 907）

H. 18.2cm

器形呈椭圆型，下部向内敛。喇叭状撇口，短流，三股把柄下缀以饰钮浮雕，上系以绳结，平底，白色瓷胎敷以白泥釉，上施薄而透明的泛黄色釉。

此器胎呈白色，胎质细密。胎体很薄，器型典雅俊美，为唐代邢窑白釉典型器。河北省临城县文物保管所藏有一件类似执壶，底阴刻"张"字款。

唐代以后，由于朝廷的提倡，佛教成功汉化，在民众中蔚然成风，实现了与中国艺术的完美结合。佛教美术在瓷器的造型、装饰上向世俗化发展。此器制作精美，在装饰上足以传神，又保持着浓厚的生活气息。

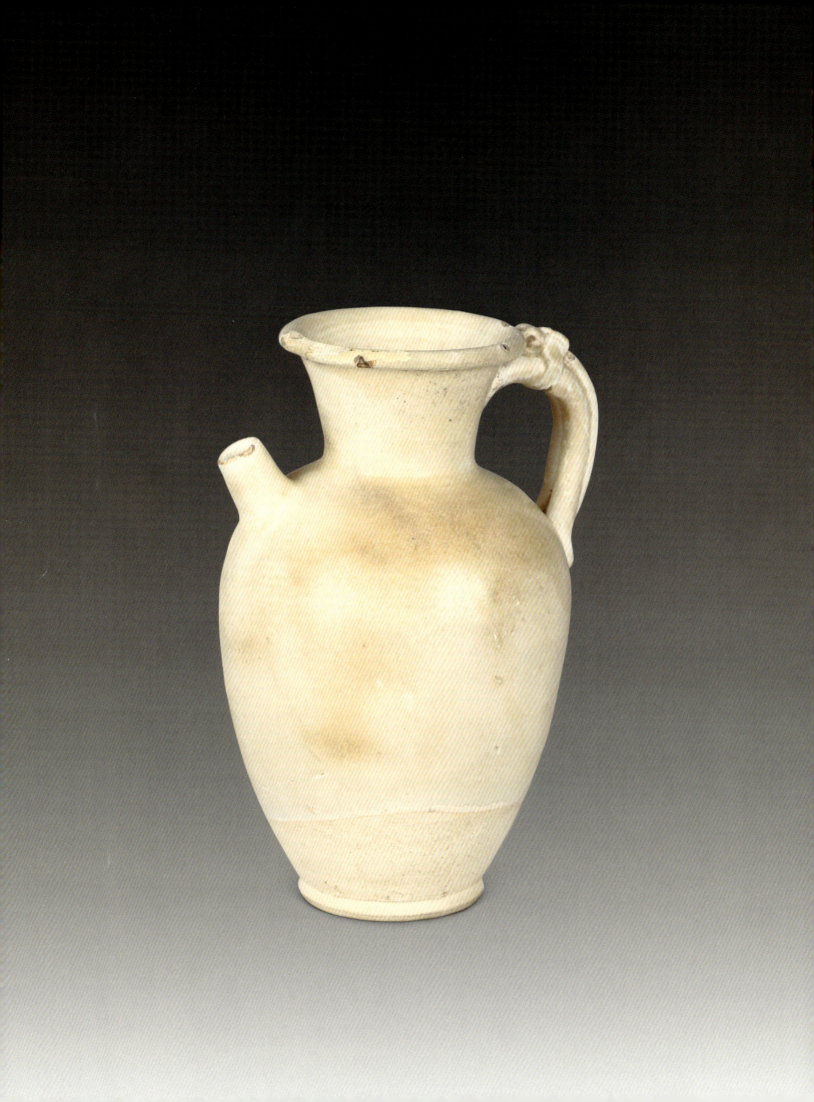

39 邢窑白釉执壶

唐代（618 ～ 907 年）

高 19.5 厘米

Xing Yao White-Glazed Ewer

Tang Dynasty,（618 ～ 907）

H. 19.5cm

椭圆形器身，下部内敛，短流，把柄为三股，作宽扁形，下缀饰浮雕，上系以绳结。饼形足，釉色奶白而莹润，白色胎。

唐代邢窑白瓷执壶是集优良的制瓷原料，优秀的制瓷技术和独特的社会人文环境所结合起来的产物。这件唐邢窑白釉执壶虽无装饰，但重胎质釉色，质地细腻，透明度高，加之其造型端庄，有鲜明的唐代风韵，距今已有 1000 多年的历史。

据说在佛教密宗中强调五种颜色，即白、黄、红、蓝、绿五种，白色为息且思纯洁。

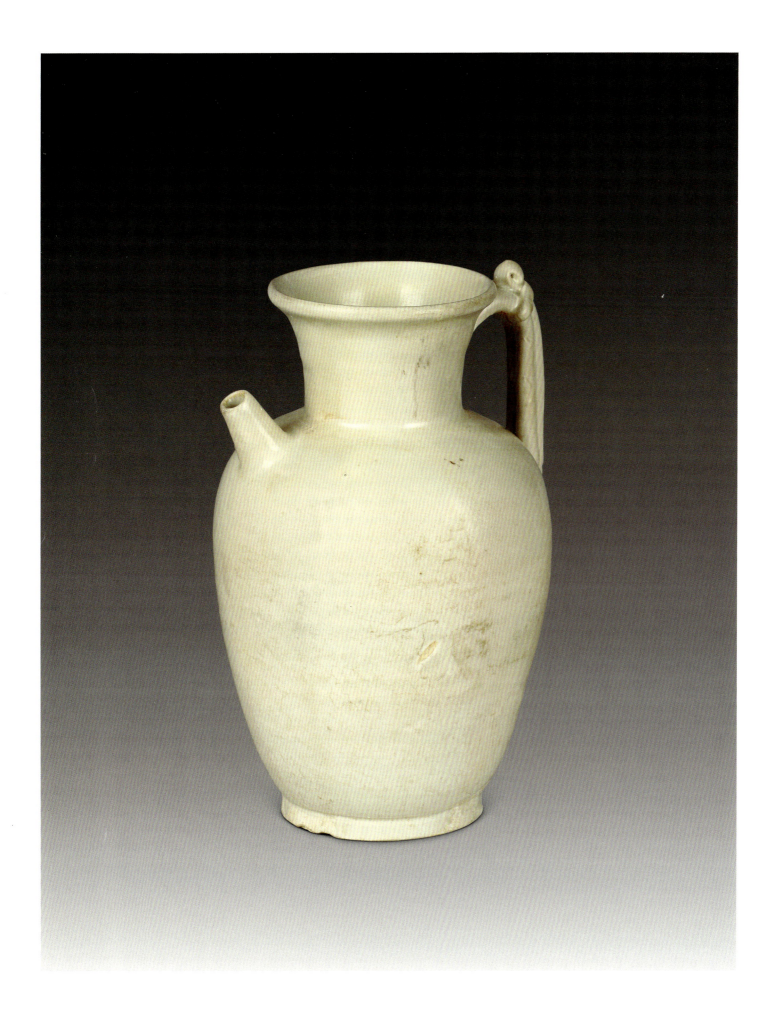

唐代（618～907 年）

高 24.6 厘米

敞口，短颈，溜肩，椭圆形腹，圆形圈足。颈部有八方形短流，曲柄。器身内外施青釉，釉色青中闪黄，莹润透彻，开有细小纹片。

越窑青瓷执壶，属唐代饮茶用的点茶器具，能盛水，能点汤。为该时期南方窑口的突出代表。

"九秋风露越窑开，夺得千峰翠色来。"这是唐代诗人陆龟蒙赞誉越窑秘色青瓷的著名诗句。说明当时越窑瓷器是以一种青翠的绿色为最。此器造型隽美，高雅大气，釉层均匀，滋润而不透明，隐露青光，有追求类玉的效果，为唐五代越窑之典型器。

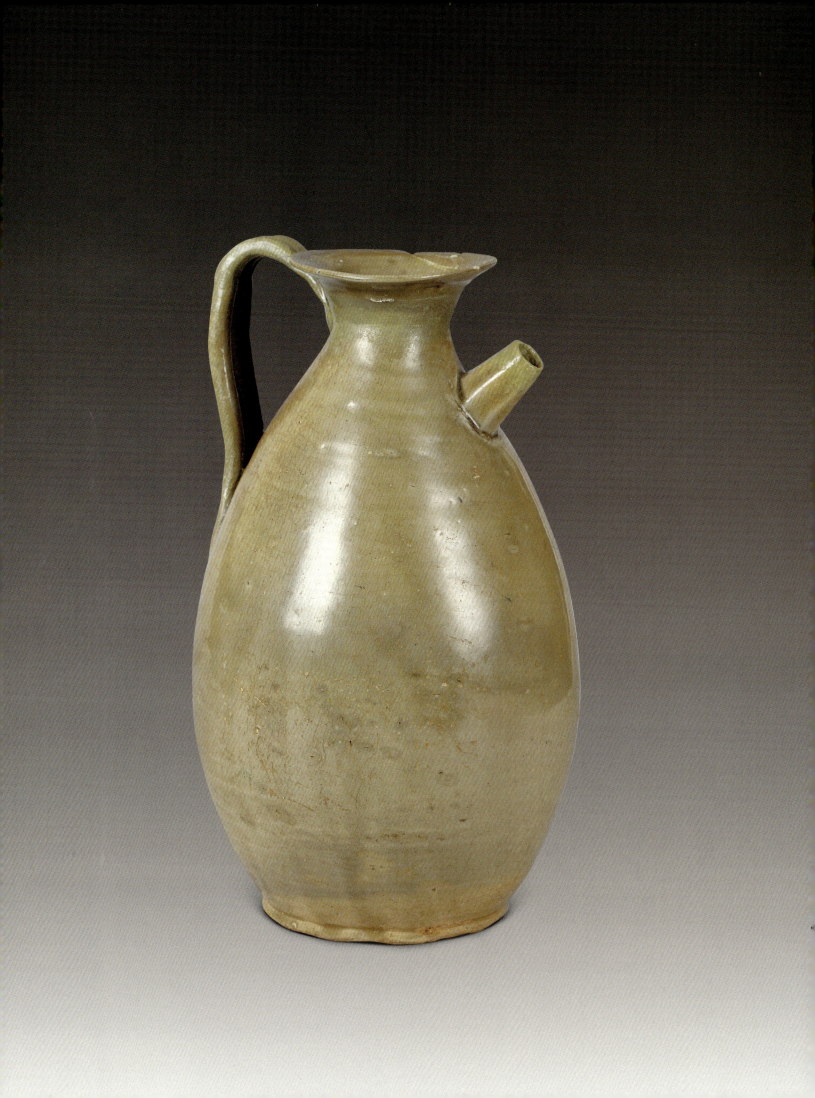

41　绿釉璎珞纹贴花执壶

唐代（618～907年）

高 18.2 厘米

Green Glazed Ewer with Appliqué

Tang Dynasty,（618～907）

H. 18.2cm

壶呈六瓣瓜棱形，器身附短流及贴花把柄，灰白胎，口沿饰弦纹二道。壶身施草绿釉，自上而下，以模印贴花方式贴塑五组宝相花、瓜型花卉纹，均与佛教纹饰有关。壶底心无釉，带釉圈足上有垫烧痕迹。

宝相花又称宝仙花。所谓宝相是佛教徒对佛的尊称。宝相花是圣洁、美丽、端庄的理想花型。可见，在佛教装饰艺术的影响下，其植物花卉题材的纹饰渗透到了陶瓷装饰艺术之中。

此器造型优美，装饰华丽，具有唐代金银器造型之特征。是当时上层社会用于敬佛、祭祀等活动之用器，灵气十足。优美的造型，复杂的工艺，令人赞叹古代先贤们巧夺天工的制瓷技术。

42　绿彩龙首角杯

唐代（618～907 年）

口径 7.5 厘米

长 18 厘米

Green Glazed Horn-Shape Cup with Dragon Head

Tang Dynasty,（618～907）

D. 7.5cm

L. 18cm

　　胎呈白色，圆口，杯身为龙首，龙首回头向背部弯曲，卷成杯柄。龙首双目圆睁，目光炯炯，生动自然。颈间浅雕，模印乳钉及线刻羽毛纹，造型精致，形象逼真。

　　此器可能受当时波斯金银器造型的影响而作，器身装饰有绿叶和点状印花，象征吉祥。龙首造型憨态可掬，充满勃勃生机。

三　五代时期的茶具（907～960年）

　　五代时期，北方的邢窑，南方的越窑，形成了"南青北白"的局面。越窑的制瓷工艺更加精湛，胎体轻薄，造型隽美，釉色碧翠，印、刻花并用。许多器皿，特别是与茶、酒文化用途有关的受唐代金银器影响，装饰工艺上呈现粗工套细工的特点，装饰上出现莲瓣纹、人物供养图等与佛教有关的纹饰。邢窑自北朝后期开始生产，初唐得到初步发展，到后唐至五代时工艺成熟。五代邢窑以白瓷著称，邢窑注壶制作规整，胎体洁白，釉层凝厚，光泽莹润，代表了邢窑的最高水平（图43）。五代时期的茶具除白色之外多呈"艾色"，浙江省博物馆陈列的相关器物与艾草接近，而称之为"艾色"。人类将植物之绿色移到茶具上，给人带来的是春天的沁人心脾的气息，自然多娇的知己。如越窑青釉瓜棱提梁壶（图45），器身呈橄榄形，通体施青釉，造型优美。

《韩熙载夜宴图》　五代　顾闳中

III. TEA SETS OF THE FIVE DYNASTIES
(907 AD ~ 960 AD)

During the Five Dynasties, Xin Kiln in northern China and Yue Kiln in southern China formed the situation of "celadon wares in southern China and white porcelains in northern China". With combination of print and engraving, porcelains of Yue Kiln features exquisite craft, light and thin body, excellent shape and green glaze. Many wares, especially tea sets related to tea and wine culture, were affected by gold and silver wares of Tang Dynasty. Combined use of crude and fine workmanship is the feature of decorative crafts, and such Buddhism-related decorations as lotus petal design, pattern of figures making offerings and so on emerged. Starting to go into production since the late Northern Dynasties, Xin Kiln realized primary development in early Tang Dynasty and obtained technical maturity from late Tang Dynasty to the Five Dynasties. Xin Kiln of the Five Dynasties was famous for white porcelain. As the high Pouring pot of Xin Kiln of the Five Dynasties features well shape, pure white body, thick glaze layer and bright and smooth color, representing the highest level of Xin Kiln. (fig.43) Except for white, many tea sets of the Five Dynasties are "absinthe green", and relevant wares displayed in Zhejiang Provincial Museum have the color similar to Asiatic wormwood. People make tea sets by adopting green color of plants, to create refreshing atmosphere of spring as well as natural beauty. For example, the Handled Celadon Pot with Melon Edges of Yue Kiln has olive shape and appealing design, covered with green glaze. (fig.45)

43 邢窑白瓷执壶

五代（907 ~ 960 年）

高 11.8 厘米

Xing Yao White-Glazed Ewer

Five Dynasties,（907 ~ 960）

H. 11.8cm

　　圆口微撇，长颈，阔肩，圆腹，腹下部渐收敛，圈足。腹外部施白釉至近足处。肩部一侧向前伸出乳流，后部曲柄与颈部相连。器底胎质细腻洁白，坚实，修胎工整。器身釉质莹白润泽，积釉处泛湖水绿色，有"类银类雪"之感。此器小型大器，端庄的造型和莹润的釉色烘托出一种凝重素净之美。

　　邢窑从北朝后期开始生产瓷器，到盛唐时工艺成熟，盛唐至晚唐生产达到鼎盛时期。此器器型敦厚，体态丰盈，庄重结合。由于受到波斯金银器影响，从唐穆宗至五代十国，之前那种粗犷雄放的风格完全让位于精巧雅致的风格。

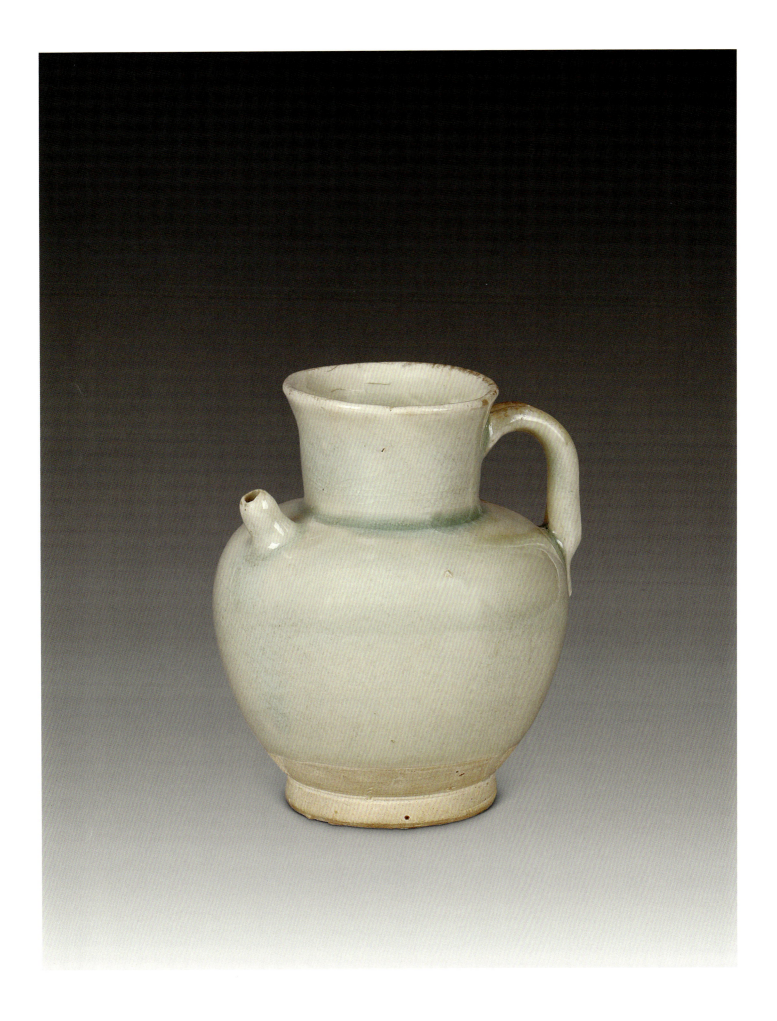

五代（907～960 年）

Five Dynasties,（907～960）

口径 9.6 厘米

D. 9.6cm

盌浅壁，口沿微敞，三个兽形足，柄呈龙爪形。器内施白釉，外部施茶叶末釉，器型古朴。

此器胎体洁白、质细、坚硬。器身内外，白褐两色，相映成趣，兽足与龙爪型柄装饰更添加了其灵动之气。

五代时期是中国佛教，特别是中国禅宗大发展的时期。这件三足盌造型，仿金银器，乃与中国传统文化结合之作。实用而审美，蕴含禅宗之气。

45　越窑青釉瓜棱提梁壶

五代（907～960年）

通高 26.3 厘米

Yue Yao Celadon Glazed Ewer with Handle

Five Dynasties,（907～960）

H. 26.3cm

　　壶呈瓜棱形，圆形钮盖，子母口，溜肩，橄榄形圆腹，圈足，外撇。肩置管状长流，两侧有两系。壶肩部连接腹部饰一弯曲"飘带"状提梁柄，造型生动。

　　五代越窑，开始有了新的风格。执壶的流开始增长，容量较大，腹部做成瓜形，式样较唐代隽美，

着重体现器形优美和青瓷釉色。此器制作精致，通体施青釉，釉色青绿，釉汁莹润，可以色诱感官。反映出先人依恋自然，追寻心理平和的理想观念。

　　（注：北京光华路五号艺术馆藏有一件类似越窑提梁壶。藏品编号：5PS1056，年代定为北宋。）

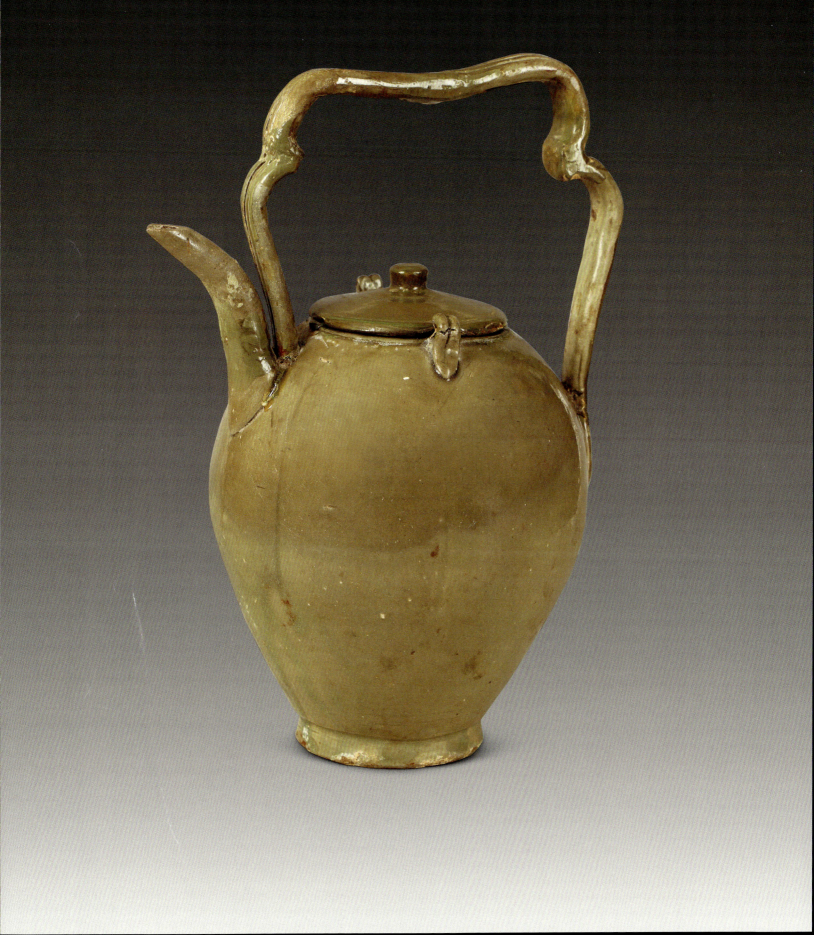

五代（907～960 年）

高 15.2 厘米

Yue Yao Celadon Glazed Ewer with Carved Peony Design

Five Dynasties,（907～960）

H. 15.2cm

　　八瓣鼓腹，直口执壶，圈足，支烧。附多切面流及双股把手。灰白胎上薄施青釉，肩部两侧有双系，饰印刻朱雀和怪兽纹。腹部八瓣开光剔刻牡丹纹饰，肩部饰莲瓣纹。

　　青瓷印刻花工艺自隋代又开始活跃，纹饰生动活泼。五代越窑青瓷承上启下，刻花技法更加成熟。这件青釉刻花壶，腹部刻牡丹纹饰，喻义富贵。肩部印刻朱雀纹（朱雀，"四灵"之一，又名朱鸟，其形象颇似凤凰）。其艺术来源很大程度上受到战国时楚文化的影响。楚人崇尚凤，凤是通天的神鸟，在他们眼里，只有它的引导，人的灵魂才能飞登九天。

　　唐五代是越窑空前繁荣的时期，其釉质青润的瓷器当时被称为"秘色瓷"，其精美者为贡品。这件越窑青釉刻花壶釉色温润优雅，装饰丰富精美，刻线活泼流畅，刀锋犀利，刚劲有力，花卉图案布局工整对称。器身做八瓣开光，器型独特，着力于造型优美，釉色及装饰工艺，是五代时期越窑青瓷中一件难得的精品。

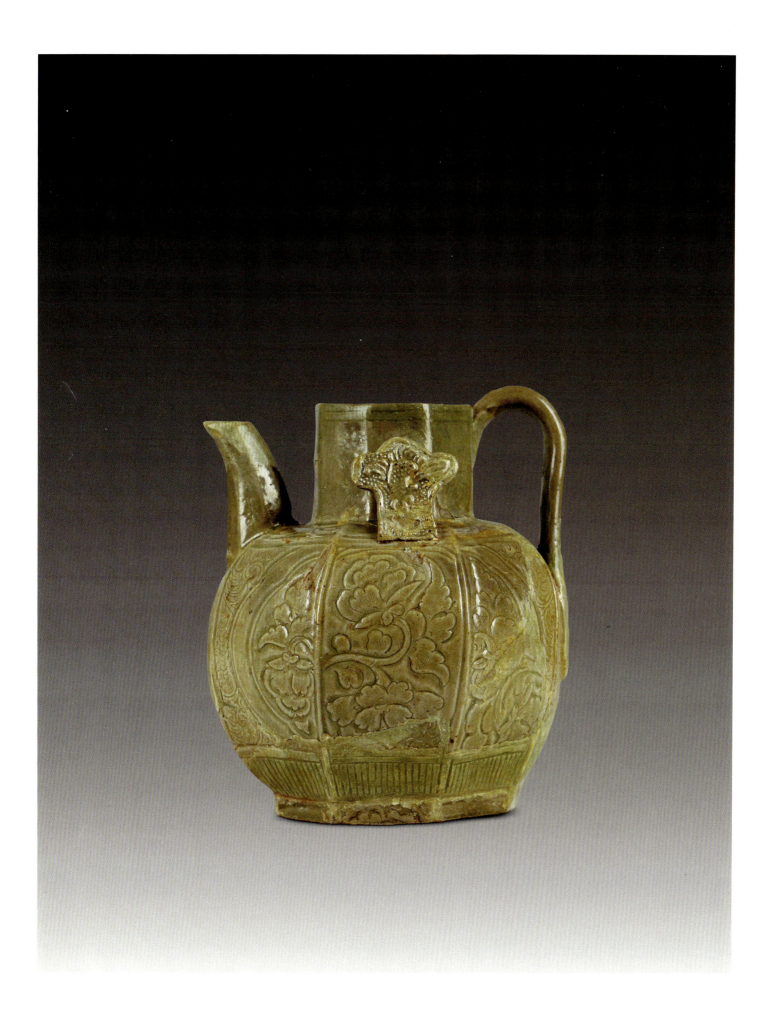

四 辽代时期的茶具（907～1125年）

　　辽代为北方游牧民族所建，辽代陶瓷从器型上分为中原形式和契丹少数民族形式。由于辽宋之间经济、文化交流，契丹人饮茶习惯深受宋人影响，中原形式的茶具在造型上与同时期的五代、北宋同类器皿没有多大区别。辽代白瓷注壶，胎细白色，外施无色透明釉，瓷化程度很高，剔划工艺风格简朴（图47）。契丹少数民族形式的器皿有鸡冠壶、凤首壶等。鸡冠壶是辽代少数民族使用的最具民族特色的器物，其造型是器体下肥上扁，上部有管状流和孔鼻环梁，便于使用和携带（图49）。辽代三彩壶也是依据唐代金银器造型和纹饰创造的，唐、宋中原人酷爱牡丹，辽人受其影响，对牡丹花也情有独钟。辽代陶器上牡丹纹饰适用的很普遍，不仅有花，还有叶，此外，还有芍茶、菊花、莲花等，一挥而就，给人以朴拙粗犷的美感。辽三彩不同于唐三彩，也有别于宋、金三彩。

河北宣化下八里辽墓壁画

IV. TEA SETS OF THE LIAO DYNASTY
(907 AD ~ 1125 AD)

The Liao Dynasty was built by nomadic nationalities of Northern China, Central Plains and Qidan nationality are the base to divide the shapes of porcelains of Liao Dynasty. Due to the economic and cultural exchanges between Liao Dynasty and Song Dynasty, the tea-drinking habit of Qidan people was deeply affected by people of Song Dynasty. The shapes of tea sets of Central Plains had no big difference with that of the Five Dynasties and the Northern Song Dynasty. Covered with transparent glaze, White Pouring Porcelain Pot of Liao Dynasty features white body and simple carving style. (fig.47) The wares of Qidan nationality include Cockscomb-Shaped Pot and Phoenix Head-Shaped Pot, etc.. As ware with the most national characteristics in minority nationalities of Liao Dynasty, Cockscomb-Shaped Pot features plump lower part and flat upper part, tubular spout and ring-shaped handle, convenient for use and carry. (fig.49) Three-colour glazed pottery of Liao Dynasty was also made based on the shape and design of gold and silver wares of Tang Dynasty. Since people living in the Central Plains of Tang and Song Dynasties had passion for peony, people of Liao Dynasty also followed their hobby. Therefore, peony patterns and designs were widely used on potteries of Liao Dynasty. Besides, there were also patterns of herbaceous peony, chrysanthemum and lotus, etc.. These floral and leaf patterns and designs present simple and rugged beauty, so three-colour glazed pottery of Liao Dynasty is different from that of Tang, Song and Jin Dynasties.

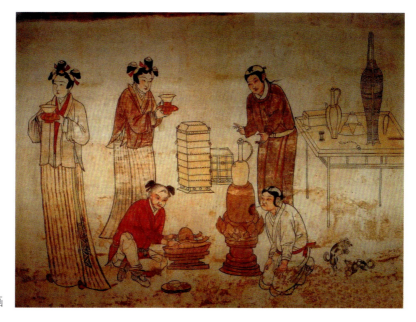

河北宣化辽墓壁画

辽代（907～1125 年）

Liao Dynasty，（907～1125）

高 18.5 厘米

H. 18.5cm

　　壶身斜肩，细颈上饰弦纹，肩部一侧置短流，另一侧与颈部连接，扁平把手模印花纹。腹部下收，刻有蕉叶纹，刻工精细，富立体感。造型秀丽，匀称。此品胎、釉、刻花工艺都学习定窑白瓷，辽金制瓷的工匠，大多来源于中原的磁窑镇和定窑。这种白釉刻花作品在内蒙古林东窑、江官屯窑均有生产。

　　在《大方等大集月藏经》中对芭蕉有如下记载："犹如幻芭蕉，亦如水中月，三界有为法，一切皆如是。"意思是说，芭蕉是没有实心的，众生往往不知世间事，也是如芭蕉一样。此器器身上简朴的蕉叶纹，除了装饰美之外，亦为后人揭示了禅宗深奥的哲理。

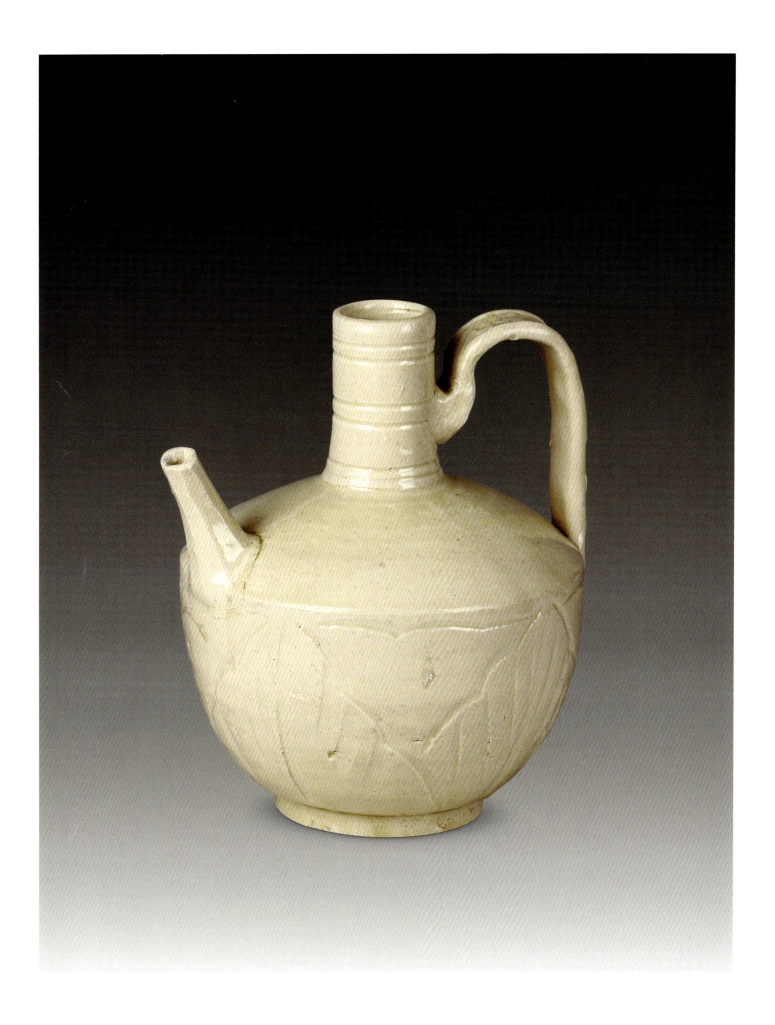

48 绿釉绳纹柄壶

辽代（907 ~ 1125 年）

高 14.8 厘米

Green-Glazed Ewer with Rope Design Handle

Liao Dynasty,（907 ~ 1125）

H. 14.8cm

　　圆肩，细颈，唇口，鼓腹，圈足。肩部一侧置流略弯，另一侧置绳纹把手。胎体轻薄，隐见旋痕，淡红色胎身上遍施鲜明草绿色釉并带有细密开片。

　　辽代陶瓷造型分中原形式和契丹形式两类，单

色釉陶瓷胎质细软，作淡红色。此器釉色单纯，趣味高雅，象征自然的葱翠绿色，给人以美感，契丹人生活习俗的汉民族化，是多民族文化交融的象征。

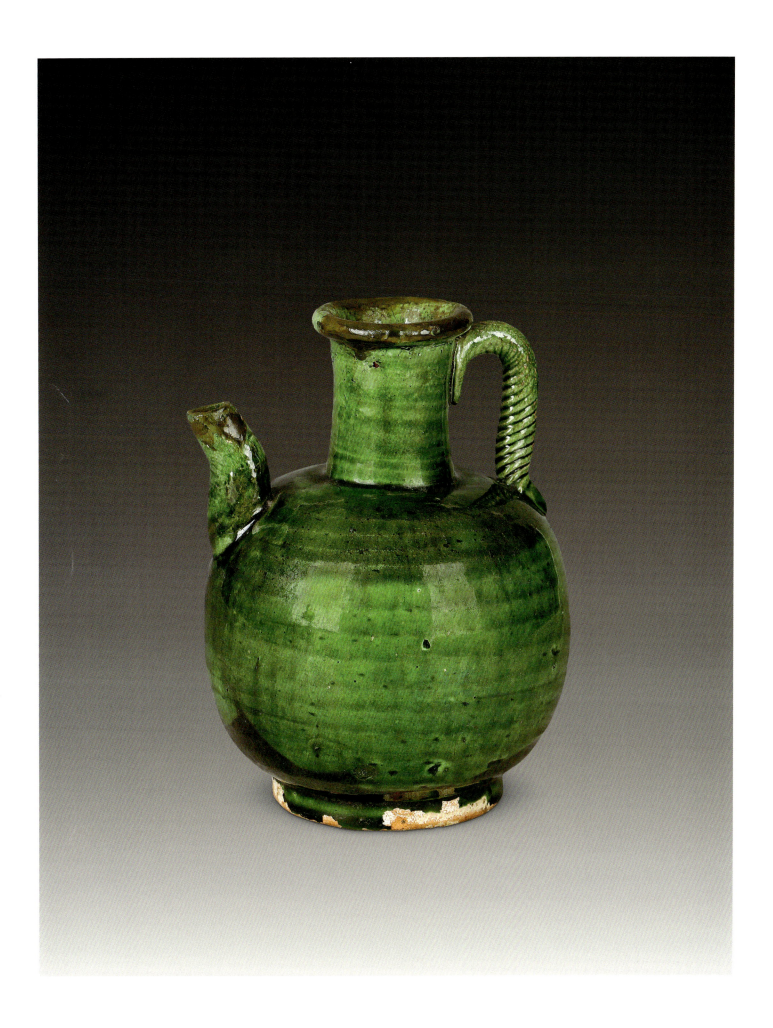

49　绿釉刻花鸡冠壶

辽代（907 ~ 1125 年）

高 23.8 厘米

Green-Glazed Ewer of Cockscomb Design with Carved Flower

Liao Dynasties,（907 ~ 1125）

H. 23.8cm

　　辽代模仿羊皮囊的圆脚平底鸡冠壶，器型扁平，上置管状流及作系绳用的双系，如同鸡冠。淡红色胎身上施草绿色釉，并伴有细密开片，两壁饰以刻划植物图案，周边环以"皮革缝针"纹。

　　辽代契丹族是古代北方鲜卑族的后裔，几个世纪以来，他们一直过着逐水草而居的游牧生活。

　　此件鸡冠壶俗称皮囊壶，为模仿辽代契丹族多游牧生活用具之各种皮囊容器而烧造，以其形似鸡冠而得名，是辽代陶瓷最具个性化的器型。早期壶身较短，下部肥硕，中期以后壶身增高，缝合痕逐渐消失。

传为宋徽宗所作《文会图》　台北故宫博物院藏

五　宋代时期的茶具（960～1279 年）

　　宋代追求的是平易质朴的风尚和禅宗深奥神秘的哲理。在艺术上则爱好幽玄苍古之趣。这种所谓文人的趣味，也必然直接影响到工艺美术领域，反映在宫廷士大夫及上流社会所崇尚和使用的茶、酒器上：讲究器皿的色调自然、单纯，细洁净润，趣味高雅，有韵味。特别是宋代宫廷御用的青、白瓷茶具，釉色淡雅含蓄，在朴素之中隐含着使人心平气静的意蕴，走进更为细腻的官能感受和情感色彩的捕捉之中。

　　宋代是我国制瓷业的又一高峰，宋代瓷器创造了崭新的美学境界，在民窑生产的基础上，出现了为皇室制作御用瓷器的瓷窑："五大名窑"，即汝窑、钧窑、定窑、官窑、哥窑。除此之外，还有龙泉窑的梅子青；耀州窑的剔、刻花；湖田窑的湖水绿；磁州窑的绘画；建阳窑的兔毫；吉州窑的玳瑁釉；壶的形制亦出现了多种变化。宋代茗茶风俗发展至大江南北，皇室贵族，文人雅士开始精心设计在备茶过程中用茶及茶具的礼仪。宋人喜欢的备茶方式是先将茶末置于碗内，以壶倾入沸水，在以茶笔伴匀饮用，这种是唐末已流行的"点茶法"。据文献及图画提供的历史资料，如宋徽宗所作《文会图》，使我们了解在奉茶礼仪中，注壶是最主要的茶具。

　　宋代河南汝州生产的一件青釉注壶，壶流细长，壶身的曲线与流、柄协调一致，腹部为瓜棱形，釉色青中泛翠绿，温润透彻，在汝釉执壶中为罕见之物（图 74）。宋代定窑执壶器型隽美，庄重；釉色白中泛黄，呈牙白色，胎土细腻（图 58）。在陕西的耀州窑器物中，青瓷深受越窑的影响，如耀州窑花瓣口盏（图 52）。

　　此时，河北及山东淄博窑生产以黑釉白线条纹的注壶，在装饰工艺上有异曲同工之处，河北黑釉线条注壶胎质较为细腻（图 93），山东淄博窑黑釉线条壶胎质更为坚质（图 66）。

　　众多茶盏形制，在宋代有所改变，以适应当时饮茶与斗茶之风。此时的耀州窑、定窑、等茶盏脱胎自宋初越窑类型，特点是薄胎，圆锥形，窄圈足。（图 57、59）。另耀州窑生产的一种口沿带白色装饰的黑釉盏，（又称为白履轮）（图 68），也有的学者认为，此器是定窑器的化身。特别一提的是定窑黑釉器中亦有一件黑釉兔毫盏，兔毫如发丝细致有度，是定窑器中之罕见之物，如图 92。"雪拉同"原自 16 世纪法国小说，描写牧羊人雪拉同与牧羊女的爱情故事，其中牧羊人的名字来自他出场时所穿的一身青色衣服，而欧洲人以此来比喻龙泉青瓷为"雪拉同"。引人注目的是，在 2004 年浙江省博物馆首次设专柜陈列冠以"龙泉官窑"名称的青瓷标本，第一次将南宋龙泉黑胎青瓷确定为"龙泉官窑"。如：南宋龙泉官窑青釉盏（图 87）。龙泉官窑中心

《撵茶图》 宋 刘松年 台北故宫博物院藏

《茗园赌市图》 宋 刘松年

窑场在大窑、溪口一带，所烧器物釉色天青，釉面温润淡雅，透明度较低，因多次素烧、施釉，乳浊感较强，开片。宋高宗南下辗转八年之后，方定都杭州，其间南宋宫廷用瓷急缺，为满足生活、祭祀活动的需要，在未设立修内司官窑之前的过渡期内，由处州府监烧贡器供宫廷使用。然而至今，见海内外拍卖中将龙泉官窑当做南宋修内司官窑瓷器拍卖的，亦屡见不鲜。

宋代茶具器表上的纹饰，所描写的人物、山川、花鸟、鱼虫，都表现着深沉的静默，与自然融为一体。茶具上无论是剔花或印花都意味着面向自然的一片空明，它是自然的结构，是青春永驻的灵魂。茶器上的一花、一鸟，让人发现无限可能，成为追求超脱世俗的影射。

V. TEA SETS OF SONG DYNASTY (960 AD ~ 1279 AD)

Plain style and abstruse Zen philosophy were popular in Song Dynasty, while mystery and antiquity dominated art. Such interest of scholars certainly had direct impact on the arts and crafts, which was reflected on the tea and wine wares used by scholar officials and upper class. These people took particular care to the nature, pureness and smoothness of hue as well as elegant taste and lasting appeal. Especially for the celadon and white porcelain tea sets used by palace, they feature plain glazing color and imply tranquil connotation, leading people to fell delicate sensation and emotional color.

Upon the creation of brand-new aesthetic realm, porcelain industry reached to another peak in Song Dynasty. On the basis of folk kilns, kilns producing porcelains for royal family appeared, i.e. "the Five Great kilns"-Ru Kiln, Jun Kiln, Ding Kiln, Guan Kiln and Ge Kiln. Besides, there were plum green glaze of Long Quan Kiln, engraved designs of Yaozhou Kiln, light green glaze of Hutian Kiln, paintings of Cizhou Kiln, design of hare's fur and tortoise-shell glaze of Jizhou Kiln, while shape and structure of pot also varied. As the tea culture developed across the county in Song Dynasty, royal family, nobility and refined scholars started to design etiquettes of tea tasting and tea sets during the preparation of tea. People of Song Dynasty liked to put tea dust into cup and then pour boiling water, mixing evenly with tea whisk before drinking. Such method is called as "infusing tea with boiling water" prevailing in Tang Dynasty. According to historical data recorded in literature and pictures, such as the Picture of Refined Scholars Gathering in Tea Party by Emperor Huizong of Song Dynasty, we can know that pouring pot is the major tea set during the tea serving rite.

Produced in Ruzhou, Henan of Song Dynasty, celadon-glazed pouring pot features long and thin spout, melon-shaped belly, jade green glaze and mild quality, while the curve of pot body is in coordination with spout and handle, so this kind of pot is rare among ewers of Ru Kiln. (fig.74) Ewers of Ding Kiln of Song Dynasty feature graceful and solemn shape, cream white glaze and fine clay. (fig.58)Among the wares of Yaozhou Kiln in Shaanxi, celadon was greatly influenced by Yue Kiln, such as Cup with Petal-Shaped Edge of Yaozhou Kiln. (fig.52)

During this period, in terms of decorative crafts, black glazed pouring pot with white-stripe pattern produced in Hebei is similar to that produced in Zibo Kiln of Shandong. The pouring pot produced in Hebei features exquisite porcelain body, (fig.93)while pot produced in Zibo Kiln features rough porcelain body. (fig.66)

In order to follow the trend of tea drinking and tea contest, shapes of many tea cups changed in Song Dynasty. Tea cups produced in Yaozhou Kiln, Ding Kiln were derived from product types of Yue Kiln in early Song Dynasty, characterized by thin porcelain body, conicalness and narrow ring

foot. (fig.57.59)For the black glazed cup with white-decorated edge of Yaozhou Kiln (also known as Bailvlun), some scholars think it represents the wares of Ding Kiln. (fig.68)Among black glazed wares of Ding Kiln, Black Glazed Cup with Design of Hare's Fur is particularly outstanding. With design of hare's fur as fine and neat as hair, it is rarity among wares of Ding Kiln. (fig.92) "Celadon" came from a French novel of 16th Century which tells the love story about shepherd Celadon and shepherdess, and shepherd was named for the cyan clothing he wore when he appeared on the scene. Therefore, European regard Longquan wares as "celadon" from then on. What's more, when celadon wares titled as "Longquan Royal Kiln" were firstly displayed in Zhejiang Provincial Museum in 2004, the celadon wares made from black clay in Longquan Kiln of the Southern Song Dynasty was firstly tilted as "Longquan Royal Kiln", such as Celadon Glazed Cup of Longquan Royal Kiln of the Southern Song Dynasty. (fig.87)Located in the area of Dayao and Xikou, the main kiln factory of Longquan Royal Kiln produced wares characterized by celeste glaze, plain and elegant surface, low transparency, strong opacification and gracked glaze due to biscuit firing and glazing for many times. Emperor Gaozong of Song Dynasty established the capital in Hangzhou after eight years of going around in Southern China. During the transition period, due to deficiency in porcelains in palace, Chuzhou government supervised the manufacturing of wares used by the palace before Xiuneisi Royal Kiln was set up, so as to meet the personal needs and demands of ritual activities. So far, it is common in domestic and foreign auction to consider porcelains of Longquan Royal Kiln as porcelains of Xiuneisi Royal Kiln of the Southern Song Dynasty.

The designs and patterns on tea wares of Song Dynasty, including figures, mountains, flowers and birds as well as fish and insects, reveal the integration of tranquilness and nature. Tea Set's decordtion and molded and applique decoration represent natural structure and forever-lasting soul, indicating ethereality of nature. You may discover infinite possibilities from the floral and bird patterns on wares, pursing extraordinary above the common.

50　越窑青釉褐彩执壶

北宋（960 ~ 1127 年）

高 26.2 厘米

Yue Yao Celadon-Glazed Ewer With Brown Spot

Northern Song Dynasty,（960 ~ 1127）

H. 26.2cm

　　壶喇叭口，高颈，球腹，矮圈足，细长圆流，扁平弯曲执把，执把上划四道深条纹，颈腹分界处饰凸棱一周。

　　此壶造型规整，器身线条优美、雅致，与常见浑圆凝重的执壶风格迥异，胎釉质地上乘，釉色青中泛黄，滋润薄亮。尤其特殊的是在腹部剔刻牡丹

纹并绘褐彩复莲瓣纹和卷云纹，生动飘逸，气势恢宏。

　　唐代以后，佛教世俗化，牡丹、莲花装饰图案有很多的寓意和丰富的内涵。此器釉色平淡含蓄，制作手法上，采用刻划和点染画法，使器身立体感强。朴素之中隐含着使人心平气静的意蕴。

51 耀州窑褐釉茶盏

北宋（960 ~ 1127 年）

口沿 14.8 厘米

YaoZhou Brown-glazed Tea Bowt

Northern Song Dynasty,（960 ~ 1127）

D. 14.8cm

　　盏呈斗笠形，撇口，矮小圈足。釉为酱色，表面无纹饰，釉色较亮。

　　耀州窑酱釉瓷器是宋代耀州瓷器中出现的一个新品种，为仿宋代漆器之作。

　　每个时代的审美都有不同的标准，每个人的色彩审美感觉也不同。此器釉色为柿红色，宋代茶汤色白，两色相衬互映极为美观。

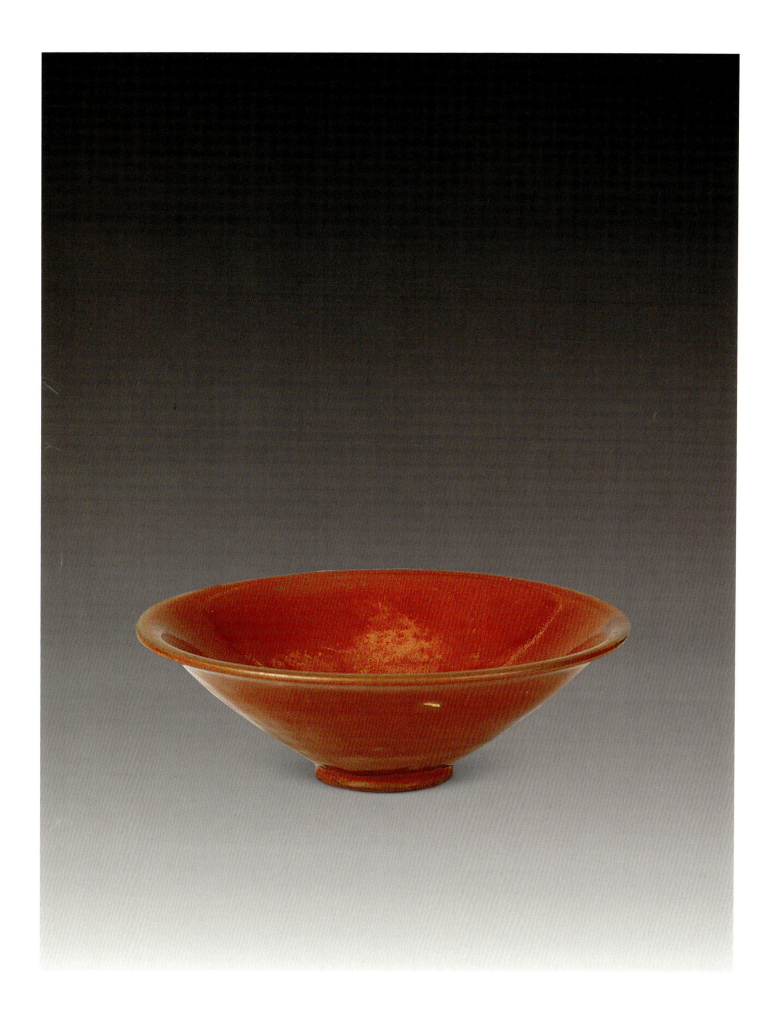

52 耀州窑六曲花瓣口盏

北宋（960 ~ 1127 年）

口径 12.3 厘米

YaoZhou Bowl with Six Petal Side

Northern Song Dynasty,（960 ~ 1127）

H. 12.3cm

　　盏为敞口卷唇，六瓣花型。里外施釉，釉色青翠，器身轻薄，高圈足，足边有姜黄色，足心有釉。

　　耀州窑装饰艺术是吸取了金银器的装饰中的錾刻工艺。六瓣花型的花卉多见君子兰和百合花，寓意吉兆和美好。此品惜残，但器型隽秀，宛如盛开的花朵，轮廓清晰，常开不败，笑傲群芳，其装饰艺术的独特性，体现了宋人对自然美的追求。

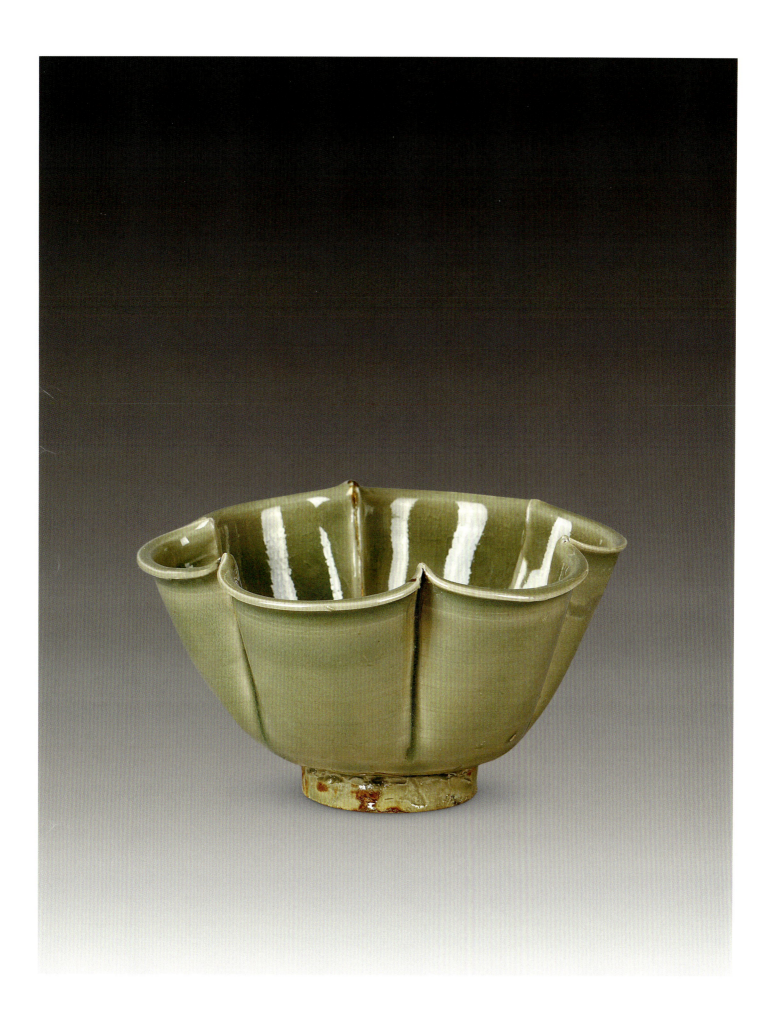

53　定窑白釉执壶

北宋（960 ~ 1127 年）

通高 21.5 厘米

Ding Yao White-Glazed Ewer

Northern Song Dynasty,（960 ~ 1127）

H. 21.5cm

　　敞口微外撇，粗颈，圆肩，腹向下收，肩置微曲流和弧形扁柄与颈相连。

　　圆足切削平整，矮而外侈，颈部有弦纹一道，全器施白釉，薄而泛黄，器型丰满，古朴典雅。定窑被誉为宋代"五大名窑"之一，其窑址位于河北曲阳涧磁村和东、西燕村。定窑创烧于唐、盛于北宋而终于元。

　　宋代由唐代的繁华绚烂过渡而来，在艺术审美和工艺上发展出了宋瓷洁净高华的气质。宋代定窑追求玉质效应，以有玉质感为上品。此器釉水莹润，朴素中富有灵动之气。

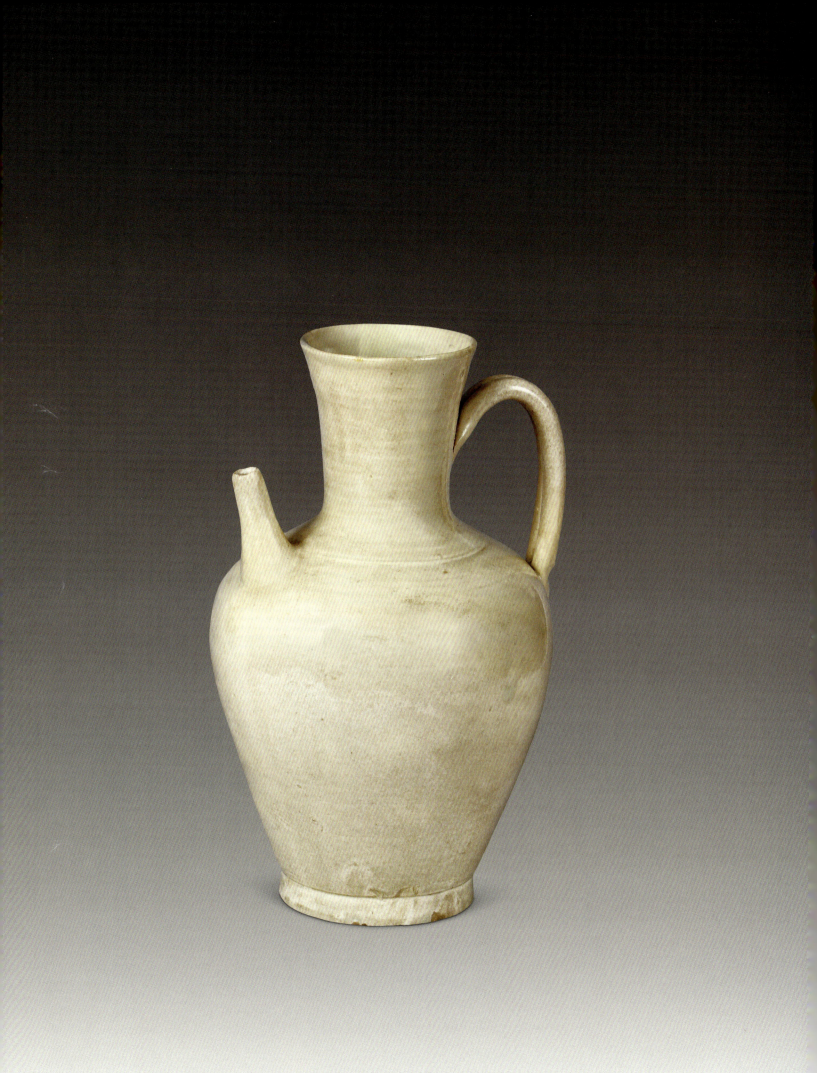

白釉敛口茶盏

北宋（960～1127 年）

直径 8.8 厘米

Tea Bowl with White Glaze

Northern Song Dynasty,（960～1127）

D. 8.8cm

敛口白釉茶盏，薄胎，矮圈足。圈足底部无釉，有墨书"高"字。

这种造型简单的定窑系茶盏，系北宋时期河北磁县窑烧制。

宋代瓷器简约素雅，沉静内敛。本器造型优雅，釉色润亮，胎、釉工艺均具有定窑产品特征，规整而美观。器底墨书，似与当时使用者"物权"有关。

55 越窑刻花青釉执壶

北宋（960 ~ 1127 年）

高 20.8 厘米

Yue Yao Ewer with Carved Peony Design

Northern Song Dynasty,（960 ~ 1127）

H. 20.8cm

越窑青瓷执壶，长颈，喇叭形口，丰肩，六瓣瓜棱，圆形腹，每瓣瓜棱均装饰竖凸线条纹，其间及肩部以细线划团花纹，笔触生动，自然。肩部两侧置弯流和曲柄。胎质灰白，圈足，外撇，周身施橄榄绿釉，器形工整，釉质莹润。

北宋越窑承袭了唐代制品在釉色和装饰工艺上的成就，尤其在针线划花技术上更有发展。此器的装饰技法及刻花风格给人视觉上一种轻松、自然的享受，文雅而宁静。

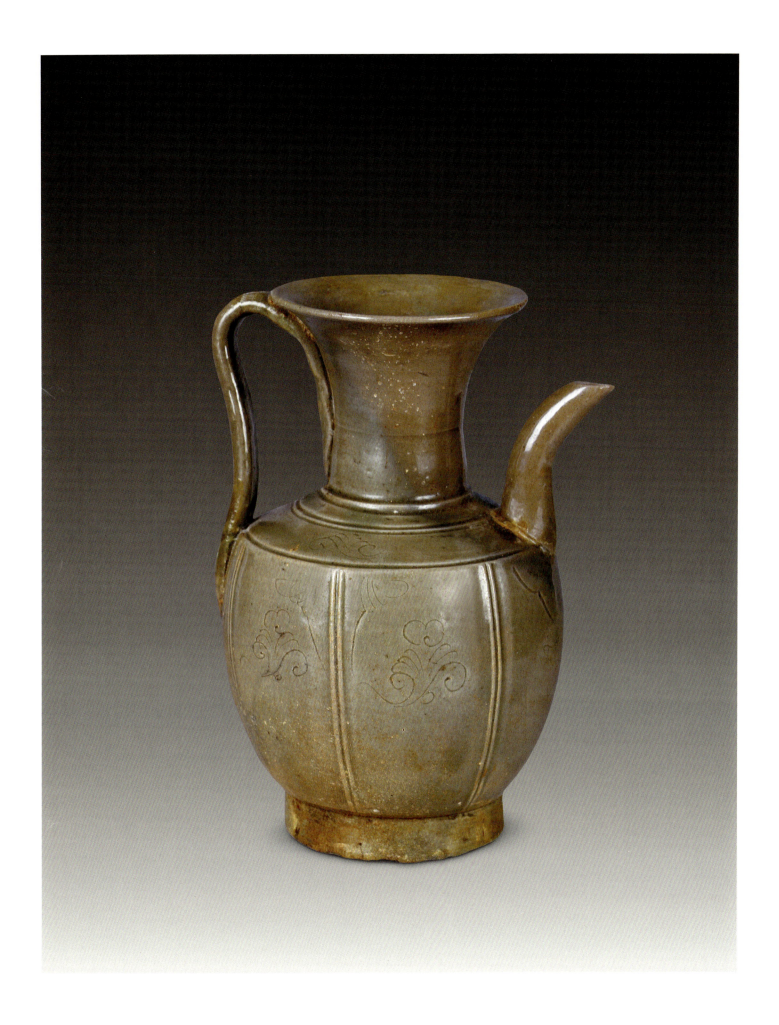

56 越窑青釉"李"字款执壶
YueYao Green-Glazed Ewer With Chacter of "李"

五代或北宋（907 ~ 1127 年）
Five Dynasties Northern Song，（907 ~ 1127）

高 23.5 厘米
H. 25.3cm

　　壶作橄榄状，长颈，喇叭型口，灰色胎身施以橄榄绿釉，矮圈足。壶身以直凹槽划为六瓣，凹槽旁起双棱脊，立体感较强。肩部附尖而弯曲流，两侧饰堆塑开光叶纹双竖耳，开光叶纹中模印"李"字，罕见。似与当时使用者权属有关。

　　唐代晚期至五代，越窑制瓷技术达到了炉火纯青的阶段。北宋早期，越窑继续繁荣发展。

　　此器造型精巧秀丽，釉色青绿、光滑，壶腹部呈六瓣瓜棱形，划花纤细，贴塑装饰，简洁清秀，折射出越窑以釉色和造型取胜的时代风尚。

57　耀州窑青釉斗笠碗

北宋（960 ~ 1127 年）

直径 13.6 厘米

YaoZhou Green-Glazed Conical Bowl

Northern Song Dynasty,（960 ~ 1127）

D. 13.6cm

口沿微敛，小圈足，足有窑渣。釉色青中泛黄，口沿呈酱色，外底足为青釉。碗呈斗笠形，内外壁素面，青色釉面温润，明亮，胎体轻薄。

此器釉色宛美如玉，有"青如天，明如镜"之特征。尤以形如斗笠，器形精巧的工艺特征，反映了宋代社会整体崇尚简约素雅的审美文化价值取向。

58 定窑白釉执壶

北宋（960 ~ 1127 年）

通高 17.5 厘米

Ding Yao White-Glazed Ewer

Northern Song Dynasty,（960 ~ 1127）

H. 17.5cm

短颈，圆肩，腹微向下收，肩置弦纹二道，微曲流，耳型曲柄与颈相连，圆形钮盖。

足底呈圆形，切削平整，矮而外侈。全器施白釉，器型呈圆曲线。胎洁白，细滑，质坚。

定窑在北宋发展为白瓷中的佼佼者，此器通体釉色白中微泛米黄，光亮肥润，造型古朴端庄，均匀纯净，为早期定窑烧制，惜有残。

宋代瓷器追求细洁静润，色调单纯，趣味高雅。此器迎合了宋人所追寻的对神、趣、韵、味的审美习俗。以及"静为依归"，崇尚自然，含蓄，平淡，质朴的观念。

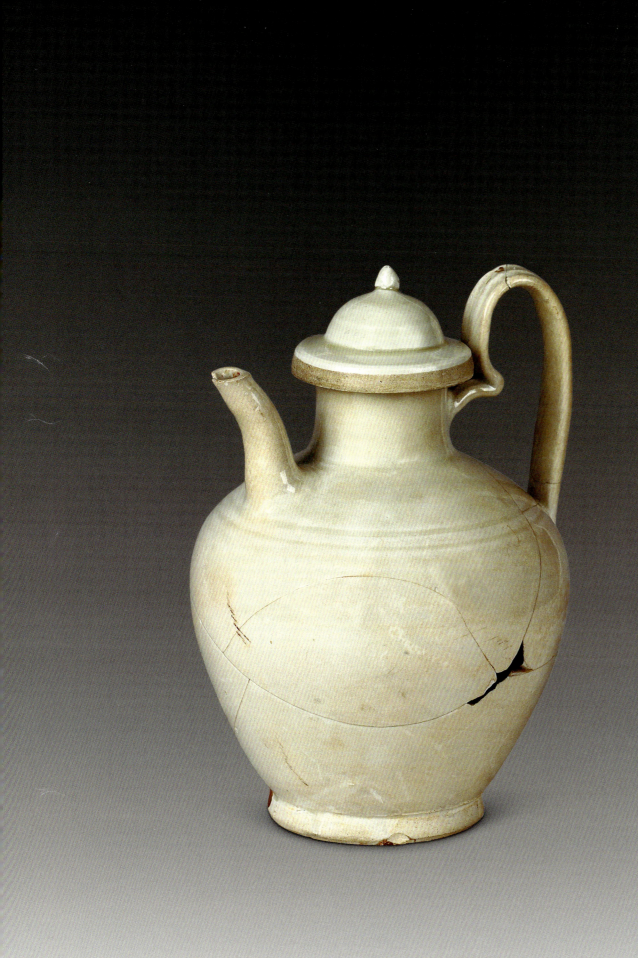

59　定窑刻花斗笠盏

北宋（960～1127年）

直径 14.3 厘米

Ding Yao White-Glazed Conical Bowl

Northern Song Dynasty,（960～1127）

D. 14.3cm

斗笠形盏，小圈足，口沿外撇，无釉。裹足满釉。胎釉细密，胎体轻薄，洁白，微显牙黄色。碗内壁刻莲花纹，花纹布局严谨，线条流畅，技艺娴熟。达到了引人注目的艺术效果。

定窑在北宋中期，釉的色调普遍显得柔和温润，即所谓牙白色。此器内壁用细线刻莲花纹，纹饰最富时代特色。

宋代的莲花纹装饰在文化内涵上产生了很大变化，受佛教世俗化思想的渗透，摆脱了强烈的宗教色彩，世俗气浓厚。莲花亦被称为"花中君子"，洋溢着独特的民族特色。

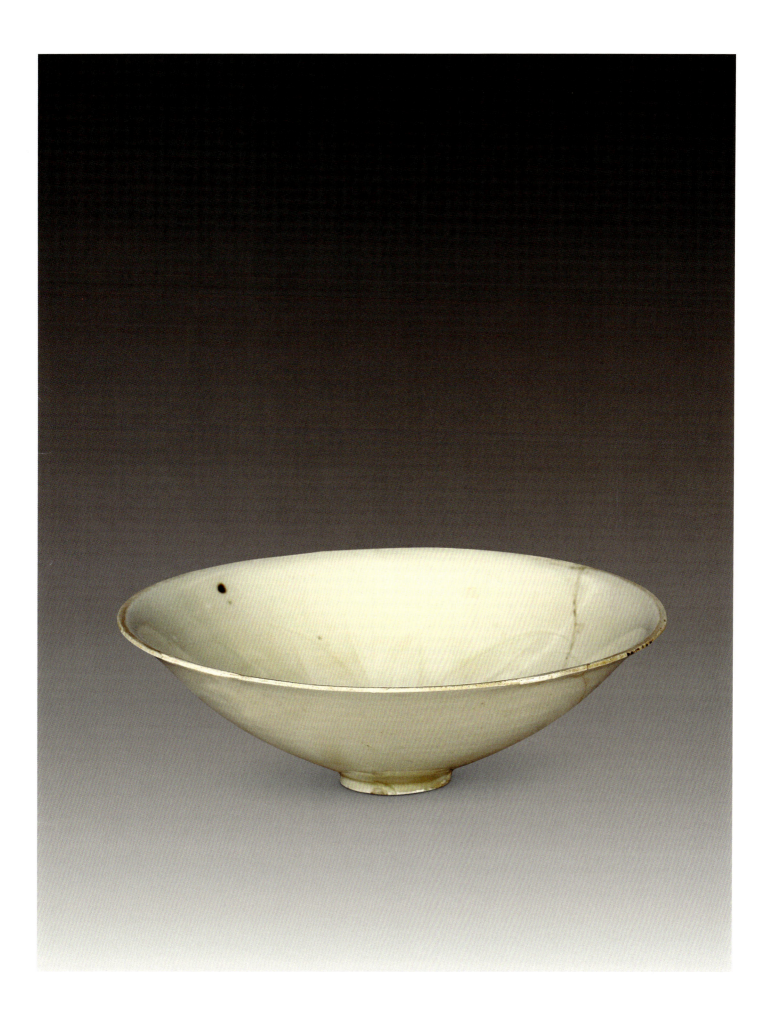

60 耀州窑黑釉执壶

北宋（960 ~ 1127 年）

高 22.2 厘米

YaoZhou Black-Glazed Ewer

Northern Song Dynasty,（960 ~ 1127）

H. 22.2cm

　　黑釉执壶，壶口薄唇，长颈，广肩，圆腹，圈足微外撇。壶肩一侧置有上细下阔弯曲形长流，另一侧置有双条并列相连的单柄把手。壶通体施黑釉，釉层较厚，近足处施褐色釉，圈足露胎呈灰色，底足施褐色釉。

　　宋代耀州窑以烧制青瓷为主流，亦烧制黑釉器。此壶系宋代耀州窑所烧的为数不多的黑釉执壶代表作，器形丰满，古朴优雅。含蓄端庄，简练大方，表现了纯朴的艺术美。

　　宋代茶壶造型大多是壶腹较大，颈细而流长。此壶嘴的出口圆而小，以求出水时呈抛物线形，出水流畅且富含线条之美，又不易"破坏"斗茶时的茶面。

61　耀州窑黑釉盌

北宋（960～1127 年）

口径 12 厘米

盌型呈墩式，敞口，腹部下收，黑釉，圈足，灰白胎，圈底足外撇，器内壁口沿下饰宽弦纹。古朴质拙，釉色乌黑如漆。

黑釉瓷生产最兴盛的阶段是在北宋中晚期至南宋时期。这是因为自宋代开始，饮茶方法已由唐时煎茶法逐渐转变为点茶法，而宋代流行的斗茶之风，又为黑釉茶具的兴盛创造了条件。

此器造型敦厚、端庄，为宋代晚期耀州窑烧制。

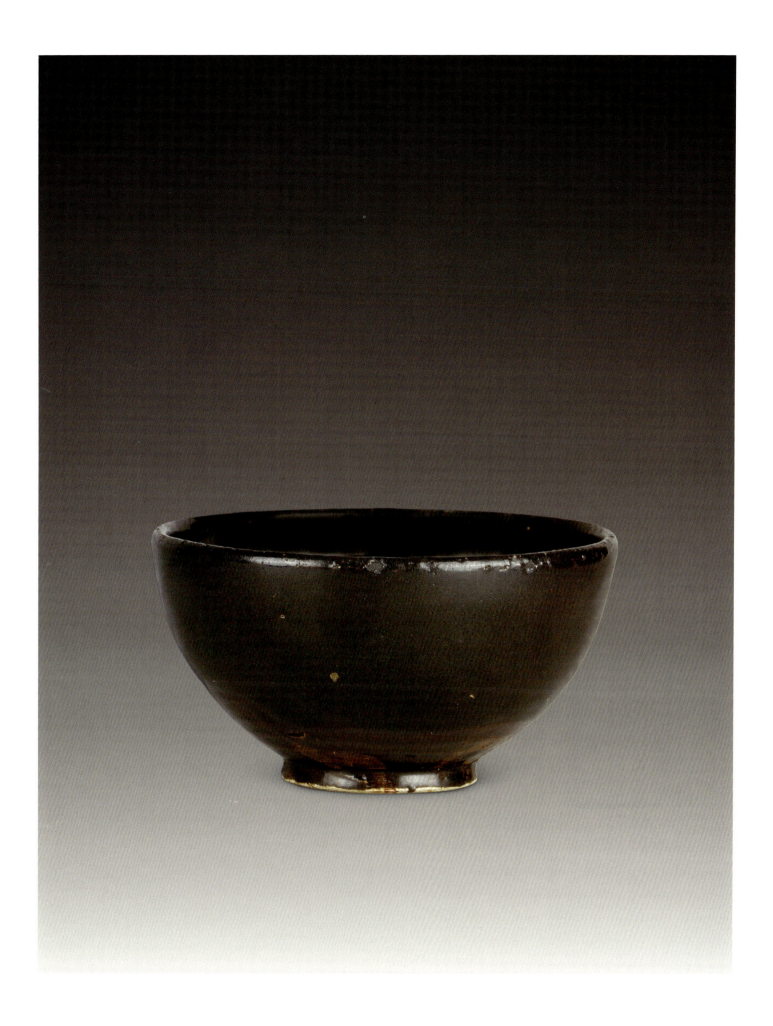

62　油滴天目盌

北宋（960 ~ 1127 年）

直径 19.7 厘米

Black-Glazed Bowl with Oil-Spot

Northern Song Dynasty,（960 ~ 1127）

D. 19.7cm

　　该器呈斗笠形，胎色灰白，胎质坚致细密。撇口，腹部斜收为小圈足，足底斜削，施有酱色护胎釉并有粘沙。釉黑如漆，凝厚莹润，盌内外壁黑釉上均匀泼洒褐黄色斑点，类如金色油滴，迎光而视，犹如在漆黑的苍穹中，满布金光闪闪的星座，与黑釉相间辉映，斑斓绚丽，华贵雍容。宋代黑釉盏多与斗茶习俗相关，此器施釉技法独特，器型硕大，亦为饮茶器，在同类油滴天目盌中所罕见。此作品微伤，但仍不失为宋代艺术之佳作。

　　此器为宋代河南当阳峪窑（李封窑）烧制，当阳峪窑位于河南省焦作市修武县西村乡当阳峪村，是我国宋、金时期北方著名的陶瓷窑口。

　　日本静嘉堂文库美术馆藏有一件建窑油滴天目茶碗，斗笠形。碗口直径亦为 19.7 厘米。（《宋磁》朝日新闻社 1999 年）可作参照。

63 磁州窑黑釉酱彩盌

北宋（960～1127年）

口径 14.7 厘米

CiZhou Black-Glazed Bowl with Brown Spot

Northern Song Dynasty,（960～1127）

D. 14.7cm

盌撇口，宽唇，圈足。内外施黑釉，上施五道褐彩，口沿处彩较宽，至盌心渐收细，俯视碗心如一朵盛开的花卉，静中怒放，神态雅然。釉质细腻，肥润，工艺精致。

黑釉酱彩，可分为酱斑和酱花两类，此器酱彩装饰系用泼洒或指弹工艺，将一种富含铁的酱釉附

着在已施黑釉的器坯上，经高温烧成后，黑釉上即出现条形酱斑。

北宋蔡襄《茶录》里"茶色白，宜黑盏，"说明宋时白色的茶汤，要以色彩浓重的茶盏衬托汤色为宜。

此器胎釉及成型工艺上具有耀州窑产品的特征。

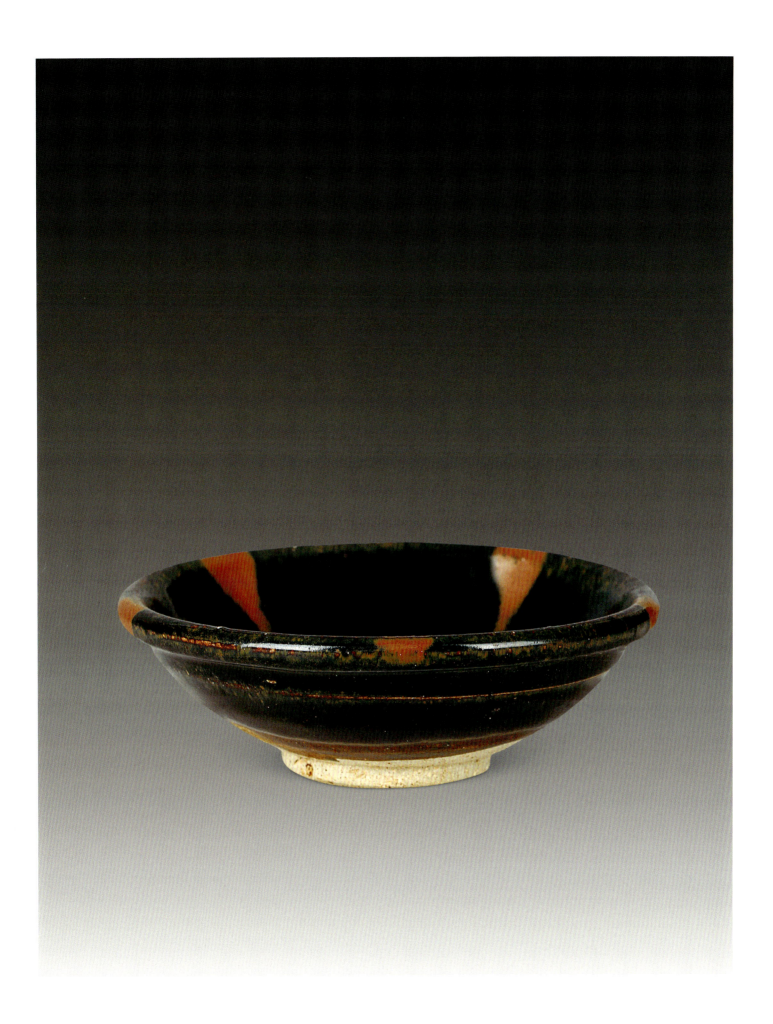

北宋（960 ～ 1127 年）

Northern Song Dynasty,（960 ～ 1127）

直径 15 厘米

D. 15cm

盏呈笠式形，浅壁，口沿外卷。圈足，胎呈灰白色。茶盏内外施褐色釉，器内壁褐红色釉地上饰银蓝色窑变。

窑变即器物在窑内烧成过程中，由于含有多种呈色元素，经氧化或还原作用，出窑后呈现意想不到的釉色效果。

此器形如斗笠，盏内褐红色釉地上饰银蓝色窑变，宛如天空中道道晚霞，色彩绮丽多姿，变化自然，令人陶醉。实为耀州窑系烧制，罕见而珍稀。

北宋（960～1127 年）

口径 14.5 厘米

YaoZhou Black-Glazed Conical Bowl spotted with Brown Color

Northern Song Dynasty,（960～1127）

D. 14.5cm

　　斗笠型，灰白胎。撇口，口沿以下渐内收，圈足。内外施黑釉，内外窑变柿红色釉，两色相熔融，呈菊瓣式花纹，韵味别具。柿色釉属酱色釉一种，是以铁为着色剂的高温釉，由于含铁量的不同和烧造时对温度之控制不一所致。本器外形优美，黑褐对比强烈，形象生动，为耀州窑烧制。

　　窑变釉也是一种艺术釉，变化多样，色彩丰富。此器内壁窑变出一朵盛开的菊花，呈柿红色，色彩斑斓，奇幻美妙，体现了先人精神境界中对"天然之美"的追求。

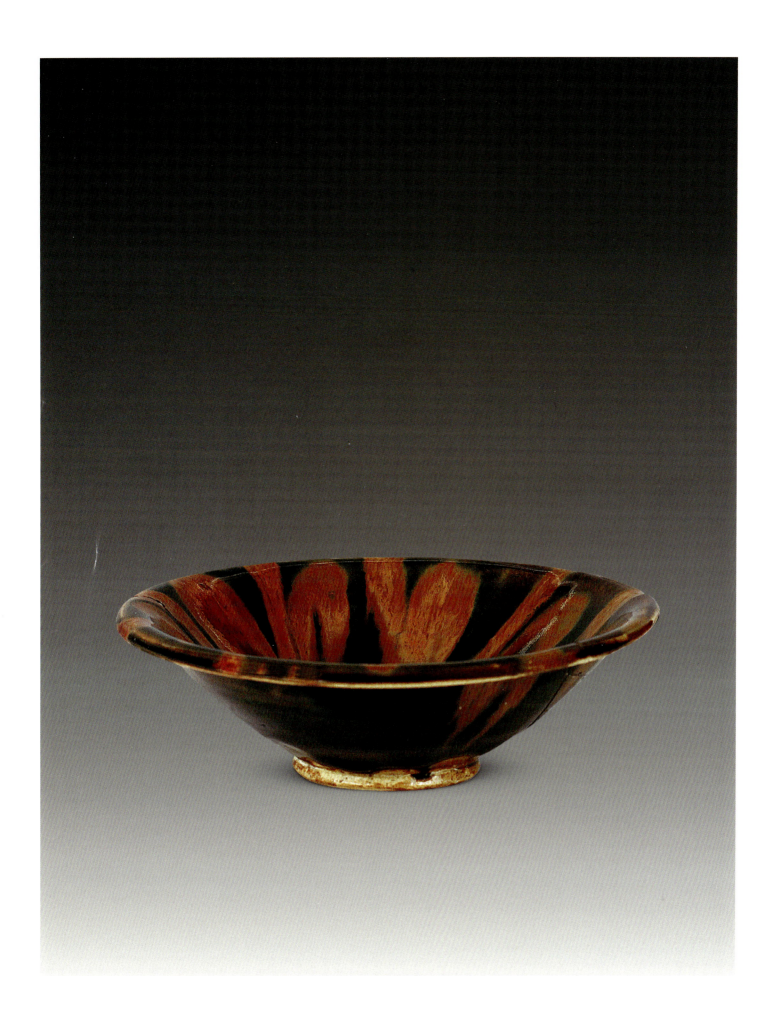

66 黑釉花系棱线条壶

北宋（960 ～ 1127 年）

高 15 厘米

Black-Glazed Bowl with Line Drawing Design

Northern Song Dynasty,（960 ～ 1127）

H. 15cm

撇口呈喇叭形，圆腹，浅圈足。在肩部置曲流，柄连接于颈。壶施黑釉，近足处露胎，釉面莹润光亮，胎体灰白致密。肩部两侧各置一花叶形系，连接于颈部，显出生机勃勃。瓷工以堆线手法在腹部装饰六组金黄色竖凸泥条，立体感极强，宛如树木的枝干深深扎根于沃土之中。

淄博窑位于山东淄博，亦称"博山窑"。唐代盛烧黑釉瓷，宋、金时烧制黑釉白线纹器，为具有特色的品种之一。此器为山东淄博窑制品。

这件黑釉线条壶釉质晶莹滋润，色黑如漆。五线一组的凸泥条装饰排列有序，疏密有致，浑圆有力。这种"出筋"的装饰手法，使壶体表面上的厚釉与出筋处的露白，产生了色差变化和棱角转折的视觉感，打破了臃肿呆板的审美格局，使之达到了和谐完美的统一，更具朴拙之美。

67　耀州窑黑釉盏托

北宋（960～1127年）

口径 12.3 厘米

高 6.8 厘米

YaoZhou Black-Glazed Stand of Cup

Northern Song Dynasty,（960～1127）

D. 12.3cm

H. 6.8cm

盏托敞口，中间盏座凸起，高足外撇，盏托及盏座施黑釉。胎质灰白，底足内满釉。

此器为耀州窑烧造，在宋代时称台盏，宋元时由盏与盏托组成的台盏兼作茶具与酒具，不仅美观而且有保温作用。当时在汝、官、定、钧、龙泉及景德镇青白瓷等窑均有生产，但完整器十分罕见。

此器如黑色髹漆制品，色泽动人，线条流畅，器型隽美。高雅之中蕴含着美妙动人韵律，是北宋时期耀州窑生产的饮茶用具，较为罕见。

耀州窑黑釉白沿盏

北宋（960～1127年）

口径 13.9 厘米

敞口，以下渐收。口一周施白釉，以下施黑釉。因黑白釉分界，日本称此种盏为"白覆轮"。白釉带成型工艺复杂，这种黑白相间的器物在宋代较为流行，它打破了单一釉色，用两种黑白分明色彩釉作装饰，别具一格。本品外形秀丽，黑釉莹润，黑白釉分界整齐，反差强烈，曲高和寡。精致，胎薄，质坚，为典型北宋耀州窑黑釉上乘之作，弥足珍贵。

目前发现烧黑釉白沿盏的瓷窑有登封窑、当阳峪窑、定窑、磁州窑、介休窑等。南方窑场也有烧制，但白釉不如北方窑的白。黑釉瓷器在宋代得到普遍发展，似和漆器的普遍应用不可分，部分黑釉瓷显然是仿漆器而作。黑釉白边即仿银扣漆器。

宋代的复古思潮和哲学思想，为这件黑釉白沿盏所蕴含的一种圆满、高贵的艺术风格奠定了理念基础。

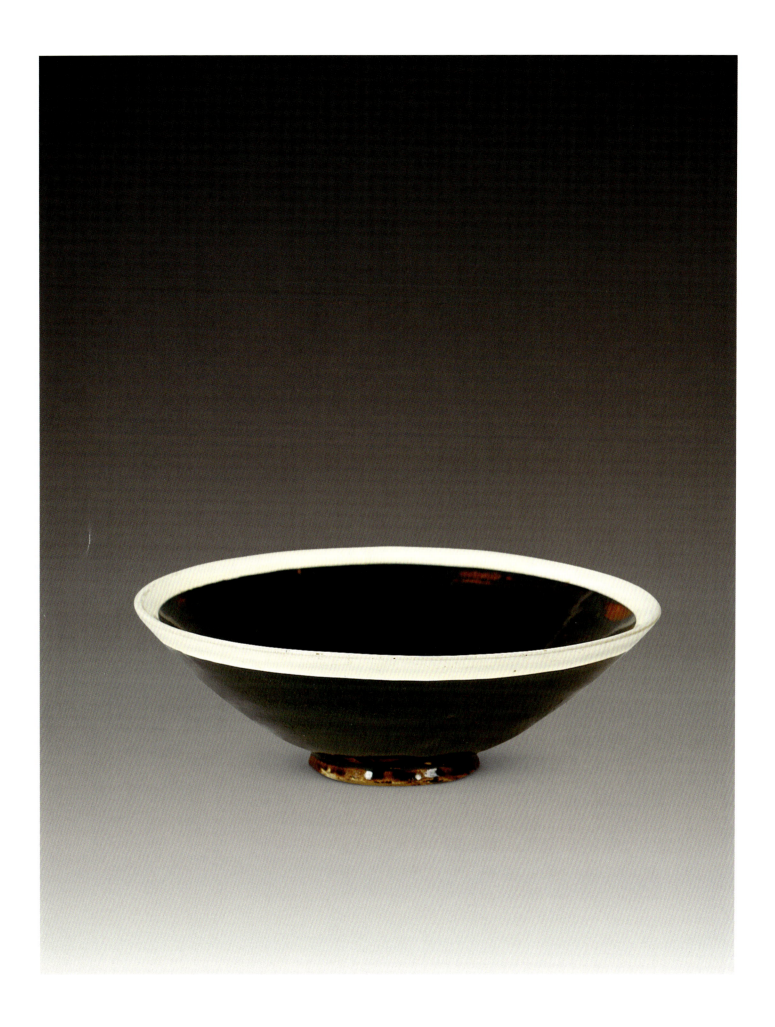

69　当阳峪窑绞胎壶

北宋（960 ～ 1127 年）

高 12 厘米

Marbled Ewer of DangYang Kiln

Northern Song Dynasty,（960 ～ 1127）

H. 12cm

壶鼓腹，直颈，丰肩，圈足，灰白胎。肩一侧置一圆形曲流，另一侧置一麻花形柄。颈口部、流、柄施白釉，腹部及底部以褐、白两色胎土烧结，呈羽毛翅状。壶上、下两色相映，色泽协调，典雅秀美，纹路自然，风格独特。

绞胎产品自唐代创烧。在中国古陶瓷史中，绞胎陶瓷占有独特地位，宋代绞胎器用两种以上不同色料胎泥揉绞成大理石、羽毛纹等，成型后上透明釉烧制而成，工艺难度很大。此器为河南修武当阳峪窑烧制。此类绞胎瓷器，尤为时人所重，据说，宋朝人对它的追求已近"癫狂"。

宋人崇尚理学，崇尚自然。绞胎瓷器在线条纹理变幻之间，完成纹样装饰，更蕴含了天地之间自然和循环的深沉哲理。这件绞胎器的羽毛纹装饰技法即源于自然界中的鸠鸟，生动自然，岂止玄妙。造型及线条具有张力，给人充满遐想空间感，从而展示出宋代陶瓷工艺中传统的人文思想。

70　当阳峪窑绞胎白边盏

北宋（960 ~ 1127 年）

口径 8.6 厘米

　　敞口，圈足，白胎，胎体坚实细密，圈足底部有三个支烧痕。口部施白釉，器身通体以白、褐两色泥交替叠擦，再轻糅合，盘卷，切割滚压，纹饰入胎。纹理出有如羽毛状花纹，成型后再施以透明釉。

　　北宋时期，当阳峪窑的绞胎制瓷工艺已十分成熟，此器口沿及足部均施白色釉，腹部内外饰白褐色泥绞成的羽毛纹，色彩交融，纹理变化无穷，出现了亦真亦幻的艺术效果，给人一种梦幻般的感觉。匠人的精心构思，将艺术美在瓷胎装饰上推向极致。

71　当阳峪窑酱釉花口盏

北宋（960～1127年）

直径 12.8 厘米

Brown-Glazed Tea Bowl of Dang Yang Kiln

Northern Song Dynasty，（960～ 1127）

H. 12.8cm

葵花六瓣口形盏，俗称"六出口"。圈足。胎白而细腻。通体施酱色釉，胎壁薄，釉色润泽。

宋代烧造酱釉薄胎撇口器见于定窑、耀州窑、河南当阳峪窑等。

此盏系河南当阳峪窑烧制。

这件酱釉花口盏质地洁白坚实，胎轻体薄，精巧秀美，制作规整。其与定窑生产的"紫定"十分相似，难分伯仲。盏口为六瓣花型，如一朵盛开的百合花，外表净洁，气质高雅。

72 黑釉茶盏

北宋（960 ~ 1127 年）

口径 11.8 厘米

Black-Glazed Tea Bowl

Northern Song Dynasty,（960 ~ 1127）

D. 11.8cm

圆锥形盏，口沿微撇，短小圈足。口沿外部施褐色釉一周，以下施黑色釉，近足处呈褐色，圈足满釉并有粘沙。盏内局部泛褐色兔毫斑，釉面莹润。

黑釉的呈色剂为氧化亚铁，当其含量在 6% 至 8% 左右，烧成后是赤褐色，如果把釉厚度增加到 1.5 毫米左右，而还原火焰又烧得很足够，釉色就呈纯黑，呈发出美丽的光泽。但如何把釉的成分和温度控制恰当，令酱、黑釉同时出现一件器物上，则十分困难了。

本器见于河南宝丰县清凉寺窑，红、黑对比强烈，釉色肥润、亮泽，布满细小综眼，两色分界如此清楚明显，十分罕有。

宋代饮茶讲究情趣。宋代赵佶在《大观茶论》中有"盏色贵青黑"的主张，其原因与宋代的斗茶有关。

玳瑁釉茶盏

南宋（1127 ～ 1279 年）

口径 15.3 厘米

Hawksbill Turtle Color Glazed Conical Bowl

Southern Song Dynasty, （1127 ～ 1279）

D. 15.3cm

盏呈圆锥形，口沿外卷，圈足呈灰色，修足工艺考究。器身内外褐色釉呈不规则放射状的金黄色窑变，流淌自然，类玳瑁纹样。

玳瑁属海龟科海洋动物，背甲光滑，具褐色和淡黄色相间的花纹。玳瑁釉器的坯体，系用含铁量较少的瓷土做成；生坯挂釉，入窑焙烧后施一次膨胀系数不同的釉，并重烧一次。由于釉层的龟裂，流动，便在黑色中形成玳瑁的斑纹。

南宋四川涂山窑有类似产品。

此器敞口，斜壁小足，具有宋代斗笠盏优美的线条。釉质深沉浑厚，明亮润泽，金黄色的玳瑁斑纹交织混合，自然垂成，千变万化。带给人一种天然美感的享受。

74 河南青瓷执壶

宋（960 ～ 1127 年）

高 20.5 厘米

Olive-Green Glazed Ewer of Henan Kiln

Song Dynasty,（960 ～ 1279）

H. 20.5cm

青瓷壶，长颈，腹部为六瓣瓜棱形，腹部前方斜出一管状流，弯曲修长，后部一侧附扁条形柄，直达颈间相连。壶底为圈足，灰白胎，采用垫饼烧制而成。

宋代壶具以纤细柔美的形制，内在的艺术美感和温润厚泽的釉色成就了其高洁的气质。此器形制优美，釉色温润优雅，传达了那个时代的世风人情，既体现闲散淡远的自然美，又符合中庸、中和等中国传统文化中的儒教思想，给人留下一种唯美的享受。

河南文物考古研究所藏有一件北宋汝窑小口细颈瓶，与此器胎釉及装烧工艺甚为相近。

参阅：河南省文物考古研究所《宝丰清凉寺汝窑址的钻探与试掘》，《文物》，1989 年 11 期，彩页 1，3。

台北故宫博物院《北宋汝窑特展》，2006 年 12 月

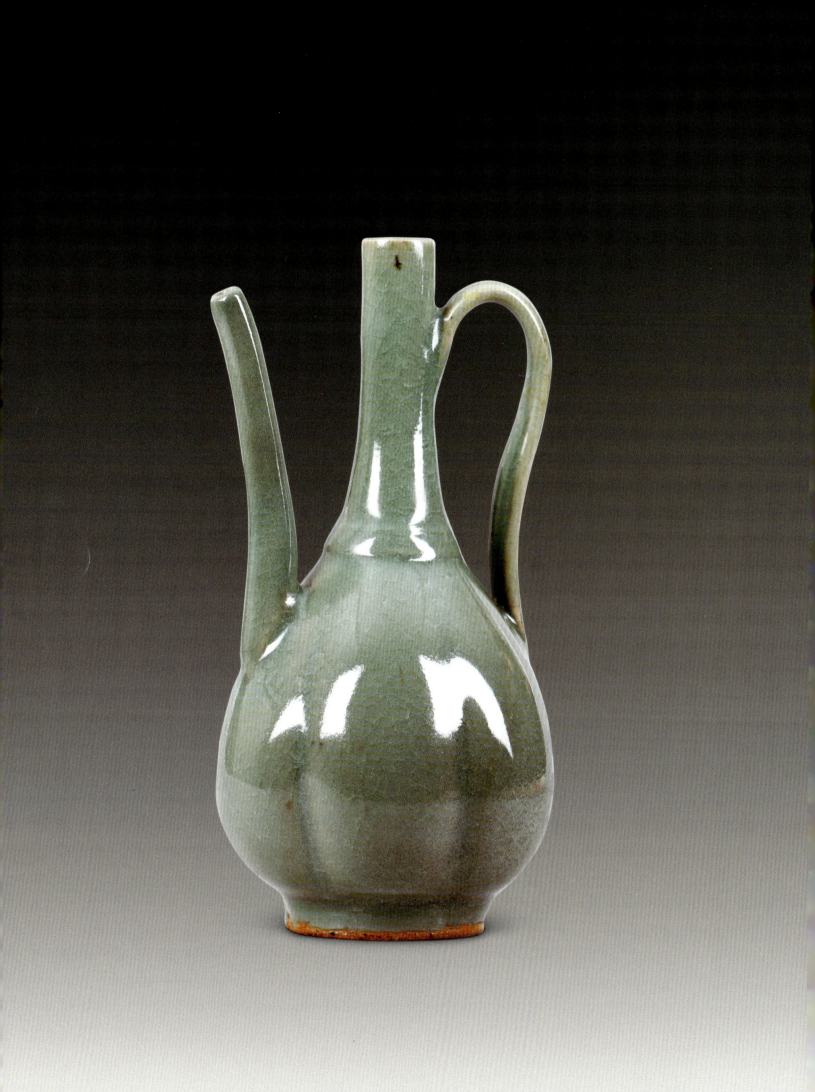

75 影青白釉执壶

南宋（1127 ~ 1279 年）

高 17 厘米

YingQing Porcelain Ewer

Southern Song Dynasty,（1127 ~ 1279）

H. 17cm

　　直颈，平口，丰肩，扁圆形腹，矮圈足，胎体呈白色，胎薄质细，釉色莹润。肩部一侧置一弯曲长流，另一侧置双股弯曲形柄，扁圆顶钮盖，盖壁有两小孔可穿绳带连接于柄。器型典雅，沉稳。

　　影青釉是人们对宋代景德镇烧制具有独特风格瓷器的名称。它的釉色介于青白之间，青中带白，白中泛青，因此被称为影青釉，习称青白瓷。在北宋前期釉面多光素无纹。

　　在宋代青白瓷中，执壶是最富有典型的器型之一。此器造型典雅，釉色青白如玉，是一件反映宋代社会生活风貌的代表性作品。

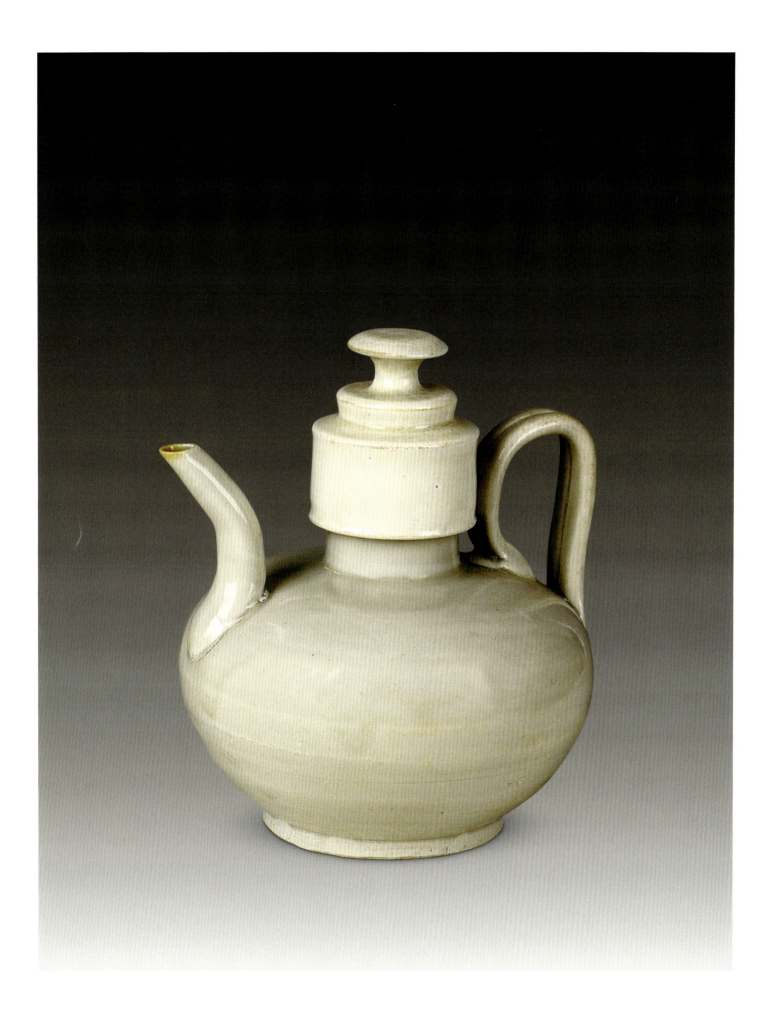

76 白釉印花凤首壶

南宋（1127 ～ 1279 年）

高 22.8 厘米

White Printed Ewer with Phoenix Head Design

Southern Song Dynasty,（1127 ～ 1279）

H. 22.8cm

　　此器口都如凤头，细颈饰弦纹三道，曲柄，溜肩，圆腹。腹下部饰一凸带，下饰瓜棱纹。平底，垫烧。肩部饰模印莲瓣纹，腹部饰印花菊瓣纹，其间为珍珠地纹饰。

　　凤首壶在初唐时开始流行，在 7 世纪到 9 世纪当中，中西交通发达，中国陶瓷在文化艺术上受西亚外来文化影响颇深。这件凤首壶形状及头、肩、腹之间堆贴纹饰即是西亚波斯一带金银器鸟首壶造型风格之演绎，生动地表明瓷器对外来文化的吸收性。

　　宋代凤首壶在广州西村窑遗址有发现，这与宋代广州贸易港对外繁盛的贸易有关。

　　此器造型奇特，富有装饰寓意，还能给人以美好的"有凤来仪"联想。

南宋（1127 ~ 1279 年）

高 7.2 厘米

Southern Song Dynasty,（1127 ~ 1279）

H. 7.2cm

鼓腹，器身上下拼接而成，盖沿平折，顶隆拱呈浅笠状，灰白胎，矮圈足，模印卷草、轮花纹并置有一孔，以系绳之用。两侧置流和柄，腹部模印规则柳条纹，工艺流畅、熟练、形象逼真。

吉州窑创烧于唐代晚期，鼎盛于南宋。此器型制古朴，器身以柳条纹装饰，与器物型制配合得十分协调，更显静中有动，具有生活气息和美感。

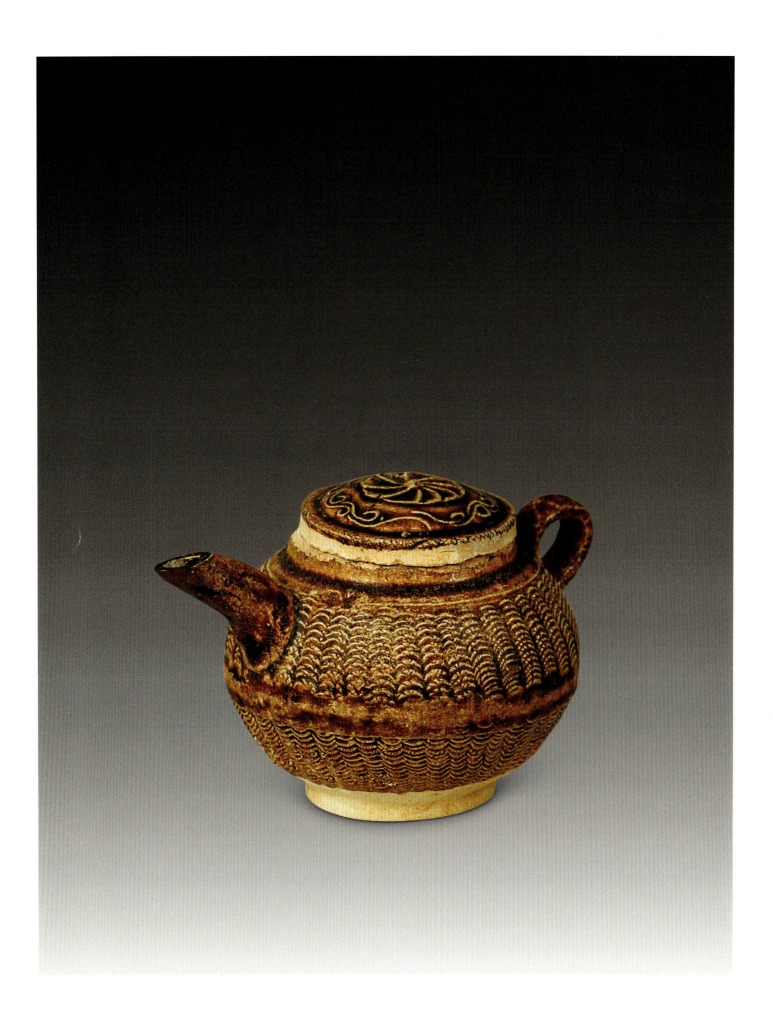

78 吉州窑黑釉彩绘盏

南宋（1127 ~ 1279 年）

口径 11.6 厘米

JiZhou Black Tea Bowl with Colors Painted

Southern Song Dynasty,（1127 ~ 1279）

D. 11.6cm

敞口，内里口沿下约 1 厘米处有凸棱，内外施黑釉，外釉至近足处。圈足内外露胎，胎呈灰白色。吉州窑是宋代著名的民间瓷窑之一，窑址在江西省吉安县永和镇。

此器采用二次施釉工艺，盏内外以浅黄色彩绘折枝梅花，纹饰简单流动，表现效果奇特，近于写意。更为此盏增添了自然，纯朴之美。品茶之余，欣赏盏上的图案，高雅的情趣自在情理之中了。

79 青白釉刻花盏

南宋（1127～1279 年）

口径 12.2 厘米

YingQing Porcelain Bowl with Carved Peony Design

Southern Song Dynasty,（1127 ～ 1279）

D. 12.2cm

　　盏口作六瓣花形，腹部微斜，青白色釉，呈斗笠形，圈足，底露胎，泛火石红并有颗粒黑斑。外壁光素，内壁刻三组花卉图案。碗心饰小月亮底，微凸，胎体轻巧，器型隽美。

　　南宋青白釉瓷刻花，由单线划花向刻划过渡，此器刻花纹样疏朗，刀痕略窄，胎壁轻薄，使整个器物显得亭亭玉立，独冠风采。表现了宋人生活的唯美情趣。

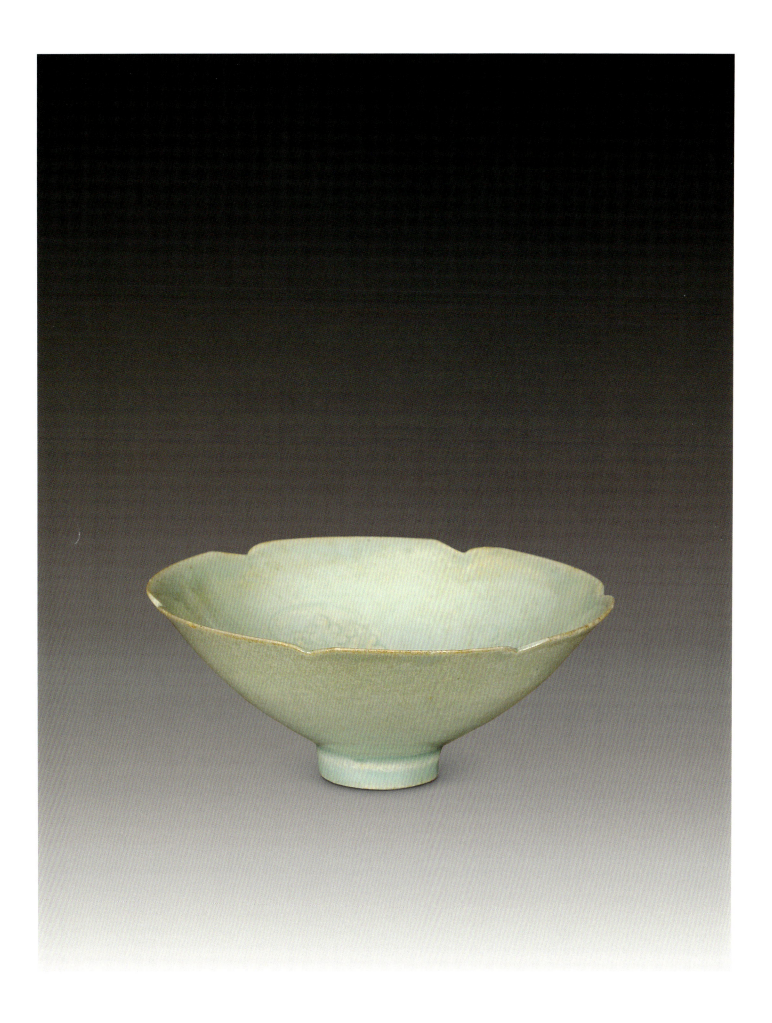

80 青白釉梨形执壶

南宋（1127 ～ 1279 年）

高 10.8 厘米

Yingqing Porcelain Ewer in Pear-Shape

Southern Song Dynasty,（1127 ～ 1279）

H. 10.8cm

壶直口，短颈，器身呈梨形，肩部一侧置宽曲柄，另一侧置一流。壶身施青白釉，釉积处为湖水绿色，腹部刻莲瓣纹，圈足，底无釉，口盖上饰弦纹二道，钮为花瓣形。器形小巧、优美，造型生动，釉色光润，如一朵含苞待放的莲花，一派清新气息。

莲瓣纹是佛教文化影响下流行的纹饰，莲花俗称"佛花"，人有了莲的心境，可禅悟佛性。

这件青白釉梨型执壶器型优美，构思精巧，如冰似玉，洁净高雅，充满了美好的祈福，使人遐想万千，显示出工匠高超熟练的创作技巧和工艺造诣。

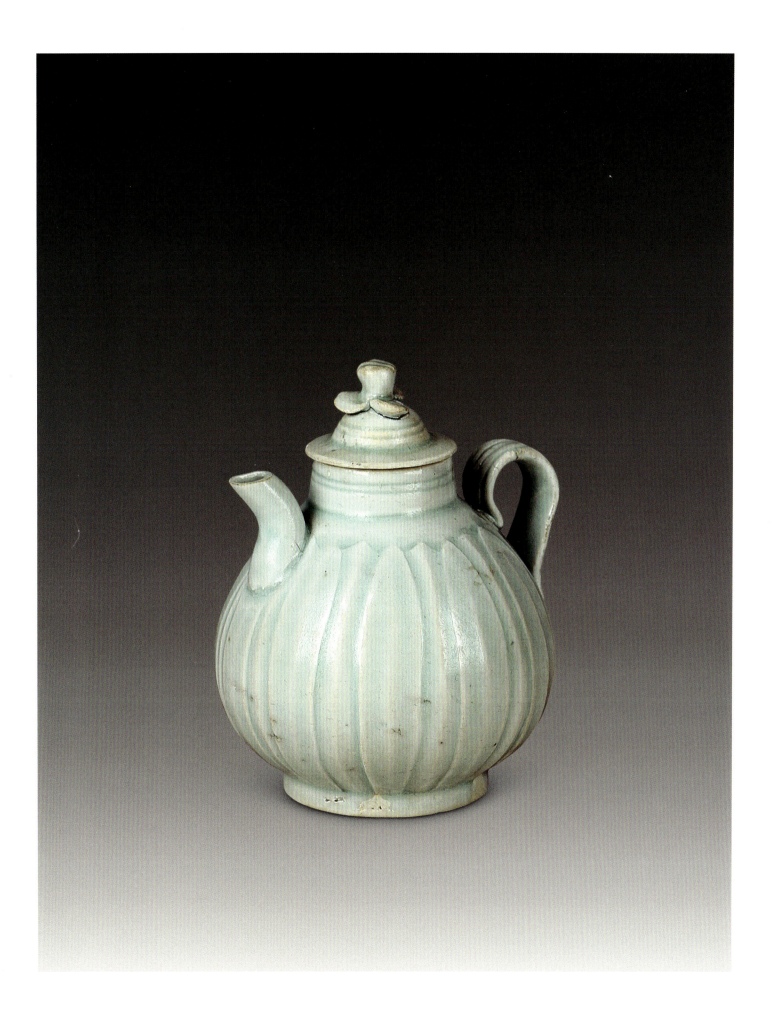

81　龙泉青釉执壶

南宋（1127～1279年）

高 20.8 厘米

LongQuan Celadon-Glazed Ewer

Southern Song Dynasty,（1127～1279）

H. 20.8cm

器身呈玉壶春瓶式，细长颈中部饰弦纹二道，撇口，高曲柄，弯长流，圈足。足内满釉，制作工艺精湛，通体施粉青釉并伴有开片，质感柔和秀美，具有南宋遗风。

龙泉窑发展形成于北宋，兴盛于南宋中晚期。南宋龙泉是青瓷骄子，釉色以粉青和梅子青为代表。

此件青釉执壶器型隽美，亭亭玉立，粉青釉光泽淡雅柔和，宛如上乘之美玉。令人引发美的遐想，获得精神上的愉悦之感。

壶的生命情调在于它的美和实用功能。瓷器型制线条优美，以明丽釉色，动人的弧线，构成匀称的壶体，符合宋人清逸典雅的审美情趣和精神。

82 龙泉窑"河滨遗范"盏

南宋（1127 ~ 1279 年）

口径 14.5 厘米

高 5 厘米

LongQuan Celadon-Glazed Bowl with Character of "He Bin Yi Fan"

Southern Song Dynasty,（1127 ~ 1279）

D. 14.5cm

H. 5cm

盏口呈五瓣花形，盏底平坦，小圈足，灰白色胎。胎体厚重，里内外施满青色釉，足内无釉。盏心印阴文"河滨遗范"四字楷书款，内壁划有五道白色花瓣纹为饰。

这种印有"河滨遗范"的铭文盏是龙泉窑特有产品。"河滨"是指山东西南部万福上游的定陶县。传说舜曾在河滨制陶，《史记·五帝本纪》即载有"舜陶河滨，器不苦窳。"

宋代龙泉窑工匠用"河滨遗范"作为吉语，来激发人们的怀古幽情，同时以舜之传人自居，展示自己的制瓷工艺和水平。此器在整体造型和布局上，以精湛的工艺和艺术构思紧密结合，阴阳相应，虚实相生，是文人情趣以瓷器艺术审美为媒介的表达和完美结合。

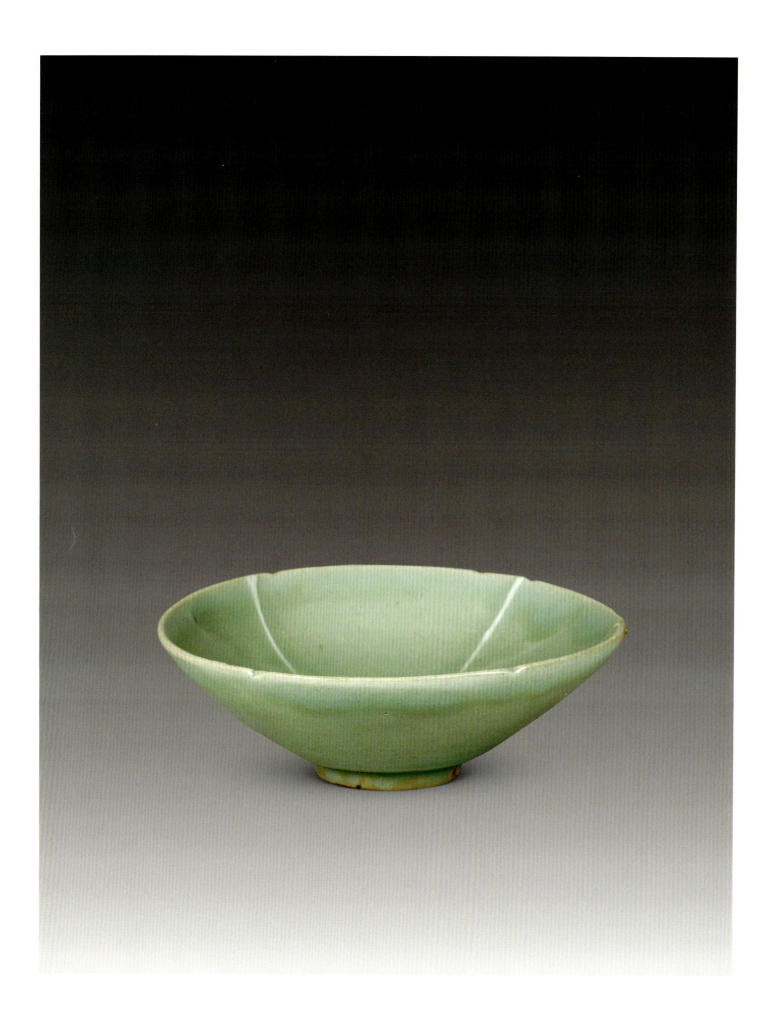

83　龙泉窑六瓣花蕾形壶

南宋（1127 ~ 1279 年）

高 9.8 厘米

LongQuan Celadon-Glazed Ewer Shaped in Flower Petals

Southern Song Dynasty,（1127 ~ 1279）

H. 9.8cm

　　花蕾形壶，直口附宝珠形钮盖，六瓣器身，灰白胎，小圈足。肩部一侧置流，一侧置耳形柄，橄榄绿色釉，釉质莹润。器型隽秀，圆润而不张扬。

　　南宋龙泉青瓷，一改以往厚重之态，壁薄轻盈，在釉色上改用石灰碱釉，耐高温，黏度大，不易流动。细品味此壶，比例和谐匀称，典雅秀美，形如花蕾，含苞待放。给人视觉上增添美好享受。

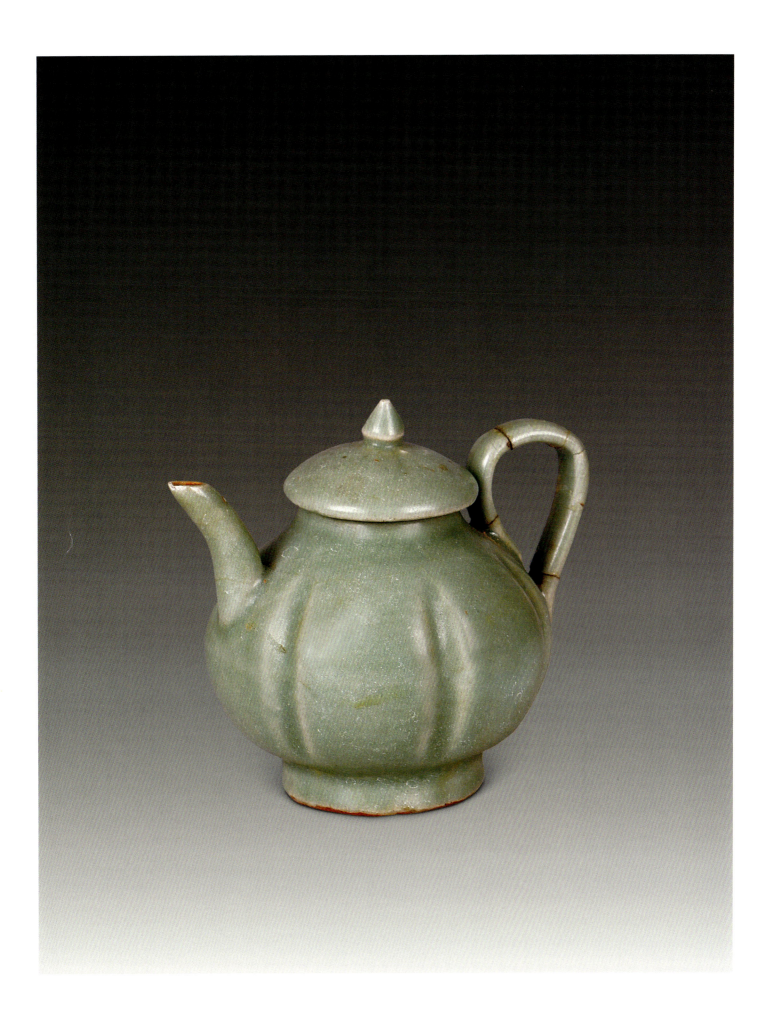

84　龙泉窑青釉莲花杯

南宋（1127 ~ 1279 年）

直径 9.2 厘米

LongQuan Celadon-Glazed Cup in Shape of Lotus Flower

Southern Song Dynasty,（1127 ~ 1279）

L. 9.2cm

圆锥形杯身，撇口，腹下渐收，高圈足内施釉，隐见乳突。灰黑胎，底足平削规整呈深褐色。器身内外施粉青釉，模印莲花瓣纹，釉色乳浊并伴有开片。

宋代的龙泉窑有为数不多的窑口烧黑胎青瓷，这主要跟宋人的摹古好雅之风盛行有关。

从北宋末年到南宋初年，溪口窑一直是具有官窑性质的特殊窑场。

龙泉窑黑胎青瓷较为珍贵稀少。此器薄胎厚釉，造型隽秀，纹片美丽。外壁浮雕仰莲花纹，犹如一朵盛开的莲花。蕴含着意趣高雅的人文气息，这是宋人生活美学的具体表现。

85 龙泉官窑青釉壶

南宋（1127～1279 年）

高 7 厘米

鼓腹壶身，小口，肩部一侧置直流，另一侧置耳形柄。深褐色短宽圈足，底足满釉。灰色胎上敷天青色釉，釉质肥润，釉面伴有大开片。

从北宋末期开始，瓷器的烧制出现了中央官窑与地方官窑并存的特有现象。溪口窑原属民窑，但又不同于一般民窑，到了北宋宣和时期，朝廷根据自己的审美和实用要求，为官窑器物制定了统一的造型、尺寸及样式，下发到中央官窑和地方官窑。于是，龙泉窑又一次为朝廷烧造贡瓷，且产品质量更加精致，精美程度不逊于临安官窑，两者难分伯仲。

这件龙泉官窑青釉壶，简约素雅，敦实拙朴；天青峻美，淡雅柔和；釉质莹润，比德尚玉；型制端庄，不失古雅；体现出儒家思想所推崇的"中和敦厚"的艺术美感，成为宋代文人的最爱。

龙泉官窑青釉把盏

南宋（1127～1279 年）

高 4.2 厘米

直径 12 厘米

LongQuan Celadon-Glazed Bowl With Handle

Southern Song Dynasty,（1127～1279）

L. 12cm

敞口，圆唇，口沿泛紫黑色一周，浅圆腹，圈足，灰黑胎。足内施釉，下凹，足墙呈深褐色。器身一侧平出一如意云头，下设环形柄。内外均施月白色釉，甚为罕见。

黑胎青瓷承载了宋人的审美底蕴。龙泉溪口，小梅窑等烧制黑胎青瓷，薄胎厚釉，釉面伴有大或小的纹片。此器古朴，素雅，高格，俱"紫口铁足"之特点，与南宋修内司官窑特征相近。从龙泉官窑（溪口窑），修内司官窑，郊坛下官窑三个窑场的异同来比较，其产品的形态和质量几乎不分伯仲。

宋代社会复古思想潮流造就了这件青釉把盏青色淡雅，简练大方，以黑胎青瓷模仿青铜礼器的造型。集宋代精致典雅和超凡脱俗的美学价值和人文理念于一身，匀称秀美，静谧空灵。釉色犹如青玉，釉汁纯净柔和。见证了古代匠人巧思神技，溢散着赵宋文士儒雅情调。

87　龙泉官窑青釉盏

南宋（1127～1279 年）

口径 8.9 厘米

LongQuan Royae Celadon-Glazed Bowl

Northern Song Dynasty,（1127～1279）

L. 8.9cm

　　敞口，弧腹，圈足，薄胎，通体施粉青釉，肥厚且优美并伴有冰裂纹状开片，开片色黑且深峻，与淡淡的青色釉互相映衬，相得益彰，极具审美。口、足处露胎呈深褐色，紫口铁足，造型秀美。

　　南宋是我国茶文化发展的鼎盛时期，龙泉官窑和南宋官窑都有追求开片纹的风尚。龙泉官窑器物的开片纹理自然，纵横有致，釉质不透明，体现出自然天成的古雅之趣，寄托着东方艺术审美的禅意。

　　这件龙泉官窑青釉盏为龙泉溪口窑所烧，器型匀称，釉色宜人，若水映晴空之色，澄澈莹润，隐透丹霞，不失温煦。片纹自然，浓淡不一。在高雅中又蕴含美妙动人之感。此品极少传世，存世精品更为稀少，她凝聚和积淀着当年使用和赏玩这件雅器的上流社会阶层的情感态度和审美旨趣。

88 青白釉印花壶

南宋（1127～1279 年）

高 8 厘米

White-Glazed Ewer with Carved Flowers

Southern Song Dynasty,（1127～1279）

H. 8cm

壶身圆腹，矮圈足。在肩部一侧置弧形长流，另一侧柄连接于肩、腹之间。器身中间印莲花装饰纹，下饰覆莲纹。盖亦饰以莲花。

古人以釉色的"青"及纹饰的"莲"相符，寓意"清廉"。与后世青花绘莲，乃异曲同工。

宋代青白釉青中带白，白中闪青，胎薄质佳。北宋初期影青器无纹饰者多，中期流行篦纹等刻花，晚期则尚印花装饰。此器型犹如一粒莲子荷包欲出，匠工手下律动的线条变化，赋予莲花静中翩然。

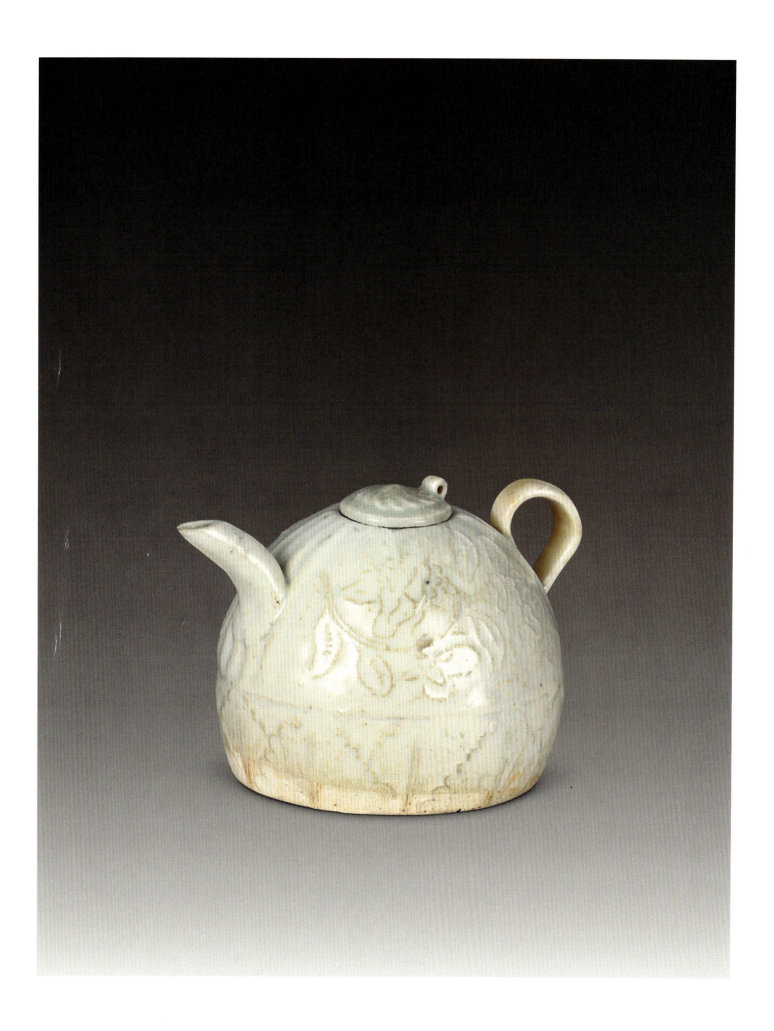

89　建窑兔毫盏

宋（960 ~ 1279 年）

口径 12.3 厘米

JianYao Tea Bowl with "Hare's-Fur"

Song Dynasty,（960 ~ 1279）

L. 12.3cm

　　盏敞口，口下凹槽，俗称"注水线"，瘦底，圈足。内外施釉，口部为酱色，以下渐为黑色，釉面有黑褐相间的细条纹，犹如兔毫。垂釉较重。近足露紫黑色胎呈细颗粒状。建阳窑采用含铁量很高的瓷土，故胎色一般为紫黑色。

　　兔毫盏是宋代建窑最具特色的代表性瓷器之一。北宋晚期因皇室盛行"斗茶"之风，为满足这种特殊需要而兴起。宋代茶具釉色与"茶面"的关系密切。建盏因其黑色釉可以反衬茶汤的白与缘。此件

　　兔毫盏的真正魅力在于盏内向外发射的兔毫纹。当茶汤注入，凝神静观，那些兔毫纹在水中交相辉映，在小小的杯盏中，变换无穷，极为美观。

　　宋代的特殊时代背景，使得社会中文人的理想与现实的差距越来越大。人们为了弥补社会理想破灭而产生的空洞，转而追求个人心灵的安逸与感观上的享受。品茗、斗茶时尚之风正反映了这 ~ 时代的追求。

六　金、元时期的茶具（1115～1368年）

　　金代瓷器沿袭了宋代北方磁州、耀州、钧窑、定窑等产品，在器物造型、釉色及烧造工艺上有些改变。

　　元代，蒙古人入住中原后，一部分陶瓷在型制上仍沿袭前代，但到了元代中后期，青花瓷却骤然发展成熟，成为陶瓷艺术的代表，其原因是蒙古族尚白尚蓝，白地蓝花的青白瓷最能体现这两种颜色时尚。蒙古族上层早期使用贵金属器皿，随着在中原居留渐久，受农耕民族浸染日深，才萌发了对陶瓷的情感。据史料记载：景德镇于元至正十五年设立了专门为朝廷督造瓷器的"浮梁瓷

《斗茶图》　元　赵孟頫

局"，成功烧制了一种釉下彩瓷，青白相映的元代青花瓷。由于元青花的外销为朝廷带来了巨额收入，匠艺精湛，明静典雅，深受海内外上流社会的喜爱。茶具生产也出现了许多新品种及纹饰，如竹菊纹、人物故事图等。如青花花卉纹葵口茶盏（图102），用国产青花料绘缠枝菊纹，淡雅而明快。当时蒙古人喜欢饮用酥油茶、马奶酒，生产一种甜白釉碗，呈折腰形，器内模印向日葵花，花中模印"枢府"二字（图96），多为当时上流社会饮酒或祭祀之用。

　　目前已知的元青花器物上绘画的人物故事多是汉文化历史题材和传统的汉族人物形象，如"昭君出塞"、"百花亭"、"西厢记"、"三顾茅庐"、"萧何月下追韩信"等。这些故事内容将"儒、释、道"精神作为其治国安邦的理念，并融入当时的社会及文化之中。

VI. TEA SETS OF JIN AND YUAN DYNASTIES
(1115 AD ~ 1368 AD)

Although porcelains of Jin Dynasty followed product types of Cizhou Kiln, Yaozhou Kiln, Jun Kiln and Ding Kiln, there were still some changes on shapes, glazing color and firing craft.

After Mongolians came to the Central Plains in Yuan Dynasty, shapes of some porcelains still followed the previous dynasty. However, during the middle and late Yuan Dynasty, blue and white porcelains gradually well developed and became the representative of ceramic art, because blue and white porcelain catered to Mongolians' pleasure since they liked white and blue. In early stage, Upper class of Mongolian used wares made from precious metals. As they lived in the Central Plains for a long time and were greatly influenced by farming culture, they started to generate feeling for porcelain. According to historical records, in Zhizheng 15th year of Yuan Dynasty, "Fuliang Porcelain Bureau" was established in Jingdezhen, supervising porcelain production for royal government, with representative works of underglazed decorative porcelain and blue and white porcelain of Yuan Dynasty. Thanks to exquisite craft and elegant quality, blue and white porcelain of Yuan Dynasty was very popular in upper class home and abroad, so the export of such porcelains generated considerable revenue for royal government. A lot of new types and patterns came into being, such as bamboo and chrysanthemum pattern, pattern of figures' story and so on. For Blue-and-White Tea Cup with Okra-Shaped Edge and Floral Pattern, (fig.102) blue and white painting material was used to paint pattern of entangled branches and chrysanthemum, to show elegance and brightness. Mongolians also produced sweet white glazed bowl with bow shape and sunflower pattern, and two Chinese characters " 枢府 "(Privy Council) were printed in the center of sunflower pattern. (fig.96) As container of buttered tea and kumiss, such bowl was used for drinking or worshiping ceremony in upper class.

Most patterns of figures' story on current white and blue wares of Yuan Dynasty are excerpted from historical themes of Han culture and traditional Han figures, such as "Zhaojun Goes beyond the Great Wall as a Bride", "Baihua Pavilion", "Romance of the Western Chamber", "Liu Bei makes three calls at the thatched cottage" and "Xiao He chases after and retains Han Xi at night", etc.. In these stories, spirit of Confucianism, Buddhism and Taoism was considered as philosophy to administer state affairs and ensure national security, integrating into society and culture of the time.

金（1115～1234 年）

Southern Song Dynasty,（1115～1234）

口径 12 厘米

D. 12cm

茶盏敛口外侈，胎薄矮圈足，灰白胎，施釉不及底。器身施黑釉，盏内壁撒满不规则酱釉斑，在鲜明的黑釉映衬下交相辉映，如鹧鸪羽斑，灿烂无比。

鹧鸪斑釉的记载始见于宋初的《清异录》："闽中造盏，花纹鹧鸪斑，点试茶家珍之"，可见，自宋初以来，鹧鸪斑黑釉盏便深得文人骚客和上层社会的喜爱。这种黑釉茶盏在福建、江西、河北、河南等窑场均有烧造，此器系宋代河南当阳峪窑烧制。

鹧鸪鸟的羽毛为赤紫相间的条纹，此件鹧鸪斑盏是釉装饰的工艺在还原焰气氛中生成。釉面窑变，斑斓夺目，晕晕自然。因烧制条件要求条件高，故成为较稀少的名贵品种。

在古代诗词里，鹧鸪的形象也有特定的内蕴。由于异族入侵，连年征战，人民流离失所。如："江晚正愁余，山深闻鹧鸪"（辛弃疾《菩萨蛮·书江西造口壁》）等，极易勾起旅途艰险的联想和满腔的离愁别绪。

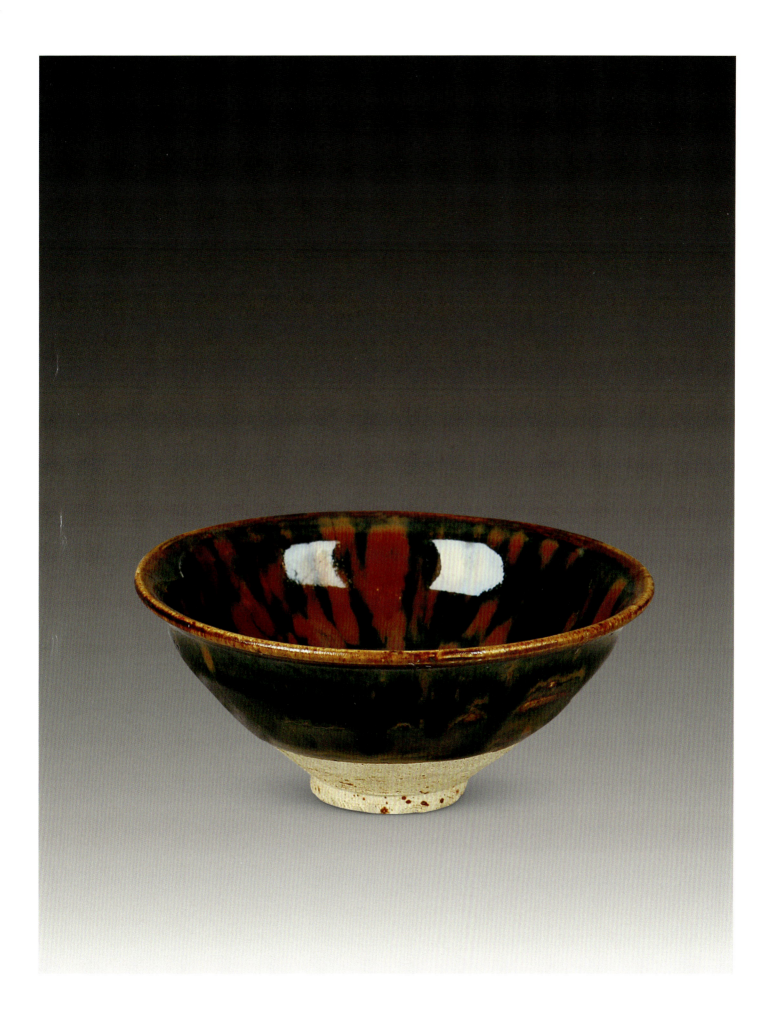

91　磁州窑黑釉白沿兔毫盏

金代（1115 ～ 1234 年）

口径 11.5 厘米

Black-glazed hare's fur bowl White Rim of Cizhou Kiln

Southern Song Dynasty,（1115 ～ 1234）

L. 11.5cm

盏作敞口状，圈足，灰白胎，釉不及底。口沿施白釉一周，以下施黑釉，有细长兔毫纹由碗心向外射出，黑白分界清晰，为磁州窑烧制。

本器造型优美，制作规整，釉面均匀。黑色器身口沿饰以白边，产生了强烈的对比和美感，细长兔毫纹窑变缤纷异常，构成柔和变化的情趣。宋瓷美学风格近于沉静素雅，不仅重视釉色之美，更追求釉的变化和质感之美，为陶瓷美学开辟了一个新的世界。

92　定窑酱釉兔毫盏

金代（1115 ~ 1234 年）

口径 11.3 厘米

DingYao Brown-Glazed Tea Bowl with "Hare's –Fur"

Southern Song Dynasty,（1115 ~ 1234）

L. 11.3cm

　　盏口微敛，深腹，弧形腹壁，圈足，胎体洁白细腻，修胎工整。器物内外为酱色釉，釉上布满细如兔丝的金毫，有如金丝铺盏，潇洒自如，高雅而奢华。

　　宋代定窑除白釉外，还生产黑釉、酱釉等品种，被称为黑定、酱定，是难得的珍品。

　　紫定是北宋和金代定窑瓷器中的褐釉品种，属酱釉瓷。明人曹昭著《格古要论》称"紫定色紫"，所谓紫定的紫色，实际是芝麻酱色而发红色调的颜色。此件酱釉兔毫盏系由定窑中心窑场生产，白胎，质地精细，胎壁很薄，金毫密布，盏内生辉，在当时已是身价不菲。

93 磁州窑线条壶

金代（1115～1234年）

高14.5厘米

CiZhou Black-Glazed Ewer with Line Drawing Design

Jin Dynasty,（1115～1234）

H. 14.5cm

喇叭形口，宽带形把手，短流，通体施黑釉，釉不及底。器腹部呈线条形装饰，此种黑釉堆线装饰多采用"立粉"工艺，出现于12世纪，自金代中期后流行。

磁州窑在今河北磁县观台镇，宋、金时代多用白化妆土技法，并将陶瓷技艺和美术揉融在一起。

此件线条器，采用线条"出筋"的装饰手法，器型隽美，寓意丰富，线条流利，自如奔放。这种装饰和色差变化使壶的器型与精美的釉色达到了和谐完美的统一。

94　磁州窑白釉褐花盌

金代（1115 ～ 1234 年）

口径 9.6 厘米

CiZhou White-Glazed Bowl Printed with Brown

Jin Dynasty,（1115 ～ 1234）

L. 9.6cm

盌口微内敛，深腹，圈足。通体施釉，外壁饰褐彩卷草纹，内壁饰双圈及弦纹，口沿及腹部饰弦纹二道，纹饰线条流畅，质朴自然，拥有鲜明的民间艺术特色。

宋、金时期，磁州窑白地黑花瓷器装饰题材多花卉，山水等。

这件白釉褐花盌器型敦厚，它的装饰技法突破了当时单色釉的局限，吸收了中国传统水墨画和书法艺术的娴熟画艺，充满浓郁的乡土气息，开启了我国瓷器彩绘装饰的新局面，不拘一格的作品令众多艺术大师叹为观止。

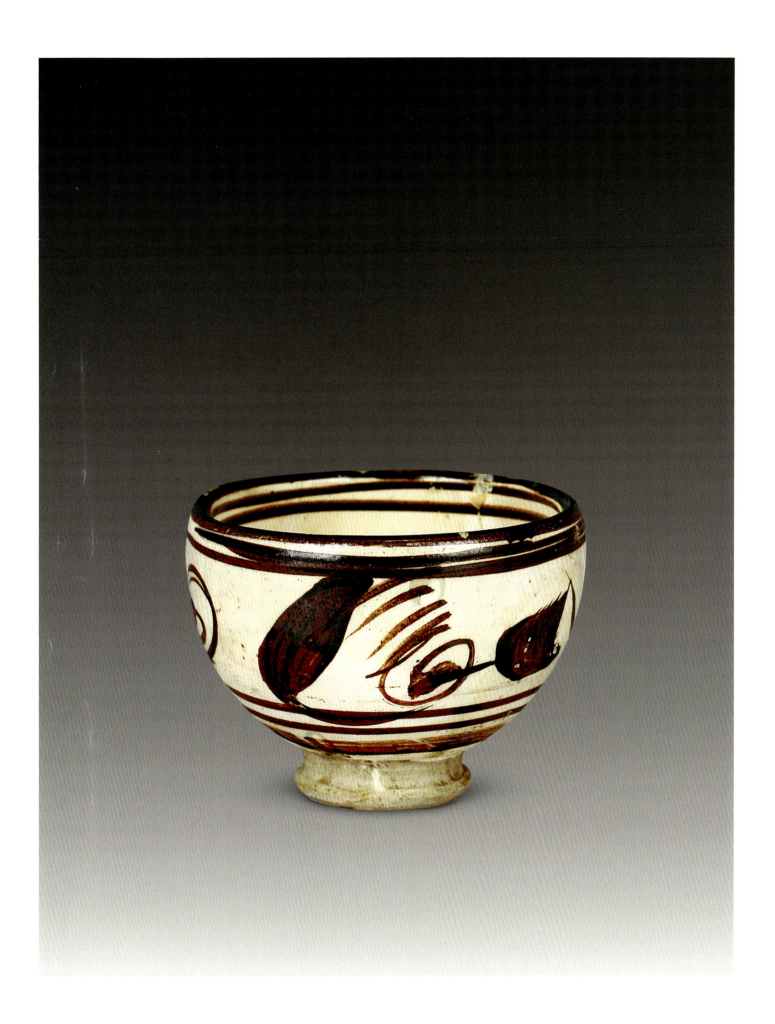

青白釉执壶

元代（1271 ～ 1368 年）

高 14.6 厘米

YingQing Porcelain Ewer

Yuan Dynasty,（1271 ～ 1368）

H. 14.6cm

壶身呈梨形，侈口，口沿微外卷似唇。腹部模印三层纹饰，为花卉，海水纹。壶身一侧为四棱曲柄，另一侧为鸟形流。胎质洁白细腻。

青白瓷是景德镇自宋代以来烧制的一种独特风格的瓷器，具有青白淡雅，明澈莹丽，仿玉逼真，透光见影的特色。

此器釉色白中泛青，晶莹碧透。壶的造型内敛别致。壶流上塑鸟形为饰，体现了人工与天工造化自然和谐的完美艺术风格。

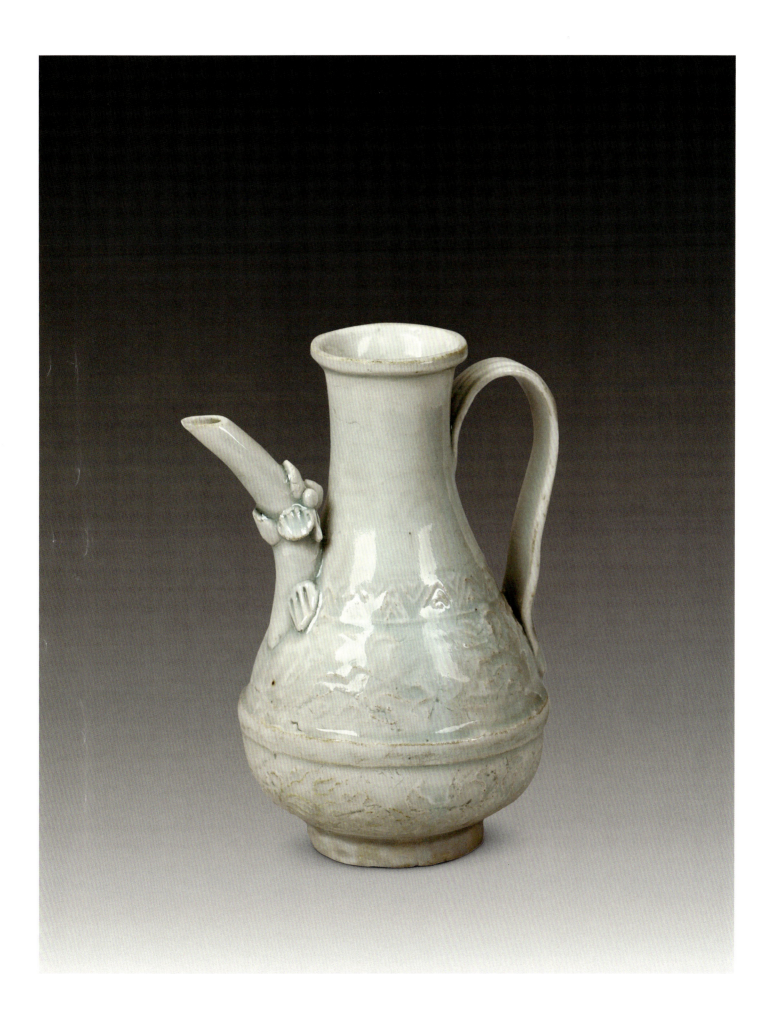

96　卵白釉"枢府"款印花牡丹纹盌

元代（1271～1368年）

口径 14.5 厘米

Egg-White Glazed Bowl with Peony Decorated (Mark of Shu Fu)

Yuan Dynasty,（1271～1368）

L. 14.5cm

折腰，斜壁，敞口，小圈足。内壁模印缠枝牡丹纹，中心两侧有相对"枢府"两字。内壁装饰回纹及仰莲瓣纹，纹样布局严谨。外壁腹部上饰凸起弦纹一道，具有元代枢府瓷"圈足小，足壁厚，削足规整，釉质细腻温润"之特点。

景德镇在元代创烧的卵白釉瓷，又称枢府瓷，是朝廷定烧的一种高档瓷器，在当时极负盛名。据考证景德镇生产枢府釉瓷器是浮梁瓷局管辖下的官窑作坊。

元人尚白。这件卵白釉印花牡丹纹盌色白微青，釉质温润而又不透明，制作规整。内壁模印缠枝牡丹纹。牡丹雍容华丽，是吉祥富贵的象征。历史上元代一些著名学者曾高度评价牡丹花，视牡丹花为富贵之花。皇家亦举办牡丹宴并以牡丹为赏赐之物。此器，将模印牡丹饰以瓷器之上，尽显华美。

97　磁州窑褐彩壶

元代（1271 ～ 1368 年）

高 11 厘米

CiZhou White-Glazed Ewer with Brown Spotted

Yuan Dynasty,（1271 ～ 1368）

H. 11cm

鼓腹，小口，短颈，椭圆形器身，灰白胎，圈足，白色釉。肩部一侧置短流，另一侧置纽绳形柄，上方以褐彩点缀花瓣，更显器物古朴之美。

金、元磁州窑的装饰风格趋于简化，元代磁州窑产品更趋向厚重，圆浑。

磁州窑是中国汉族民间的陶瓷窑系。元代磁州窑产品在装饰上主要采用黑白对比的方法。此器肩部以褐彩花卉点染，具有活力，表现了匠人独特的创造性，具有生动多姿和引人入胜的艺术魅力。

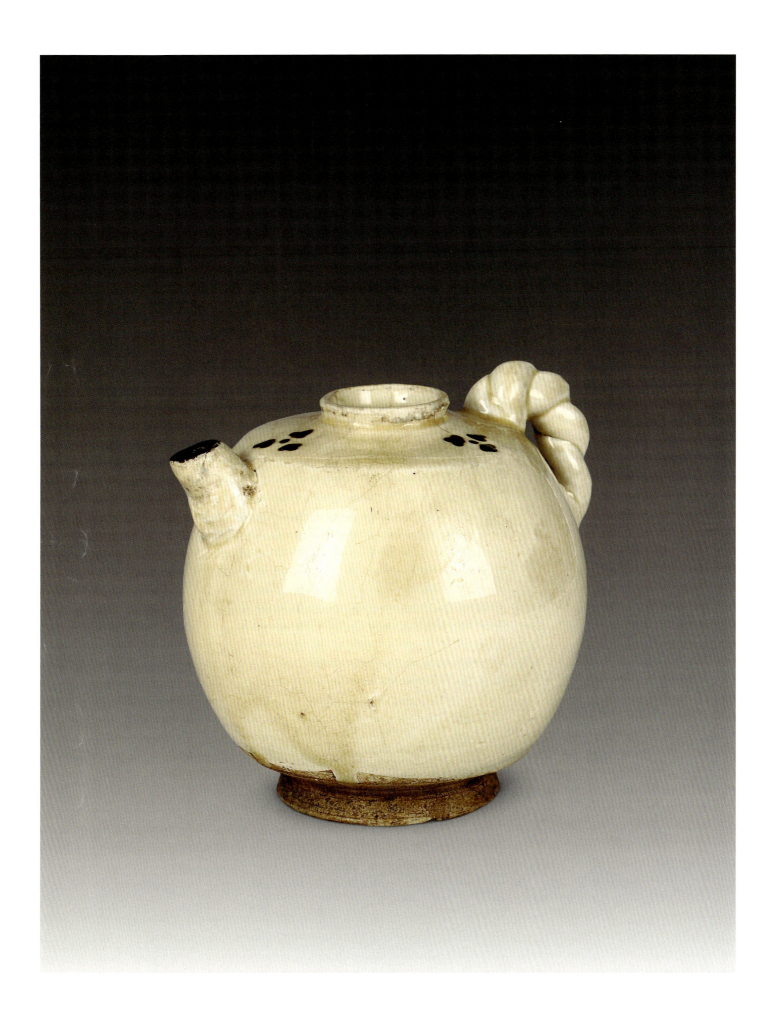

元代（1271 ~ 1368 年）

高 14.3 厘米

Jun Blue Ewer with Gourd Shape

Yuan Dynasty,（1271 ~ 1368）

H. 14.3cm

元代钧窑天蓝釉注子，器身呈葫芦形，米色胎，下部梨形，部分向上倾斜连接鼓腹上部，短颈直口。双棱把手连接器身。器身两侧有窑变玫瑰紫色斑纹各一块，紫色斑纹浑散融入天蓝色釉中均匀而跳动，增加了器物静中的动感。

钧窑为宋元时期北方瓷窑，为宋代五大名窑之一。钧瓷铜红釉的烧制成功，极其复杂的窑变机理，更为其他窑口所不及。此件执壶在钧瓷中存世量极少，虽有修复，但器型独特，绚丽多彩，窑变奇特，红蓝相映，显得秀丽动人。元钧窑变色斑为一时代特点。

葫芦是中华民族最原始的吉祥物之一，"葫芦"与"福禄"谐音，人们常用葫芦代表福禄，寄托人们的美好愿望。

99　钧窑敛口茶盏

金代或元代（1115～1368 年）

直径：13.5 厘米

Jun Bowl with Spreading Sides

Jin or Yuan Dynasty,（1115～1368）

L. 13.5cm

敛口茶盏，矮小圈足，近足处施酱釉，足内底微突。器身内外施天青色釉，釉质莹润并有棕眼。器内壁窑变玫瑰紫斑成"C"形，并闪有绿色斑点。

钧窑在烧成上采用素烧和釉烧两道工序，瓷坯经素烧稍冷后上釉正烧，釉层较厚，由于钧瓷釉采用氧化铜青色剂，由于铜的还原作用，使其出现美丽、风格独具的艺术效果。

此器釉色青中带"C"形红斑，如蓝天中的一轮明月，暮沉霞飞，窑变尤象，妙景竟生："春风又绿江南岸，明月何时照我还"（王安石《泊船瓜洲》）。使人联想当时北方汉族人民在金代少数民族统治下的忠义品质和思想。这件钧瓷窑变中形成的独一无二的绝妙奇观调动着人们的审美情趣，引人遐思无穷。

100　钧窑托盏

金代或元代（1115 ～ 1368 年）

盏直径 8.5 厘米

托直径 11 厘米

Jun Stoneware Cup and Stand

Jin or Yuan Dynasty,（1115 ～ 1368）

D（cup）.8.5cm

D（saucer）.11cm

　　盏直壁，圆口，小圈足，俗称"罗汉碗"。托盘平口，圈足，盘心下凹，内有一抹窑变玫瑰紫斑。托盏施天蓝色透明釉，釉层厚并伴有细小开片。

　　这组钧窑托盏出自河南禹州，它以粗放的线条勾勒出敦厚丰润的体态，器型古朴端庄，雍容华贵，灵动透语。瓷釉晶莹剔透，光滑温润，扶之如玉。

　　钧瓷独特的美学价值，来源其于独特釉层结构与呈色机理。观其神韵色，听其开片声；其色可赏，其声如泉。此乃钧瓷在色彩以外，另具神韵之处。故有"纵有家财万贯，不如钧瓷一片"之盛誉。

　　钧瓷的观赏价值之高，艺术魅力之大，征服了一代又一代华夏子孙。

101 哥窑茶盏

元代（1271 ~ 1368 年）

口径 7 厘米

Ge-type Tea Bowl

Yuan Dynasty,（1271 ~ 1368）

L. 7cm

　　口内敛，圈足，灰胎，底足下凹，满釉，釉呈灰青色。近足露胎处施咖啡色护胎浆，呈铁足状。器身内外开黑色冰裂纹片，其间伴有金色纹状，即谓之金丝铁线。

　　这种传世哥窑瓷器是元人孔齐《至正直记》所记载的"旧造"哥窑瓷器，大多采用垫烧工艺，个别用支钉烧造。胎呈黑灰，釉为失透的乳浊釉，釉色以灰青为主，釉面均有开片：为大纹片呈黑色，小纹片呈黄色的金丝铁线。

　　此器型制优美高雅，灰青釉色沉厚细腻，釉面肥腴，滋润如酥，冰凉柔滑，如同凝脂。金丝铁线互相交织。有不施粉黛，洗去铅华之自然美。

102　青花花卉纹葵口茶盏

元代（1271 ~ 1368 年）

口径 8 厘米

Blue and White Porcelain Cup

Yuan Dynasty,（1271 ~ 1368）

L. 8cm

　　茶盏葵口，口沿微撇，圈足，近足处呈明显火石红一道。器壁上绘青花缠枝菊纹，口沿内饰卷草纹一周。此器器形隽美，发色鲜艳明快，呈色稳定。

　　蒙古人在元代时期使用金银器比较多，元代金银器的饰纹，以牡丹、莲花、菊纹等植物纹为主。此件青花瓷葵口茶盏乃仿金银器之作。菊花傲霜，坚贞不屈，反映出当时社会的审美情趣，以及元代文人、贵族所追求的雍容华贵的社会时尚。

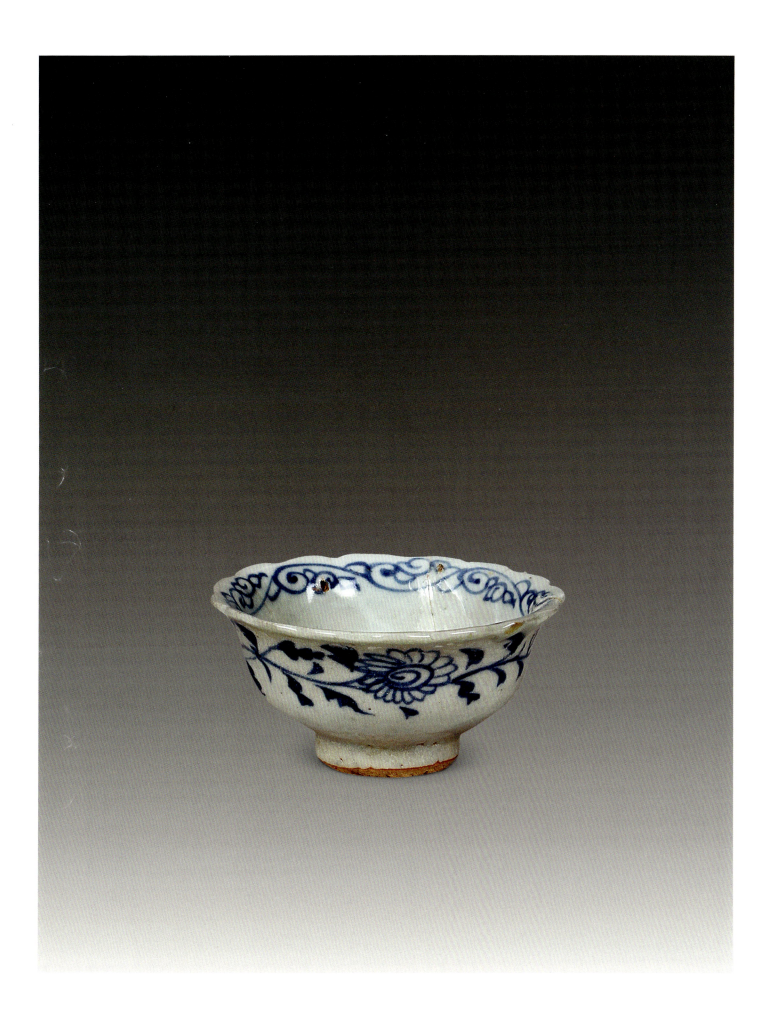

103 青花花卉纹把盏

元代（1271～1368年）

直径 7.6 厘米

Blue and White Porcelain Cup with Handle

Yuan Dynasty,（1271～1368）

L. 7.6cm

盏浅壁，口微敛，平底。器一端置龙身为柄，釉呈卵白色，器内外以青花钴料绘月影梅纹，青花发色深沉厚重，墨彩梅花，楚楚动人。

元代青花瓷开辟了由素瓷向彩瓷过渡的新时代。其作品富丽雄浑，画风豪放，与中华民族的审美情趣大相径庭，是中国陶瓷史上的一朵奇葩。

此器上的梅花装饰画法，采用单纯的青花和清淡野遗的笔致，生动地传达了梅花清肌傲骨。寄托了生活在元代的文人雅士，"不要人夸好颜色，只留清气满乾坤"的孤高傲岸的情怀。

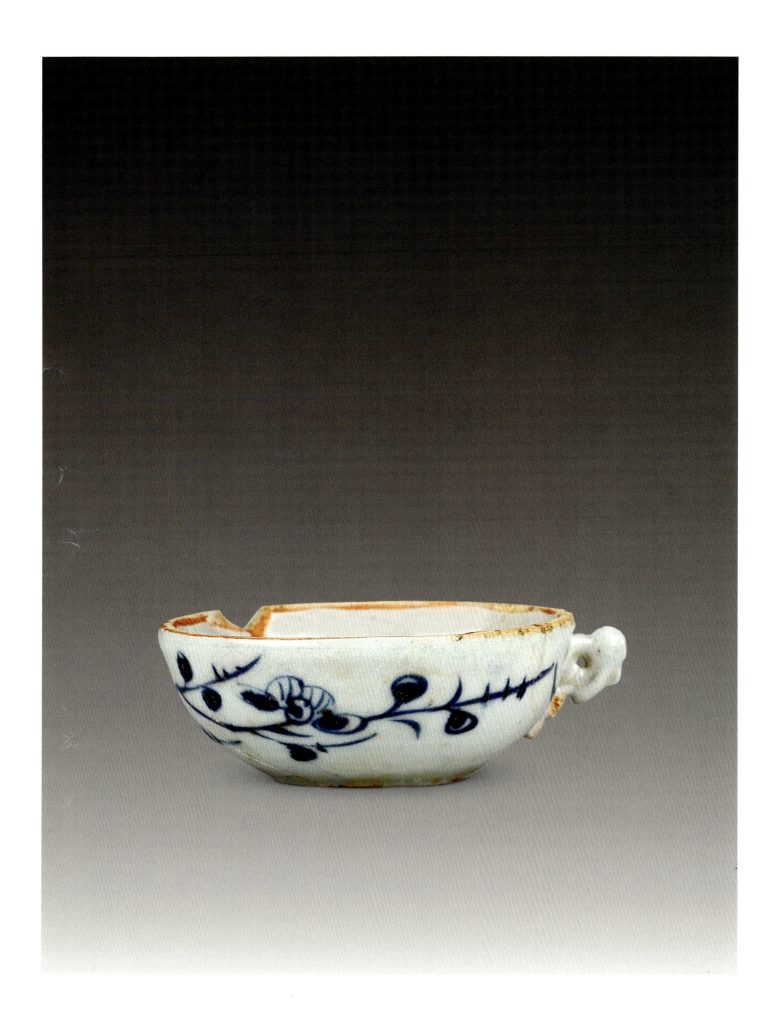

七　明代时期的茶具（1368～1644年）

　　明代是我国陶瓷史上的辉煌时期。宫廷尊崇儒家文化，"读书做官"和"高官厚禄"是明代社会的科举制度，此时又是青花瓷发展的鼎盛期，青花瓷画的人物纹饰很多反映的是这个主题。有的纹饰直截了当，有的纹饰曲折隐讳，有的通过吉祥如意的内涵，表现出封建文人们的理想追求。青花瓷的烧制虽有官窑、民窑之分，繁简粗细之别，但主题纹饰及纹样依然反映着民族信仰中的儒家思想，保存下民族的文化精神和艺术形式。一幅幅幽倩素雅的青花瓷画，无不包含着人们良好的愿望，吉祥的祝福，美好的追求，心灵的期待。

　　古人认为，饮茶是雅事，所以一起喝茶的人亦不能太俗。明人徐渭称："煎茶虽微清小雅，然要须其人与茶品相得。"另在明人表现的画卷中可以看出，明代人士往往把品饮活动置于大自然的环境中，独揽山水之胜，饱尝林泉之趣，颇合于天地之道。这里向我们传达是明代"礼"（感思于自然）与"和"（人与人

《惠山品茗图》　明代　文徵明

之和睦）的精神理念。器物上的人物，青花染绘笔触多样，舒畅流动，使茶器上的纹饰感染文人的品茗氛围。

明代官窑青花与单色釉壶、杯、盏传世极少，官搭民烧制品中不乏精美之作，明早青花葫芦壶器身以青花饰缠枝瓜瓞纹，瓜瓞为民俗吉祥物，藤蔓绵长，寓意家族兴旺，子孙繁衍。民间用壶胎质较为粗糙，如明代早期青花番莲纹壶（图106），所绘花卉多有美好寓意。"莲"寓意"一品清廉"、"喜得连科"之意。明初，精美的瓷器除了供宫廷使用或陈设外，还大量作为礼品赠与外国统治阶层及前来朝贡的外国使臣。此时期的龙泉窑青釉瓷也不乏精美之作，如明早期龙泉窑青釉刻花执壶，撇口、圆唇、短直径、圆腹、圈足。腹部四个菱形开光内剔刻四瓣草叶纹和"美酒清香"四字（图104）。浙江枫洞岩窑场为明初奉旨烧造宫廷用瓷的窑场之一，此器为明代早期枫洞岩窑烧造之产品。

《茶录》中说："壶，宜瓷为之，茶交与此。"明代才有了正意义上的茶壶，这与明代进入了一个散茶撮泡的品饮时代有直接关系。

VII. TEA SETS OF MING DYNASTY (1368 AD ~ 1644 AD)

Ming Dynasty is a splendid period in porcelain history. Under the imperial examination system of "studying to become officials" and "high post with matched salary", emperor and officials of Ming Dynasty advocated Confucian culture, while blue and white porcelain prevailed in this period. Therefore, most patterns on porcelains reflect such theme. Some of these patterns have direct meaning, while others obscure, and some implies auspiciousness and shows scholars' pursuing for ideal. There are differences between royal kiln and folk kiln, and workmanship can be divided into complexity and simpleness, but the themes of patterns and designs still reflect Confucianism, cultural spirit and artistic form of the nation. Every elegant pattern on blue and white porcelains carries people's best wishes, blessing, pursuit and expectation.

Ancient people thought drinking tea was a graceful activity, so people who drank tea also should have refined tastes, as Xu Wei of Ming Dynasty once said: "Although making tea is not a big deal, people who drink tea must have elegant taste" . From the paintings of Ming Dynasty, we also can see that people used to hold tea-drinking activities in natural environment, so as to appreciate landscape and nature charm as well as integrate into the heaven and earth. These paintings reveal philosophy-feeling for the nature and harmony between people. The figure patterns and blue and white paintings on wares are diversified, which can influence the tea-tasting atmosphere.

Few blue and white or single glazed pots and cups produced in Royal Kiln of Ming Dynasty have been handed down, but most wares produced in folk kilns with official ware base are exquisite works. For example, blue and white gourd-shaped wares of early Ming Dynasty were painted with patterns of entangled branches and melons. In folk custom, melon is mascot, and its entangled vines imply thriving and large family. The folk ware base is relatively rough, such as blue and white pot Painted with Lotus of early Ming Dynasty. (fig.106) Most floral patterns have good implications, and lotus pattern implies incorruptness and Successful official career. During early Ming Dynasty, exquisite porcelains not only served as utensil or decorations in palace, but also served as presents given to foreign ruling class and envoys paying tribute to China. In the meantime, many green glazed porcelains of Longquan Kiln also were exquisite works, such as Green Glazed Ewer with

Engraved Designs of Longquan Kiln of early Ming Dynasty, which features flared edge, round mouth, short diameter, round belly and ring foot, with four Chinese characters " 美酒清香 "(good wine) and four-leaf grass design engraved in the rhombus pattern on belly. (fig.104) This ewer was made in Fengdongyan Kiln of early Ming Dynasty. (Fengdongyan Kiln of Zhejiang was one of the kiln factories producing porcelains for royal court in early Ming Dynasty)

As stated in the Record of Tea: It's better to make tea with porcelain teapot. Since the era for loose tea started in Ming Dynasty, tea pot came into being.

104 龙泉窑 "清香美酒" 铭文执壶

明代早期（1368 ～ 1464 年）

高 18 厘米

LungQuan Celadon Ewer with "Qing Xiang Mei Jiu" Decorated

Early Ming Dynasty,（1368 ～ 1464）

H. 18cm

壶束颈，圆唇外翻，椭圆腹，圈足外撇。圈足底无釉，呈紫红色。肩与上腹间一侧置流，一侧置把手，把手弯曲呈耳形。外腹壁肩部及腹底部各凸印弦纹两道，各以八朵凸印梅花点缀，肩颈部模印牡丹折枝花卉，腹部凸印棱形开光四个，开光内分别凸印草书"清香美酒"，开光外饰折枝花卉，下部刻木叶纹，刻工娴熟，刀法流畅，器胎较厚重，施翠青色釉，釉面滋润肥厚，呈半透明状，有乳浊感。此器为明早期龙泉产品较稀有。

2005 ～ 2006 年浙江省文物部门在龙泉大窑风洞岩发现大明处州龙泉官窑遗址，内中出土大量标本，包括该类刻花厚釉梅子青器。

这件龙泉窑执壶在装饰风格与纹样上体现出精心的艺术构思与灵活性。葱绿滋润的釉色和精美的纹饰，凝结着匠师们在人类陶瓷文明上表现出的无穷智慧和辛劳，体现了此件执壶不凡的品质和特征。

北京故宫博物院亦藏有一件"清香美酒"铭文盖罐，通体施青灰色厚釉并置有圆形荷叶式盖。（《龙泉窑青瓷》朱伯谦主编，艺术家出版社，1998 年 9 月）

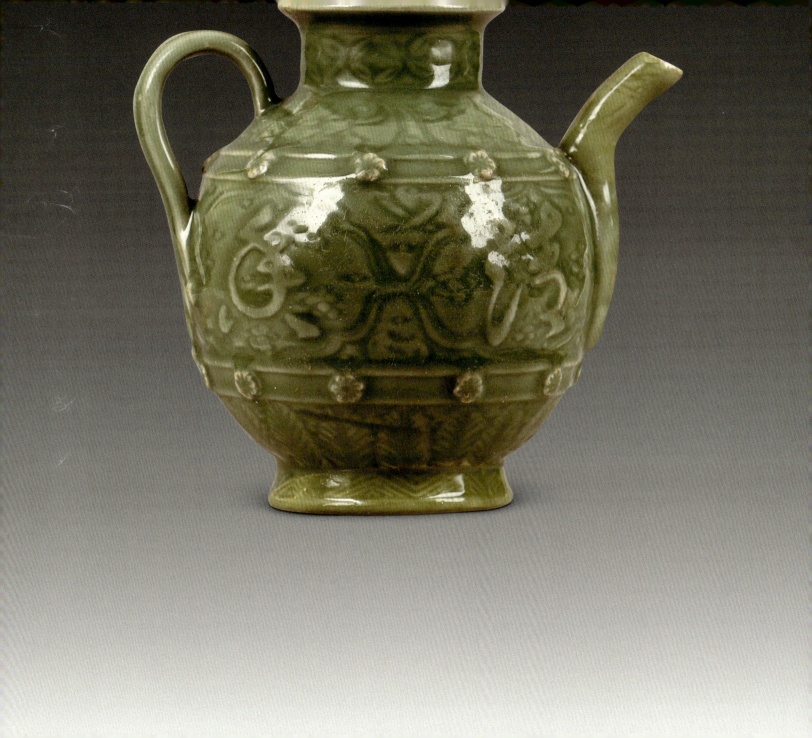

105 龙泉窑青釉托盏

明代早期（1368 ~ 1464 年）

杯直径 7.8 厘米

托直径 15.6 厘米

Longquan Celadon-Glazed Cup and Stand

Early Ming Dynasty,（1368 ~ 1464）

D（cup）. 7.8cm

D（samcer）. 15.6cm

盏杯直壁，口微外撇，腹下渐收，圈足，底足无釉。托作花瓣形五瓣葵口，口沿外卷，盏座中间置开口中空拱台，底足施釉有乳突。托、盏通体施青釉，釉色青中泛翠绿，更显清新淡雅。

瓷盏托始于东晋，南北朝时开始流行，唐代以后随着饮茶之风而盛行。宋辽时期以后的盏托，托口较高，中间呈空心盏状。

明代茶制改变，茶风极盛，茶器亦随之变化。由宋时的煎茶、点茶改变为冲泡。此套龙泉青釉托盏造型美观，比例匀称，适用于用条形散茶的冲泡法饮茶。

明代早期（1368～1464 年）

高 10.5 厘米

Blue and White Ewer Painted with Lotus Spray

Early Ming Dynasty,（1368～1464）

H. 10.5cm

壶呈梨形，圈足，底内施釉，曲柄，弯流，壶身以青花饰折枝莲花纹，颈部回纹，青花色泽深沉，浓艳，系明代早期制品。

梨形壶又称梨式壶，型制始于金、元时期，以明早期最多，官窑及民窑均有烧制。明代，饮茶器最突出的特点是小茶壶的出现。"壶小则香不涣散味不耽搁"。无论是品种及造型都表现出穷极精巧

的特征。

莲花作为装饰纹出现在瓷器上，自古就有品德高尚，高洁清廉之寓意。由于佛教文化在东汉时期传入兴起，便以莲花作为佛教标志。在明代早期，莲花图案由元代的繁复走向疏朗、简练的风格，直接影响到瓷器的装饰手法和时代审美趣味，备受人们的推崇。此器古朴典雅，绘画生动而引人入胜。

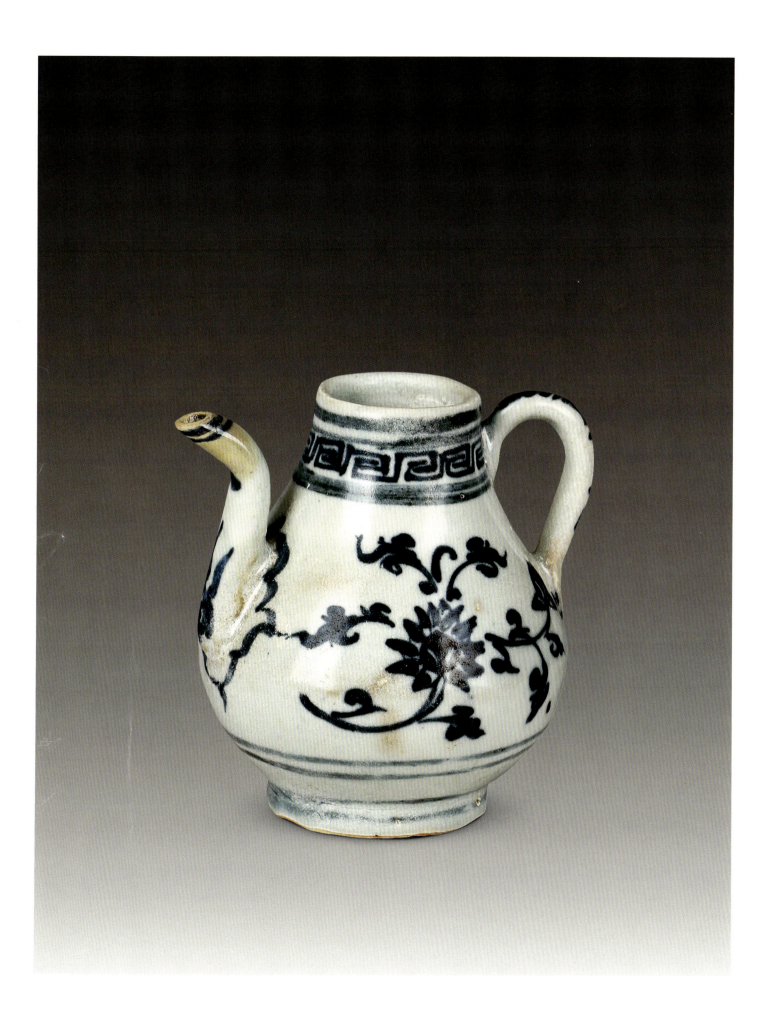

107 青花折枝花卉执壶

明代早期（1368 ~ 1464 年）

高 10.5 厘米

Blue and White Ewer Painted with Sketchy Lotus Spray

Early Ming Dynasty,（1368 ~ 1464）

H. 10.5cm

器身呈圆柱形，斜肩，小口，圈足，壶身一侧置小流，一侧置龙形扁柄，柄端一小系，扁平盖为后置。器身饰青花折枝花卉纹，肩部饰卷草纹，青花色泽发灰，呈结铁锈斑现象，釉面泛青，釉质肥厚，并伴有自然开片纹，花卉以一笔点画方法绘就。

胎质灰白，圈足下方泛有火石红，足底有积釉现象。

此壶器型古朴庄重，纹饰典雅，龙形仿生扁柄端庄，龙鼻端被装饰呈"如意形"而强化了其吉祥含义。为明代早期景德镇窑烧制。

108　青花栀子花纹执壶

明弘治（1488～1505年）

高 13.2 厘米

Blue and White Ewer Painted with Gardenia

Ming Dynasty, Hongzhi period,（1488～1505）

H. 13.2cm

　　执壶呈，长颈，口杯状，一侧环形高身把上有一小圆环作系盖用，另一侧形如卷草纹的撑连接长弯流与器身。颈部及肩部以青花饰蕉叶纹，腹部饰青花栀子纹，平底，无釉。此器束腰，形似葫芦，器型上下比例协调和谐，高雅优美。明代成化、弘治时期瓷器，胎体秀美。砂底有些呈褐黄色，俗称"米糊底"。

　　栀子为茜草科或小乔木，初夏开花，花色素白，花气清芬。南朝时期，栀子进入审美视野，南宋时期，栀子又成为文人的参禅之友，是文人雅士钟爱的"清玩"。

　　这件青花栀子花纹执壶系明代成化弘治年间景德镇窑产品，胎质细腻纯洁，釉质肥厚。装饰纹样轻灵典雅，层次分明。青花栀子花卉用平涂法装饰，只分浓淡而不分阴阳，更无渲染烘托，与洁白温润的胎釉相衬分外脱俗。其中隐藏着深刻的文化属性。

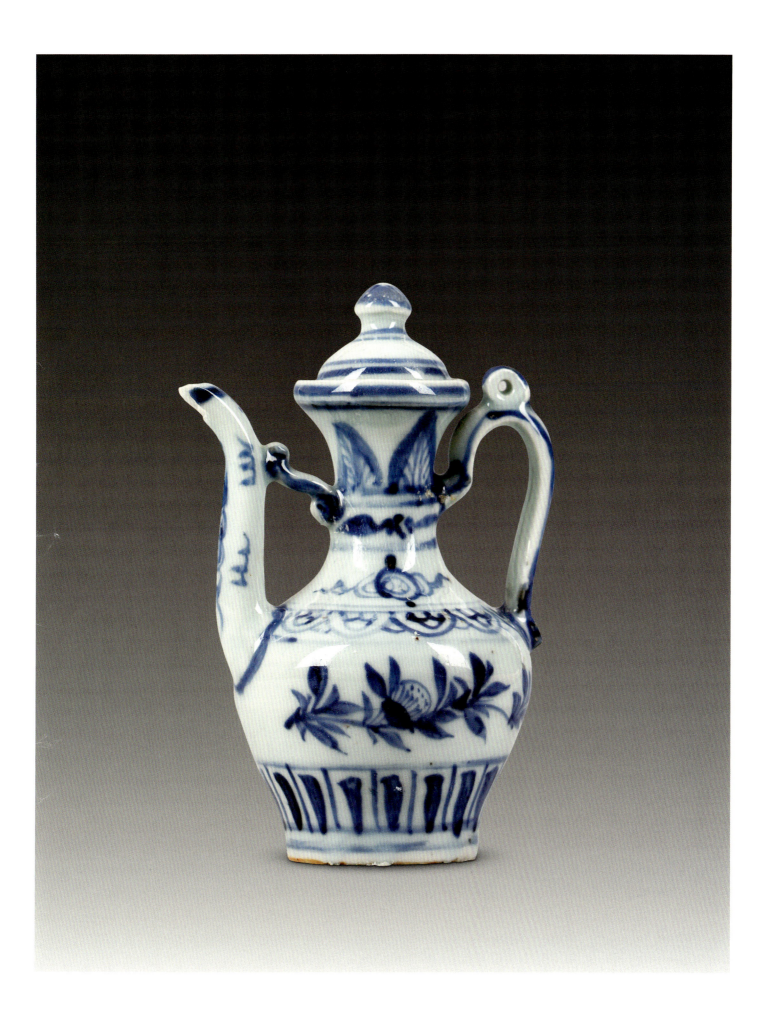

109 哥釉高桩杯

明成化（1465～1487年）

口径 6.2 厘米

Ge-type Porcelain Cup

Chenghua period,（1465～1487）

L. 6.2cm

　　杯为收口高桩型，矮圈足，器型隽秀小巧，月白色，工艺精湛，釉质肥润，平整光洁，并有酥油光，开片纹自然，器口、器足施以黄酱釉。

　　成化时期，继承前制，并形成自己的时代风格。这件仿哥釉高桩杯系景德镇窑烧制。装饰典雅，釉面肥润，虽缺少宋哥"酥润含蓄"之美，但釉质匀净光亮，玲珑俊秀，制作精巧，器口与足端涂酱色釉，以模仿传世哥窑"紫口铁足"的效果。代表了明代中期高超的制瓷水平。

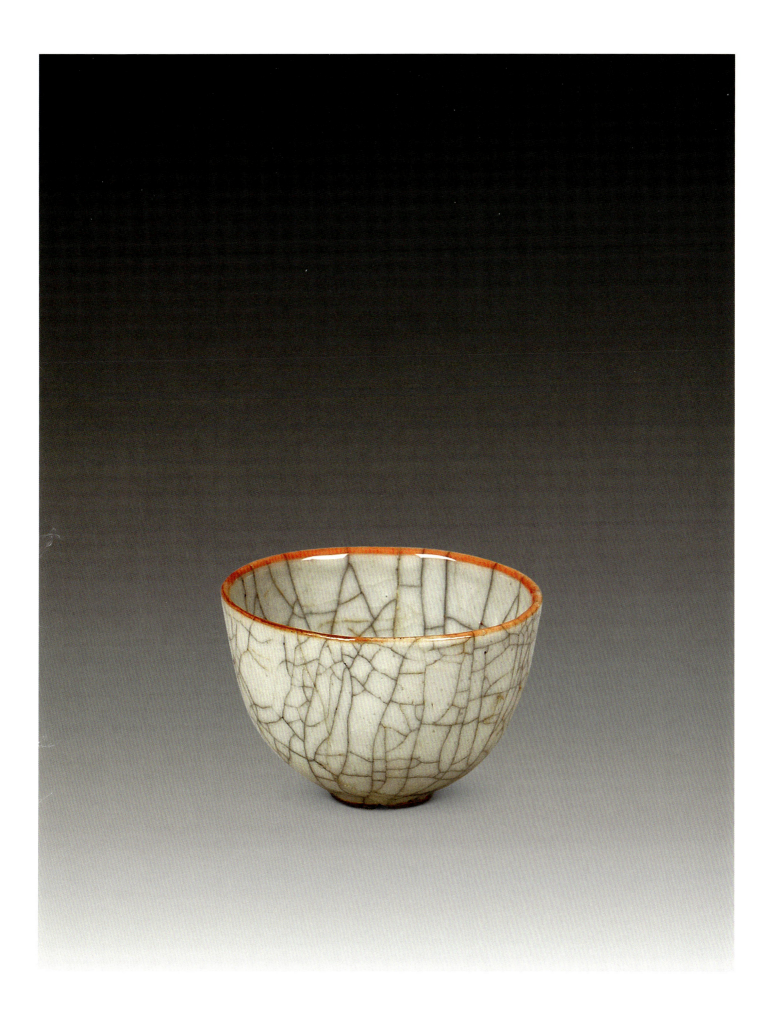

110 青花白描人物执壶

明万历（1573 ～ 1619 年）

高 14.1 厘米

Blue and White Ewer Painted in Figures

Ming Dynasty, Wanli period,（1573 ～ 1619）

H. 14.1cm

景德镇窑产品，圆口，深腹，圈足。弯流置于腹部，柄连接于肩与腹之间。腹部两侧开光，内绘白描"月下闲吟图"高仕人物，技法娴熟，构图淡雅，寓意丰富。

科举选官制度从隋代开始，经过唐代的完善，宋代的发展，元代的跌落，到明代达到鼎盛时期。"读书做官"这一科举制度对社会的深刻影响在青花瓷上亦有充分的反映。

这件青花白描人物执壶，绘高仕于月下闲吟，月夜的表现与传统中国画方法一样，青花淡描，绘画淡雅幽婉，表现意境深邃。用如此富含文化意境的茶器饮茶，自然其乐融融。

111 青花折枝花卉纹注壶

明万历（1573 ～ 1619 年）

高 9 厘米

Blue and White Ewer Painted with Sketchy Prony

Ming Dynasty, Wanli period,（1573 ～ 1619）

H. 9cm

　　壶身形似南瓜，龙柄，弯流，壶底宽圈足，底足满釉，壶身以青花勾勒牡丹花卉纹饰，发色深沉，造型别致。

　　万历青花所呈现的色调，早、中、晚期有明显区别，中期产品蓝中闪灰。此器线条流畅简洁，再加以渲染填色，图案颇有水墨画的效果。

　　牡丹花历来被视为"雍容华贵"的象征，所谓"国色天香，花之富贵者也。"明代晚期瓷器纹样的画意大多离不开表现"吉祥祈福"的内容，这反映了当年统治者的思想。

　　此器呈瓜型，寓意瓜瓞连绵，子孙万代，各种吉祥花卉纹样组合在一起，充满感情色彩，也体现了当时人们对生活的美好追求。

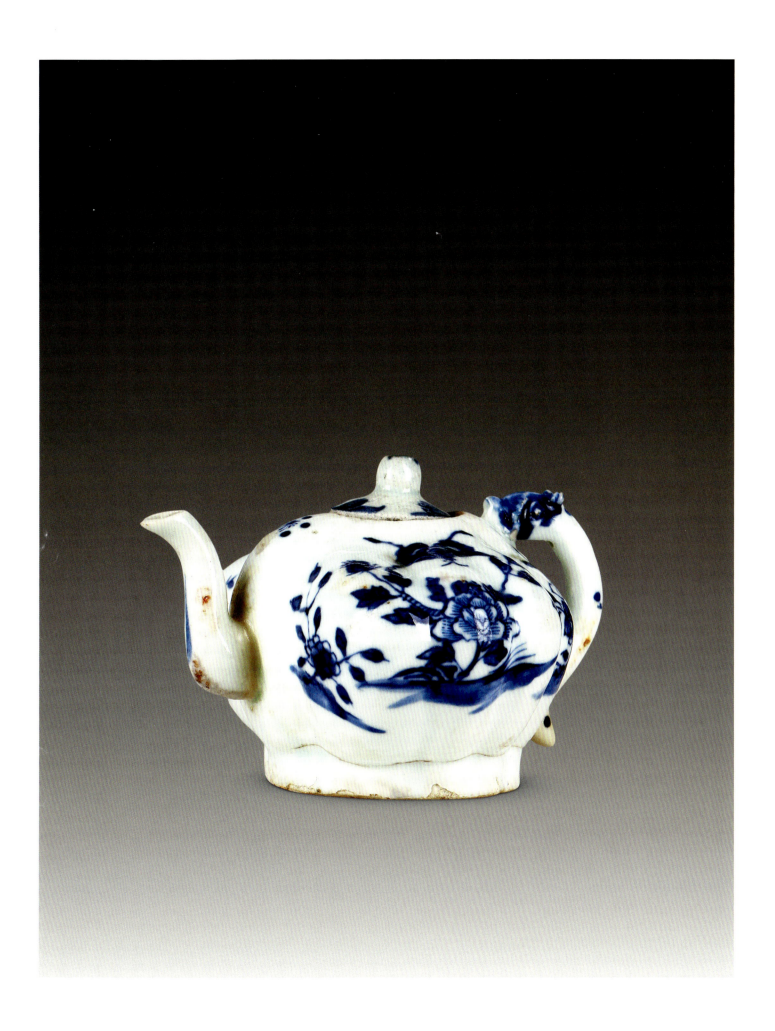

《溪泉品茶图》 清 程致远

八　清代时期的茶具（1644～1911年）

　　清王朝统一中国后，为了长治久安，采取了若干治国安邦的措施。此时，处于康、雍、乾盛世的景德镇瓷器生产，达到了历史上的最高水平。康熙皇帝在位61年，他总结并借鉴明代兴亡的历史教训，潜心学习汉文化、儒家理念以及引进西方工艺，制瓷也得到较快地发展。爱新觉罗·弘历（1711～1799年）既是大清的乾隆皇帝，又是一位酷好品茗的行家。他曾六下杭州，为龙井茶题字赋诗。传说当他85岁让位于嘉庆帝时，一位老臣不无惋惜地说："国不可一日无君！"乾隆幽默地说："君不可一日无茶啊！"乾隆一生注重养生，嗜茶与修身养性。

　　康熙朝（1662～1722年）的陶瓷在质量上有很大提高，瓷器器型浑厚古拙，青花呈色青翠明亮，胎质细腻，青花紧皮亮釉，绘画采用中国画"分水"、"皴染"技法，纹饰层次分明。期间茶叶已大量地远销欧洲，茶具亦增加出口，高档外销瓷制作工艺水准可与当时的官窑比美，但绝大部分样式及绘画都是中国传统题材。康熙中期制品，胎质细腻，釉质莹润，青花翠蓝，纹饰上多用莲瓣纹、朵莲做装饰，意寓背后的佛教文化。

　　雍正朝（1723～1735年）的瓷器博采众长，精益求精，仿宋代五大名窑及明永、宣之器，种类繁多精细，粉彩制品有很大发展。粉彩是清早期发明的一种釉上彩新品种，一些粉彩器物上以不同层次的粉色，衬托花卉、人物及山水题材，美而不艳，赏心悦目，可为饮茶之人提供极高的精神享受。本书（图113）的粉彩壶，壶身彩绘盛开的莲花，周围还饰有牡丹、菊花等花卉，色泽温润柔和，线条精细流畅，可与官窑瓷器媲美。

　　乾隆朝（1736～1795年）的瓷器造型精美、色彩缤纷、图案新颖、华缛多姿，令人叹为观止。同时更具有文人气。壶的器型融和青花，粉彩，色釉，五彩等，以诗人、绘画反映历史故事和人物。仿制宋代"五大名窑"作品，淡雅宜人。粉彩堆塑莲纹壶（图122）釉色逼真，工艺高超，体现出工匠们的智慧和创造力。

　　自嘉庆朝始至光绪朝，清代中、晚期的瓷器，仍崇尚和沿袭乾隆时期的传统风格，许多茶具是模仿乾隆及以前的器物。

　　清代许多画家以山水、花卉小品在茶具上绘画居多，常以壶寄情，记花言志，虚中有实，实中有虚。

　　宣统一朝仅三年，景德镇御窑场仍继续烧造宫廷使用的粉彩瓷器。

VIII. TEA SETS OF QING DYNASTY (1644 AD ~ 1911AD)

After unification of China in Qing Dynasty, many good measures had been taken to maintain prolonged stability. Due to flourishing age during the reign of Emperor Kangxi, Yongzheng and Qianlong, porcelain production of Jingdezhen reached the highest level in history. With reign of 61 years, Emperor Kangxi summarized and drew lessons from the rise and fall of Ming Dynasty, studied Han culture and Confucianism as well as introduced western technology, so porcelain industry developed fast as well. Aisin Gioro·Hongli was not only the Emperor Qianlong of Qing Dynasty (1711 AD - 1799 AD), but also an expert in tea tasting. He used to go to Hangzhou for six times and write poem for Longjing tea. It was said that when he abdicated and gave sovereign authority to Emperor Jiaqing in his 85 years old, an old minister felt sorry for it: "A country cannot survive a day without emperor", while Emperor Qianlong replied humorously: " I cannot live a day without tea." . Emperor Qianlong not only liked tea, but also attached great importance to health maintenance and self-cultivation.

During the reign of Emperor Kangxi (1662 AD - 1722 AD), porcelain quality was greatly improved, and the porcelain features vigorous and unsophisticated shaped, bright blue and white color, delicate porcelain base and bright glaze. Due to adoption of "painting material dilution" and "wrinkle method" used in Chinese painting, the patterns are well layered. In the meantime, as a large quantity of tea was exported to Europe, the export of tea sets also increased. With craftsmanship comparable to that of Royal Kiln, shapes and patterns of most high-end export porcelains were derived from Chinese traditional theme. During middle stage of the reign of Emperor Kangxi, porcelain products feature delicate base, smooth glaze, and bright blue and white color. In terms of pattern, lotus petal pattern and entire lotus pattern were mostly used, to show the Buddhist culture.

Through imitation of wares produced by the Five Great Kilns of Song Dynasty as well as wares of Yongxuan period of Ming Dynasty, porcelains made during the reign of Emperor Yongzheng (1723 AD - 1735AD) tended to be more absorbing, tolerant to diversity and excellent. In the mean time, pastel products, as an overglaze color invented in early Qing Dynasty, had greatly developed. In order to present such themes as flower, figure and landscape, multi-layer pastel was painted on wares, pleasant to the eye of people drinking tea. As for the pastel pot referenced in this book, due to the painting of blooming lotus, peony, chrysanthemum and other flowers, this pot features gentle and moist in tinct and smooth lines, which can be comparable to porcelains of Royal Kiln. (fig.113)

During the reign of Emperor Qianlong (1736 AD - 1795 AD), porcelains featured exquisite shape, multi colors, novel designs and magnificent patterns, which were extremely amazing and literary. With integration of porcelain shape, pastel, colored glaze and five colors, poem and paintings on the porcelain describe historical stories and figures. Through imitation of wares produced by the Five Great

Kilns of Song Dynasty, these porcelains are elegant and fascinating. With life-like glazing color and superb craftsmanship, the Pastel Pot with Embossed Lotus Pattern reveals the wisdom and creativity of craftsman. (fig.122)

From the reign of Emperor Jiaqing to Emperor Guangxu, i.e. the middle and late Qing Dynasty, traditional style prevailing during the reign of Emperor Qianlong was still advocated and followed, so many tea sets were made by imitating wares produced in that period or even longer before.

By painting landscape, flowers and sketches on tea sets, many painters of Qing Dynasty tried to express their feeling and aspiration with pots and flowers, to integrate virtual and actual situation.

Since Xuantong period only lasted for three years, Jingdezhen kiln factory still produced pastel porcelains used in royal palace.

112 青花月夜泛舟图提梁壶

清康熙（1662～1722 年）

高 15.5 厘米

Blue and White Ewer Painted with Design of "Go Boating on Moonlit Night"

Kangxi period, Qing Dynasty,（1662 ～ 1722）

H. 15.5cm

壶身呈钟形，短颈，曲流，弧形提梁。壶盖上钮部塑成牌楼状，壶身双面开光，一面绘有苏轼夜游赤壁图，另一面录咏赤壁七言诗。

康熙时期社会稳定，带来了文学艺术的繁荣。此器构图生动，图中绘苏轼头戴方巾坐在船中，前有童子奉茶，船尾艄公摇橹，一轮明月映照着两岸的山石树木，给人一种悠然自得的休闲景象。映射出人民安居乐业的盛世时代特色。

这件康熙青花月夜泛舟图提梁壶，修胎规整，缜密如玉，造型敦重古拙。绘画风格仍宗法于宋、元时的绘画技法。釉面厚润，青花浓艳，为康熙朝典型器。

113　粉彩描金花卉壶

清雍正（1723～1735 年）

高 13.5 厘米

Teapot Painted in Famille-Rose and Gilt

Yong zheng period, Qing Dynasty,（1723 ～ 1735）

H. 13.5cm

　　景德镇窑产品，圆盖，圆口，短颈，深腹，圈足，直流置于腹部，柄连接于肩与腹之间。盖中央置尖圆钮，正面绘山石，菊花。壶腹部两侧绘飞舞的蝙蝠、蝴蝶、菊花、牡丹、牵牛花等吉祥花卉置于山石之上，寓意"长寿富贵"，描金工艺使纹饰清雅艳丽，更为豪华。

　　这件雍正粉彩描金花卉茶壶，秀美而端庄，给人以高雅之感。画面构图疏朗，设色浅淡，简洁清

新，用笔苍润，雅拙，瓷绘渲染错落有致，层次分明，表现了意境之美。

　　清代康熙、雍正、乾隆三朝的工匠们已不满足于传统陶瓷单一的色釉装饰，开始用纯金加工提炼的金粉，在彩瓷上施金色，达到陶瓷更加金碧辉煌的艺术效果，这种装饰工艺的改变，自然会带来美感的变化，从而满足上层社会及外销瓷的需要。

114 粉彩花卉纹茶盏

清雍正（1723 ~ 1735 年）

口径 9.8 厘米

Tea Cup in Famille-Rose Style

Yong zheng period, Qing Dynasty,（1723 ~ 1735）

L. 9.8cm

　　该器撇口，弧腹，圈足，胎质白而细腻，上绘粉彩折枝菊花及牡丹纹，色彩艳丽，圈足底部饰青花双圈"大清雍正年制"六字楷书款，釉面细腻光亮，圈足修胎精细，呈鲫鱼背形，粉彩发色温润中浓艳，纹饰简洁而不失典雅。雍正粉彩素以细腻精巧著称于世，具有富贵高雅，艳而不俗，细而不凡的美感和文化内涵。

　　《饮流斋说瓷》有论"硬彩（五彩）华贵而深凝，粉彩艳丽而清逸。"粉彩工艺采用渲染没骨的技艺，富于国画风格，一经问世，就很快取代了五彩。

　　此件雍正粉彩花卉纹茶盏，器形隽美，粉彩牡丹花纹饰采用"玻璃白"打底，再用"渲染法"进行彩绘，花卉纹饰细腻，色调淡雅，花头柔丽，立体感强，艺术水准高超，为清代其他各朝所不及，从而盛行至今。用此茶盏盛茶、饮茶不失是一种高尚的享受。

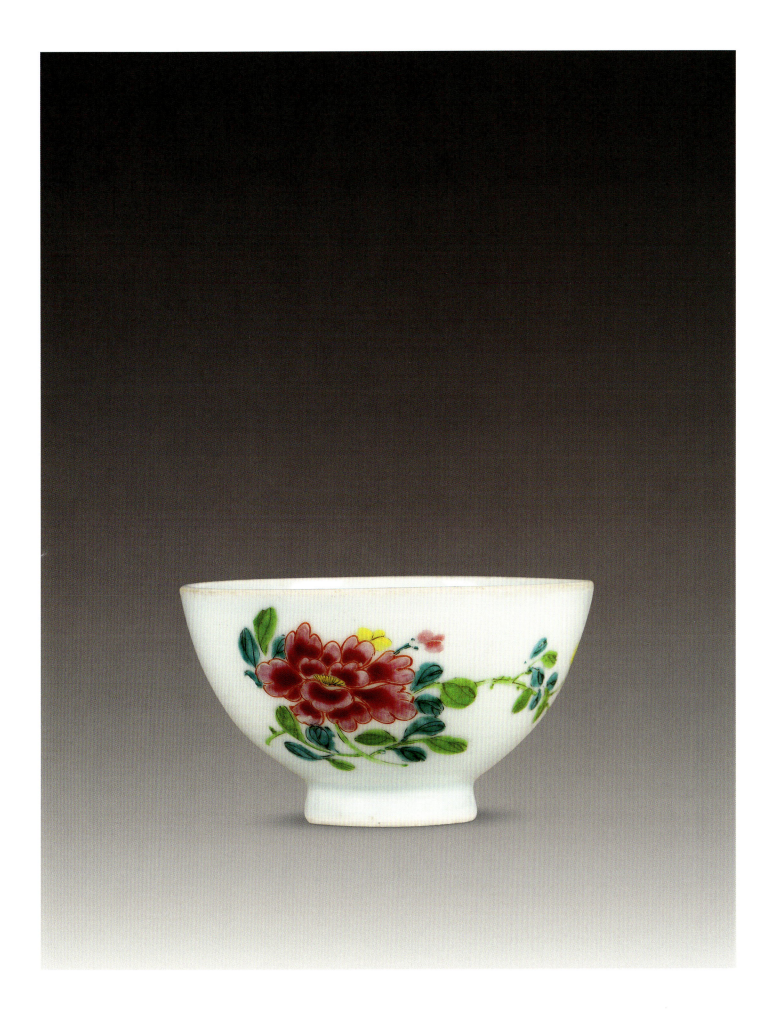

115 青花瓜瓞纹葫芦形执壶

清雍正（1723～1735 年）

高 12 厘米

阔 12.6 厘米

Blue and White Ewer Gourd-Shaped with Vine

Yong zheng period, Qing Dynasty,（1723 ～ 1735）

H. 12cm

壶呈葫芦形，卧足，唇口微撇。耳形圆柄连接壶身上下两部分，上半段出曲形流。器身以青花饰瓜瓞纹，苏料青花浓艳，釉质莹润。

瓜为蔓生植物，其藤蔓绵长，结实累累，寓意家族兴旺，福禄万代，子孙繁衍。

雍正时期，经济发展。雍正皇帝的审美情趣，对这时期瓷器的风格和技艺起到了决定性的作用。

在仿古方面体现了高超的制瓷技巧，仿烧永宣瓷器达到了"仿古暗合，与真无二"的程度。瓷器的造型和纹样，素有"线条美"之誉。

此器器型圆柔纤丽，工艺轻巧俊秀，青花发色艳丽，洁净无瑕，蓝中藏青，略有晕散，匀润而雅致。可与以纤细秀丽著称的明代永宣瓷器相提并论，实是茶具中难得的精品。

116 青花松竹梅纹杯

清雍正（1723 ~ 1735 年）

口径 6.8 厘米

Blue and White Cup painted with Pine Tree, Bamboo and Chinese Plum

Yong zheng period, Qing Dynasty,（1723 ~ 1735）

L. 6.8cm

撇口，深弧腹，圈足。器身外以青花绘松竹梅纹饰，青花发色淡雅。足底书青花"大清雍正年制"六字楷书款。

此器瓷土选料精细，胎体坚白细润，釉面莹润，器形隽秀尔雅，画面自然随意，优雅娴静。青花用色深沉而淡雅，是一件典型的雍正青花饮茶用具。

松、竹、梅合称"岁寒三友"，是中国传统文化中高尚人格的象征。古代文人喜爱借物舒情，借此表现自己理想品格和对精神境界的追求。

117 紫砂彩釉开光壶

清雍正～乾隆（1723～1795 年）

高 19.6 厘米

YiXing Teapot with Enamel Decoration

Yong zheng–Qianlong period, Qing Dynasty,（1723 ～ 1795）

H. 19.6cm

紫砂胎，短颈，深腹，圆盖，肩部一侧置流，另一侧柄置于肩与腹部之间。壶身重彩泥绘，颈肩部以黄彩饰如意纹一周，腹部四面开光，绘竹木和山水楼阁图，蓝地白彩，自然和谐，以外绘花草附托，显富贵，高雅之风格。底部篆书"方南制"款。

清代雍正年间吸收了漆画中的描金和彩绘技法，将紫砂壶装饰得如神似画，精美异常。

此壶造型大气，四面开光构图饱满，开光内绘山水树木及亭台楼阁，画笔精细，采用"界画"手法白描出一幅山水画，清新雅致。纹饰上吸收了外来的装饰手法，画面凸出于底色之上，因而富有立体感。这种加彩挂釉的紫砂壶在清代只风行一时，很快就停止烧制了，其代表着紫砂发展史上的一种新格局。

118 青花折枝花执壶

清乾隆（1736 ~ 1795 年）

高 15.2 厘米

Blue and White Ewer Painted with Sketchy Peony

Qianlong period, Qing Dynasty,（1736 ~ 1795）

H. 15.2cm

壶直身筒状，斜肩，曲流，附方形提梁，平盖上钮呈牌楼状，壶身绘折枝牡丹花纹，肩部饰卷草纹，近底部绘莲瓣纹。

乾隆一朝六十年，瓷器生产空前繁荣。器物装饰工艺极为丰富，构图及画工严谨，图案纹饰满密而繁缛。

此器器型典雅，施釉肥厚，白中泛青，壶身以青花绘牡丹、卷草纹并以仰莲纹装饰，组成一幅寓意"连生富贵"的图案。这一时期的纹饰，带有时代的鲜明烙印，常用谐音、隐喻等艺术手法来寓意吉祥，反映出先人美好的愿望。

119 青花矾红彩宝相花杯

清乾隆（1736～1795年）

口径 8 厘米

Blue and White Cup Painted with Iron-Red Flower

Qianlong period, Qing Dynasty,（1736～ 1795）

L. 8cm

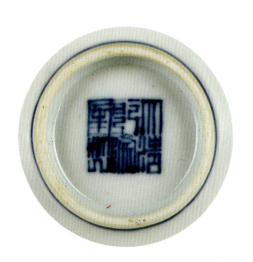

撇口，敛腹，圈足。器型外壁对称排列四朵宝相花，以青花绘叶，花用矾红彩绘，合而称之为"地涌金莲纹"做工精细，胎质细腻，画风流畅。

宝相花纹饰是魏晋南北朝以来伴随佛教盛行的流行图案，它集中了莲花、牡丹、菊花的特征，经过艺术处理组合而成，象征佛法之纯净无染。

乾隆皇帝一生嗜茶如命，亦经常设"茶宴"来招待群臣，此时期彩绘官窑茶具，在质量上达到历史的顶峰。此器以矾红彩绘制宝相花卉，画工细腻，图案新颖精美，华缛多姿，更富禅意，令人叹为观止。

120 青花开光人物壶

清乾隆（1736～1795 年）

高 18 厘米

Blue and White Ewer with Figures decoration

Qianlong period, Qing Dynasty,（1736～1795）

H. 18cm

　　壶身呈椭圆形，短颈，圈足，胎质细腻。肩部以兽头状四系装饰，曲流。腹部两侧绘青花开光人物，分别为"进宝图"和"郭子仪拜寿图"，另二侧分别绘"福、禄、寿"字，青花呈色浑厚、稳定，纹饰清晰。

　　郭子仪为中唐名将，戎马一生，屡建奇功。相传郭子仪有七子八婿，每逢寿辰，七子八婿均携子来贺。世人遂将此场景绘成画作，以祈富贵长寿、子嗣兴旺。

　　此器青花发色深沉，画工流畅，画工采用开光的手法，画面构图严谨，画中主人脸庞丰满，发髻高耸，慈眉善目，端庄稳重，神采奕奕，活灵活现，具有较高的艺术效果，是一件富有时代特色的佳作。

　　乾隆时期青花瓷画面里的文人雅士，喻义深远，在一定程度上反映出太平盛世，人民安居乐业的时代特色。

121 广彩描金开光人物壶

清乾隆（1736 ~ 1795 年）

高 13.8 厘米

Teapot with Figure Scenes in Enamels Added

Qianlong period, Qing Dynasty,（1736 ~ 1795）

H. 13.8cm

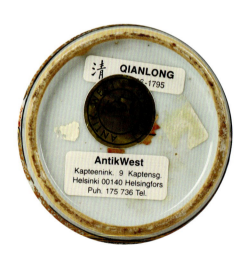

广州地区加彩产品。壶鼓腹直流，拱形盖。在锦地开光内以矾红彩、胭脂彩、紫蓝、绿等粉彩绘五个人物。宫廷庭院中，贵夫人旁有两个仕女侍候，宫廷当差奉上新鲜水果，表情十分虔诚，恰一太子闻声从内屋跳出。壶身另两侧开光花鸟风景图，表现春意盎然。

广彩是广州地区釉上织金彩瓷的简称，多为外销或来样定烧。此器图中人物绘画生动，用笔细腻，色彩艳丽，彩金的运用极富装饰性，表现了清代宫廷上层人物的生活情景，以及广彩绘画的工艺水平。

这件乾隆广彩描金人物壶，装饰工艺上的改变，在于广泛吸取外来文化和西方艺术的装饰手法，将其融入中国传统文化之中，使其更为华丽丰满，博大清新。

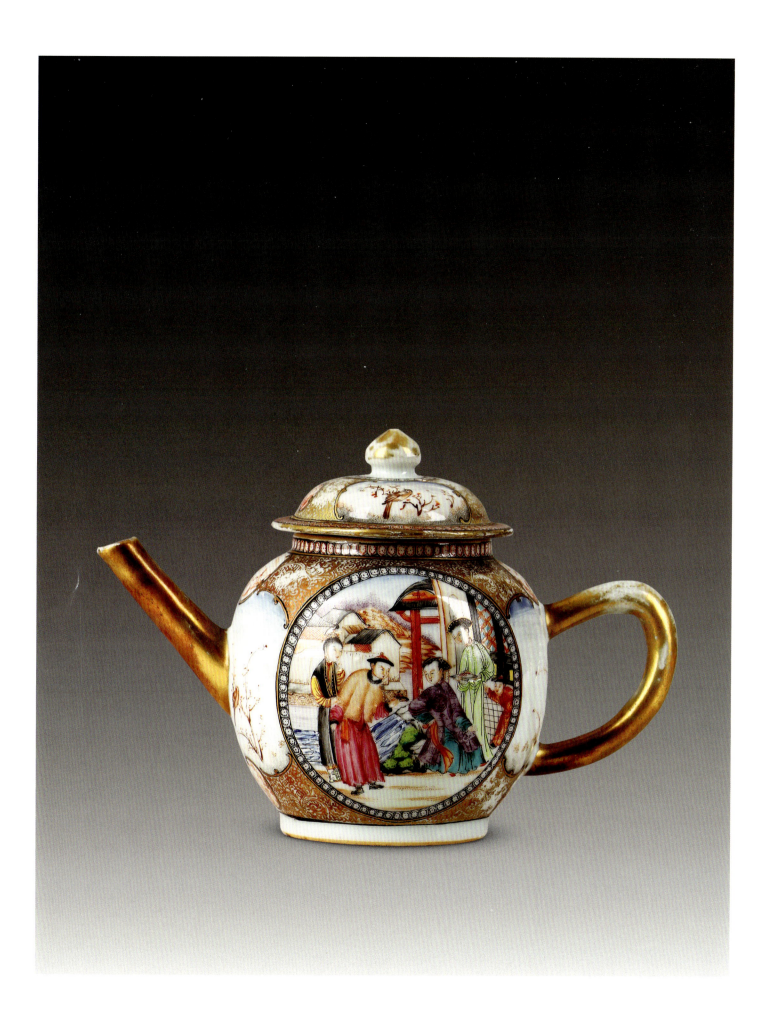

122 粉彩堆塑石榴纹壶

清乾隆（1736～1795 年）

高 14 厘米

Teapot enameled with Pomegranate Design

Qianlong period, Qing Dynasty,（1736～1795）

H. 14cm

　　景德镇窑产品，壶鼓腹附以直流，拱形盖。壶身及盖以象生莲花蕾为原型，采用模印工艺作壶并施以彩绘，宛若一枝秋天盛开的果树，硕果累累。莲花、石榴堆塑在同一器物上，寓意"连生贵子，多子多福"。

　　粉彩瓷始创于康熙，在乾隆朝瓷器中占有较大比重，效果与中国传统绘画技艺"没骨法"渲染有异曲同工之妙，但在色彩上往往借用西洋画里的阴阳突出，浓淡分明的技法，生产大量外销瓷器，有众多创新品种。

　　此件粉彩壶采用了堆贴的制作技巧，器型秀丽雅致，胎质洁白，工艺精致，粉彩柔和见长，相映成趣，富有立体效果。静心观赏，也不失是一种高雅享受。

123 青花山水凤首嘴盖壶

清乾隆（1736～1795年）

高 14.3 厘米

Blue and White Teapot with Landscape Design

Qianlong period, Qing Dynasty,（1736～1795）

H. 14.3cm

　　景德镇窑产品，深圆腹，圆口，圆盖，短颈，圈足。壶一侧置模压凤首曲流，另一侧置模压柄。壶盖、腹以浙料青花分水绘制远山、近水、渔人泛舟、拱桥楼台，无不尽收眼底。

　　乾隆一朝是清代社会发展的鼎盛时期，当时的景德镇云集了名师巧匠，所制瓷器在造型和装饰上都已达到清代瓷业的顶峰。

　　这件清乾隆青花山水茶壶，器型隽秀，风姿聘婷，制作精细。青花山水画面吸收宋、元绘画的传统技法，山石采用斧劈皴，皴法浓淡相宜，色泽柔和不艳。山石的远景和近景层次丰富。自宋代起，画山水的目的是借景抒情，借山水来表达自己的审美情趣，与寄以山林隐逸的自我追求。此器画面饱满，疏密有致，并具延展性，可谓景自天成。

124 粉彩婴戏牡丹纹盌

清乾隆（1736～1795年）

口径 11 厘米

Bowl with Enamel Decoration of Chicken and Peony Scene

Qianlong period, Qing Dynasty,（1736～1795）

L. 11cm

　　撇口，器身正面以粉彩和料彩绘洞石花卉，牡丹与子母鸡，公鸡昂首，庭院中俏皮可爱的顽童趣斗公鸡。整体结构和谐，粉彩艳丽，栩栩如生。另一侧以墨书绘制诗文，落款"乾隆丙申御题"字样，足底为青花六字印章款："大清乾隆年制"。

　　此器的瓷质洁白精细，造型规整，器型古朴优美，绘画工细，内容生动而高雅。惜口沿有磕，先人以铜口镶之，以示珍惜。

　　乾隆时期的瓷器制作工艺达到了空前的水平，这一时期有许多摹古之作。婴戏牡丹纹盏，历朝均有绘制。此件粉彩婴戏牡丹纹盌，粉彩牡丹华贵富丽，清秀古雅的山石与大段的诗文；可爱的童子与颇为呆萌的公鸡同居一景，气韵生动，情景相容，呈现出乾隆时期的侈靡和绮艳风气，从世俗生活折射出太平盛世的社会景象。

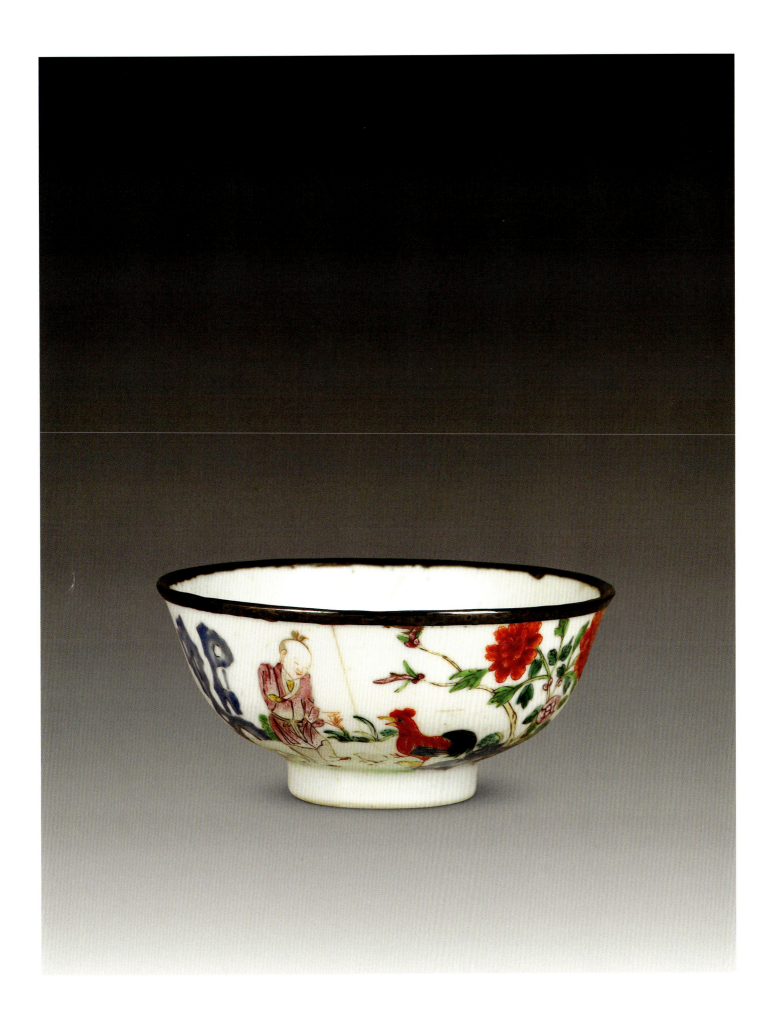

125 青花人物八方提梁壶

清嘉庆（1796～1820年）

高 23 厘米

Blue and White Ewer with Overhead Handle and Figures Design

Jiaqing period, Qing Dynasty,（1796 ～ 1820）

H. 23cm

　　壶作八方型。提梁为青花雕龙形柄，龙首口中含珠，周身施以釉下青花，一侧为郭子仪拜寿图，一侧为献宝图。器身顶部绘有"和合二仙"图。寓意"吉祥"和"福寿绵长"。

　　史称郭子仪"权倾天下而朝不忌，功盖一世而主不疑。"乾隆时期，常把封建伦理和历史典故的画面用在瓷器上。瓷器的人物绘画，重在表达先人

的观念情感，畅神，寄兴。借物寓意以示志节和意趣。这些都体现了工匠们卓越的智慧和创造力。

　　这件青花人物八方提梁壶，器形独特，青花色泽淡雅，构图清晰，笔墨生动，人物各具情态，恬然自在，带有鲜明时代的烙印。另见有清乾隆器型相近的青花（纹饰为花鸟纹）八方提梁壶，藏于瑞典哥德堡市博物馆。

126 浅蓝地青花花鸟纹壶

清嘉庆（1796 ～ 1820 年）

高 10 厘米

Teapot with Birds Design in Blue-Glazed

Jiaqing period, Qing Dynasty,（1796 ～ 1820）

H. 10cm

圆口圆腹，凹足，曲流，弓形把，带钮平盖，纽侧一通气圆孔，通体施淡蓝色釉，胎质细腻，圈足。顶盖上饰青花蝙蝠五只。弯流置于腹部，柄连接于肩与腹之间。腹部以青花绘盛开的牡丹与白头翁鸟，寓意"富贵白头"。

"蓝上蓝"釉瓷，创烧于清康熙期间，这件"蓝上蓝"执壶色彩妩媚柔和，高雅华贵。白头翁鸟与牡丹纹饰，线条用笔洒脱，动静相宜，形神兼备，画面佈局疏密相间，错落有致。其纹样寓意沿袭前朝，象征五福临门，富贵荣华，白头偕老和人们追求美好盛世的愿望。

127 红釉桃形倒流壶

清嘉庆（1796 ~ 1820 年）

高 14.8 厘米

Red-Glazed invert Ewer in a shape of Peach

Jiaqing period, Qing Dynasty,（1796 ~ 1820）

H. 14.8cm

　　执壶桃形，足外撇，流与柄塑成树枝状。此壶以象生手法制作，叶与芽塑造生动。底有一孔，用以注水入壶，故称作倒流壶。外人称作"卡多根茶壶"。

　　宋、元、明、清时期，倒流壶一直都有制作，保留下来的实物尤以清代为多。倒流壶采用的原理为虹吸原理，它巧妙奇特的内部设计和制造，充分体现了古代能工巧匠的智慧和创造。

　　《神异经》中云："东方树名曰桃，令人益寿"。传说中，桃是神仙吃的果实。吃了头等大桃"可与天地同寿，与日月同庚"。此器作桃形，红色宜人，使人见物生情，祈求吉祥。

128 青花花卉纹执壶

清嘉庆（1796～1820年）

高16厘米

Blue and White Porcelain Ewer

Jiaqing period, Qing Dynasty,（1796～1820）

H. 16cm

此壶直长颈，直口，圆钮字母盖，壶身一侧置弯曲柄，一侧置曲流，颈部绘青花蕉叶纹，腹部呈圆球状，用蓝地留白方法绘竹叶纹，更显出文雅之气。

竹是中国美德的物质载体，是君子的象征。竹子四季常青，象征着顽强的生命，青春永驻；竹子空心代表虚怀若谷的品格；其枝弯而不折，是正直清高，柔中有刚的做人原则。

此器以竹纹构图，线条用笔洒脱，形神兼备。纹样寓意沿袭前朝，富有很强的艺术魅力。表现了古代文人追求的留白、虚心与高节。

129 青花茶盌

清光绪（1875 ～ 1908 年）

口径 10 厘米

Blue and White Tea Bowl

Guangxu period, Qing Dynasty,（1875 ～ 1908）

L. 10cm

敞口，鼓腹，圈足，底足有"康熙年制"青花款，盌一侧饰耳柄。器外部以青花饰"松、竹、梅"岁寒三友，口部饰如意纹。画意生动自然。

"松、竹、梅"岁寒三友，因为这三种植物在寒冬时节仍可保持顽强的生命力而得名，借此比喻忠贞的友谊。此器造型隽秀，胎体轻薄，画笔精细，以单线平涂、一笔点画的技法，在洁白光润的白地上绘几支盛开的梅花，突出了梅花不畏严寒，傲霜斗雪的高风亮节，画面栩栩如生。

光绪青花瓷渐失康、雍、乾朝时的古雅趣味，但由于此时饮茶成为一种特别嗜好而风行于世，出现了大量"康熙年制"寄托款的茶具，制作及绘制工艺亦十分精妙细致。

130 粉彩"福、禄、寿"杯连托碟

清光绪（1875 ~ 1908 年）

杯直径 6.7 厘米

碟直径 8.2 厘米

Two Teacups and Sauces in Farmille-Rose Style with "Fu, Lu, Shou" Design

Guangxu period, Qing Dynasty, （1875 ~ 1908）

D.（cup）6.7cm

D.（stand）8.2cm

杯身呈圆锥形，斜壁，胎身薄如蛋壳，圈足，外壁以矾红描金绘"福、禄、寿"，其间以瓜纹相衬，寓意瓜瓞连绵之意。碟内绘蝙蝠与寿字，寓意福寿双全。

金彩绘瓷器，是清代的创新品种之一，最早出现在康熙年代。此类茶器耗资较大，多见于小件器物。此器造型精巧，矾红鲜而沉着，描绘工细，纹饰，华丽而夺目，具有美好的寓意和艺术效果。

131 斗彩开光方形壶

清光绪（1875 ~ 1908 年）

高 13.1 厘米

Teacup with Colored Enamels in shape of Square

Guangxu period, Qing Dynasty, （1875 ~ 1908）

H. 13.1cm

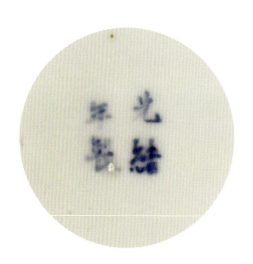

壶身呈四方形，直口，肩上置两系，做提梁用，腹部一侧置一曲流，平盖顶上饰寿桃。底部置四个角足，壶底书"光绪年制"四字青花楷书款。

壶身腹部两侧开光，以青花彩金绘博古纹，另两侧以青花、粉彩绘灵芝、瑞果，蝙蝠，盖钮用寿桃装饰，寓意"福、禄、寿"。釉下青花与釉上粉彩相互"斗"映成趣。

光绪朝，封建享乐风气盛行，朝野文人雅士特别推崇前朝瓷器，刻意摹古。此器上彩绘描金十分生动细致，博古纹饰追求康熙、雍正时的古雅趣味，因绪守旧，富有时代特色。

132 斗彩莲花纹盖杯连托

清光绪（1875～1908 年）

杯直径 10.6 厘米

托直径 11 厘米

DouCai Teacup and Stand with Lotus Flower Design

Guangxu period, Qing Dynasty,（1875～1908）

D（cup）. 10.6cm

D（stand）. 11cm

　　杯口外撇，杯盖成倒放托碟状，托碟足微外撇。杯身，杯盖，托碟以斗彩描金绘莲花纹。杯内以粉彩绘金鱼海藻，杯盖以青花书"大清光绪年制"款。

　　斗彩，创烧于明朝成化年间，符合明人审美情趣。清代晚期已失去原有清秀飘逸的风采。清光绪时期茶具的制作与日俱衰，器型大多沿袭前朝式样，工艺趋于简单，纹饰上也因绪守旧，瓷胎往往采用半机械模具"拓坯"生产，陶瓷业处于低潮。此器亦称盖碗，其釉料配方以及制作，画工已难与官窑相比，不过制作精美，为民窑之精品。

　　据说，当年慈禧太后特别喜爱盖碗，盖碗茶具盖为天、托为地、碗为人。清代晚期的盖碗做得优美精致，一直流行至今。

九　民国、近现代时期的茶具（1912年~）

　　辛亥革命推翻清王朝，建立中华民国后，御窑厂停办，成立了一些瓷业公司。民国初期，为了适应海内、外市场需求，涌现出大量仿古瓷。上至两晋青瓷，下至唐、五代、宋代五大名窑以及明清御窑几乎无不仿制，而且是有较高的水平。并大量流传于市，至今被海内、外一些机构及收藏爱好者收藏。同时，民国时期的粉彩茶具（包括墨彩）也十分流行。

　　20世纪50年代，民族工业开始恢复，反映人民当家做主和"农、林牧、副、渔"发展的纹饰开始出现，50年代初期由景德镇生产的一件粉彩茶壶（图135），壶腹部一面用粉彩绘画农业大丰收的情景，一农民手捧稻谷，脸上流露出丰收后的喜悦之情；另一面墨书"和

20世纪30年代茶馆（话剧《茶馆》剧照）

平人民，福好友乐"字样。壶盖钮饰菊花纹，并书"世界和平"四字，反映出新中国人民对和平的追求与渴望。我国人民对和谐、平衡的认识与追求正是儒家崇尚的"中庸之道"，亦是我国人民的智慧结晶。20 世纪 50 ~ 70 年代，中国经历了史无前例的"文化大革命"，景德镇、醴陵等一些瓷窑相继制作了大量反映"工、农、兵"和"忠"字题材的产品，茶具上出现了"敬祝毛主席万寿无疆""毛泽东选集"等纹饰（图 136）。1975 年，被誉为新中国官窑的中南海用瓷，由于制作工艺精湛而闻名于世。纵观近现代具有代表性的精品同样具有良好的收藏价值。

20世纪六七十年代茶馆

IX. TEA SETS OF THE REPUBLIC OF CHINA AND MODERN TIMES（1912 ~）

After the Revolution of 1911, Qing Dynasty had been overthrown and the Republic of China was established, and then royal kilns were replaced by porcelain companies. In early Republic of China, due to the domestic and foreign demands, a large number of antique-looking porcelains came into being, including celadon of the Western and Eastern Jin Dynasties as well as porcelains of Tang Dynasty, the Five Dynasties, the Five Great Kilns of Song Dynasty and royal kilns of Ming and Qing Dynasties, and imitation technique achieved high level. Now, many of these porcelains are collected by domestic and foreign organizations and collectors. In the meantime, pastel tea sets (including grisaille-painted tea sets) were also very popular in the Republic of China.

Since national industry started to recover in 1950s, patterns and designs of "farming, forestry, animal husbandry, by-product and fishery" emerged, symbolizing that people started to be the master of their own life. In early 1950s, Jingdezhen produced a pastel teapot. (fig.135) On one side of the teapot, there is pattern describing agricultural harvest: With paddy in hand, peasant looks delightful due to good harvest, while on the other side, there are eight Chinese characters " 和平人民，福好友乐 "(people live in peace and happiness). There are chrysanthemum pattern and four Chinese characters " 世 界 和 平 " (world peace) on the knob of pot cover, which reflects the desire of Chinese government and people for peace. In the course of pursing harmony and balance, Chinese people show the "golden mean" advocated by the Confucianists as well as wisdom. From 1950s to 1970s, China underwent the Great Proletarian Cultural Revolution. Therefore, kilns of Jingdezhen and Liling produced many wares reflecting theme of "worker, farmer, soldier and loyalty", and some patterns, such as Chinese characters " 敬祝毛主席万寿无疆 "(long live Chairman Mao) and " 毛泽东选集 " (Selected Works of Mao Zedong), appeared on tea sets. (fig.136) In 1975, produced in so-called official kiln of new China, Zhongnanhai porcelains were renowned for exquisite workmanship. Elaborate works representative in modern times also have good value for collection.

133 浅绛彩人物壶

20 世纪 30 年代

高 9.5 厘米

阔 15 厘米

Famille-Rose Ewer with Figur Design

1930s, 20th century

H. 9.5cm

L. 15cm

景德镇窑产品。壶呈钟形，圈足，曲流置于腹部，柄连接于腹上下之间。盖上绘兰草并书"清心"两字，壶身一面浅绛彩绘小舟垂钓图，另一面书"泊舟苇岸意清茗"。

浅绛彩瓷是清朝末年景德镇具有创新意义的釉上彩新品种。它是从同治到民国初年流行的一种以浓淡相间的黑色釉上彩料绘出花纹，再染以淡赭和水绿，使瓷画与传统的"诗书画"完美结合的产物。

此器以浅绛彩绘制一幅小舟垂钓情景，巧妙地把文人雅士与自然景色融合描绘在一起。表达了人们对安居乐业以及美好生活的追求与向往。其间山水、人物，生动而朴实，文化气息更加浓郁，足可媲美纸绢丹青。

134　墨彩"寒江独钓图"壶

20 世纪 40 年代

高 8.6 厘米

阔 17 厘米

Teapot Painted with Fishing Scene in Ink Color

1940s, 20th century

H. 8.6cm

L. 17cm

壶身鼓腹，下部敛收，直短颈，附圆钮盖书"可以清心"，肩部用墨彩绘草花纹，两侧置曲柄和曲流。腹部一侧以墨彩、白粉绘"寒江独钓"图，另一侧书"寒江独钓"，"丙戌年春月写意珠山"。

墨彩始见于康熙朝中期，一直延续到民国时期。

此器为我们展示了一幅舒适安逸的景色，"寒江独钓"图绘冬日风景，楼阁山石，一翁泊舟独钓，风欲止，水无痕，钓者斗笠蓑衣，悠然自得，尽情

享受大自然的和谐宁静，令人羡慕不已。或许，此时正座在岸边楼阁里品茶的文人雅士，如同老翁一样，也在享受自然，品味人生。山水含禅，禅寓山水。画面和谐宁静，清新秀润，墨彩浓淡相宜，景致有近有远，洁净素雅，绘画技巧，颇具生机。这件茶壶的装饰工艺和文化气息进入更高的审美境界，为人们所珍视喜爱。

景德镇窑产品。圆盖，圆口，短颈，折肩，深腹，圈足，曲流置于腹部，耳柄连接于腹上、下之间，口、肩部饰回纹及印花纹。圆形盖上墨书 "世界和平"，腹正面以粉彩绘农民及大丰收景象，另一面墨书 "和平人民福好友乐长寿" 字样。

1949 年新中国成立后，中央政府稳步推进土地改革，恢复农业生产。农业的发展，为顺利完成国民经济的恢复打下了基础。这件粉彩 "丰收图" 表现了当时的时代风貌。

此器胎体轻薄，洁白细腻，器型秀美，无橘皮纹，彩色明丽丰满，无论在光泽、色彩等方面都吸收了近代画的营养，在民国瓷器发展基础上创新，达到了相当高的水平，有着极为重要的史料价值。

136 白釉印"忠"字纹茶壶

20 世纪 60 年代

高 14 厘米

阔 18.5 厘米

White-Glazed Ewer with Mao's Slogan

1960s, 20th century

H. 14cm

L. 18.5cm

　　壶呈椭圆型，圆口，圈足，一侧曲流置于腹部，另一侧宽形耳柄置于腹上、下之间，圆盖上红彩绘"东方红"纹样，壶身上部绘有一轮红日，以下书"敬祝毛主席万寿无疆"，"毛泽东选集"。下部以地球、向日葵为背景绘红旗及三个"忠"字，在当时，寓意"三忠于"。底敷白釉，矾红彩向日葵及楷书"醴陵力生，1969"字样。

　　所谓"文革瓷"是指 20 世纪 60 年代中期至 70 年代中期，十年间各地陶瓷厂生产制作的带有"文革"色彩和风格的瓷器。它们在制作工艺、图案纹饰、题款铭文等方面，带有浓郁的政治色彩。"文革"时受大环境影响，创制人员大多当做"光荣的政治任务"，制作者大都不落款。

　　此件"万寿无疆""文革瓷"茶壶烧制于中国近代名瓷产地湖南醴陵。造型端庄规整，瓷质洁白，釉面光泽滋润，粉彩彩料精细、匀和而稳重，装饰纹样主题突出，反映出强烈的政治色彩。此器因其鲜明的时代特征而独具魅力，为中国陶瓷发展历史留下了颇堪回味的一页。

137 五彩十二花神杯 "大清康熙年制" 款

20 世纪 80 年代

高 5 厘米

直径 6.5 厘米

Twelve Cups in Famille - Verte Style Mark of Kangxi

1980s, 20th century

H. 5cm

L. 6.5cm

杯身极薄，形似仰钟，分别绘制有十二个月份代表的花卉，画工细腻，纹饰以黑彩勾勒，以花草水石作衬景。杯身背面以青花书五言或七言诗句。

青花五彩花神杯，是清代康熙官窑瓷器中的名品，匠心独具，精妙绝伦，堪称"绝世之作"。雍正、嘉庆、光绪、民国等历朝均有仿制。康熙青花五彩十二花神杯，器型优美，胎体细腻洁白，纯净无瑕，外壁分别用一年十二个月中不同的花卉装饰，每杯

一花一诗，一面绘画，对应面题诗钤印，融画、诗、印于一体，胎薄玲珑，构思巧妙。其艺术语言表现力极为丰富，平添了茶具的文化内涵和艺术之美。

这套五彩十二花神杯是 20 世纪 80 年代初江西景德镇生产仿清代康熙朝的作品，在器型和纹饰上沿用传统式样，釉面青白纯净，绘工细柔，工艺精美。既恢复了古代传统工艺，亦可满足百姓的需求，因此具有永恒的生命活力。

（a）　　　　　　　　　（b）　　　　　　　　　（c）

（d）　　　　　　　　　（e）　　　　　　　　　（f）

（a） 一月：梅花　January: Plum Blossom
　　　 素艳雪凝树，清香风满枝

（b） 二月：杏花　February: Apricot Blossom
　　　 清香和宿雨，佳色出晴烟

（c） 三月：桃花　March: Peach Blossom
　　　 风花新社莺，时节蜇春农

（d） 四月：牡丹　April: Tree Peony
　　　 晓艳远分金宁露，暮香深惹玉堂风

（e） 五月：石榴花　May: Pomegranate
　　　 露色珠廉映，香风粉辟遮

（f） 六月：荷花　June: Lotus
　　　 根是泥中玉，心承露下珠

（g）　　　　　　　　　　（h）　　　　　　　　　　（i）

（g）七月：月季花　July: Rose
不随千种尽，独放一年红

（h）八月：桂花　August: Osmanthus
枝生无限月，花满自然秋

（i）九月：菊花　September: Chrysanthemum
千载白衣酒，一生青女香

（j）十月：兰花　October: Cymbidium
庚荻清香发，高台远吹吟

（k）十一月：水仙花　November: Narcissus
春风弄玉来清画，夜月凌波上大堤

（l）十二月：腊梅　December: Winter sweet
金英翠萼带春寒，黄色花中有几绿

（j）　　　　　　　　　　　（k）　　　　　　　　　　　（l）

21
074

22
076

23
078

24
080

25
082

26
084

27
088

28
090

29
092

30
094

31
096

32
098

33
100

34
102

35
104

36
106

37
108

38
110

39
112

40
114

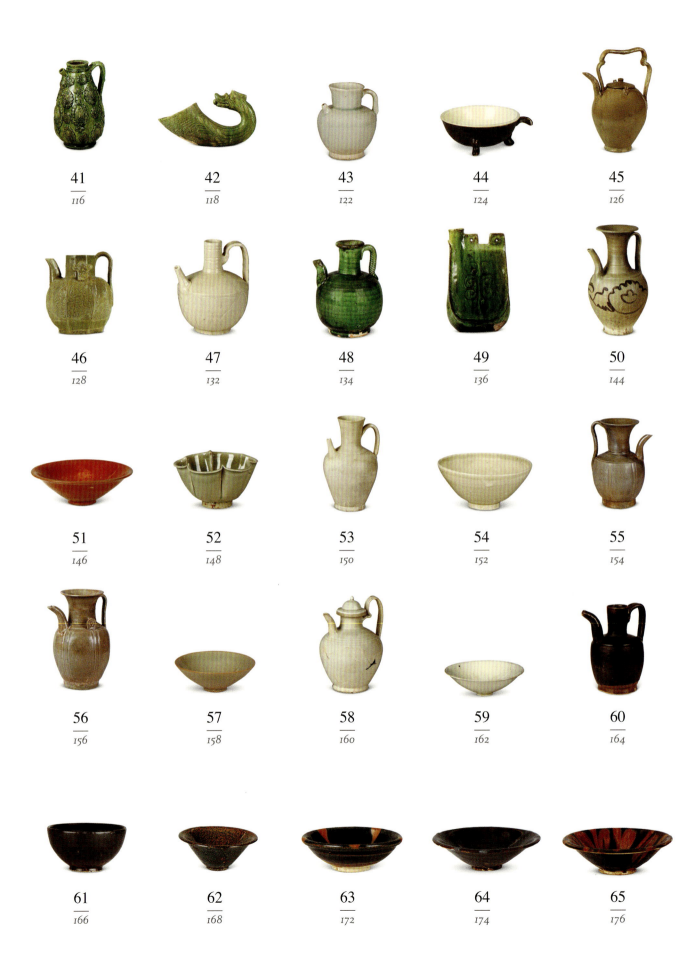

41
116

42
118

43
122

44
124

45
126

46
128

47
132

48
134

49
136

50
144

51
146

52
148

53
150

54
152

55
154

56
156

57
158

58
160

59
162

60
164

61
166

62
168

63
172

64
174

65
176

66
<u>178</u>

67
<u>180</u>

68
<u>182</u>

69
<u>184</u>

70
<u>186</u>

71
<u>188</u>

72
<u>190</u>

73
<u>192</u>

74
<u>194</u>

75
<u>198</u>

76
<u>200</u>

77
<u>202</u>

78
<u>204</u>

79
<u>206</u>

80
<u>208</u>

81
<u>210</u>

82
<u>212</u>

83
<u>214</u>

84
<u>216</u>

85
<u>218</u>

86
<u>220</u>

87
<u>222</u>

88
<u>226</u>

89
<u>228</u>

90
<u>232</u>

91
————
234

92
————
236

93
————
238

94
————
240

95
————
242

96
————
244

97
————
246

98
————
248

99
————
250

100
————
252

101
————
254

102
————
256

103
————
258

104
————
264

105
————
268

106
————
270

107
————
272

108
————
274

109
————
276

110
————
278

111
————
280

112
————
286

113
————
288

114
————
290

115
————
292

116
—
294

117
—
296

118
—
298

119
—
300

120
—
302

121
—
304

122
—
306

123
—
308

124
—
310

125
—
312

126
—
314

127
—
316

128
—
318

129
—
320

130
—
322

131
—
324

132
—
326

133
—
332

134
—
334

135
—
336

136
—
338

137
—
340

中国历代年表
Chronology of Chinese Dynasties and Periods

		BC 公元前	AD 公元
XIA PERIOD	夏	2070 ~ 1600	
Period of Erlitou Culture	二里头文化	1900 ~ 1600	
SHANG PERIOD	商	1600 ~ 1046	
Zhengzhou Phase	郑州阶段	1600 ~ 1400	
Anyang Phase	安阳阶段	1300 ~ 1046	
ZHOU PERIOD	周	1046 ~ 256	
Western Zhou	西周	1046 ~ 771	
Eastern Zhou	东周	770 ~ 256	
Spring and Autumn Period	春秋	770 ~ 476	
Warring States Period	战国	475 ~ 221	
QIN DYNASTY	秦	221 ~ 206	
HAN DYNASTY	汉	206	220
Western Han	西汉	206	9AD
Xin Dynasty（Wang Mang）	新（王莽）		9 ~ 23
Eastern Han	东汉		25 ~ 220
SIX DYNASTIES PERIOD	六朝		220 ~ 589
Three Kingdoms	三国		220 ~ 280
Western Jin	西晋		265 ~ 317
Eastern Jin	东晋		317 ~ 420
Song	宋		420 ~ 479
Qi	齐		479 ~ 502
Liang	梁		502 ~ 557
Chen	陈		557 ~ 589
Sixteen Kingdoms	十六国		304 ~ 439
Northern Wei	北魏		386 ~ 534
Western Wei	西魏		535 ~ 557
Eastern Wei	东魏		534 ~ 549
Northern Qi	北齐		550 ~ 577
Northern Zhou	北周		557 ~ 581
SUI DYNASTY	隋		581 ~ 618
TANG DYNASTY	唐		618 ~ 907
FIVE DYNASTIES	五代		907 ~ 960
LIAO DYNASTY	辽		907 ~ 1125
SONG DYNASTY	宋		960 ~ 1279
Northern Song	北宋		960 ~ 1127
Southern Song	南宋		1127 ~ 1279
JIN DYNASTY	金		1115 ~ 1234
YUAN DYNASTY	元		1271 ~ 1368

		BC 公元前	AD 公元
MING DYNASTY	明		1368 ~ 1644
Hongwu	洪武		1368 ~ 1398
Jianwen	建文		1399 ~ 1402
Yongle	永乐		1403 ~ 1424
Hongxi	洪熙		1425 ~
Xuande	宣德		1426 ~ 1435
Zhengtong	正统		1436 ~ 1449
Jingtai	景泰		1450 ~ 1456
Tianshun	天顺		1457 ~ 1464
Chenghua	成化		1465 ~ 1487
Hongzhi	弘治		1488 ~ 1505
Zhengde	正德		1506 ~ 1521
Jiajing	嘉靖		1522 ~ 1566
Longqing	隆庆		1567 ~ 1572
Wanli	万历		1573 ~ 1619
Taichang	泰昌		1620 ~
Tianqi	天启		1621 ~ 1627
Chongzhen	崇祯		1628 ~ 1644
QING DYNASTY	清		1644 ~ 1911
Shunzhi	顺治		1644 ~ 1661
Kangxi	康熙		1662 ~ 1722
Yongzheng	雍正		1723 ~ 1735
Qianlong	乾隆		1736 ~ 1795
Jiaqing	嘉庆		1796 ~ 1820
Daoguang	道光		1821 ~ 1850
Xianfeng	咸丰		1851 ~ 1861
Tongzhi	同治		1862 ~ 1874
Guangxu	光绪		1875 ~ 1908
Xuantong	宣统		1909 ~ 1911
REPUBLIC OF CHINA	中华民国		1912 ~ 1949
PEOPLE'S REPUBLIC OF CHINA	中华人民共和国		1949 ~

后 记

　　我自幼生活在北京。听长辈讲，曾祖父曾在宫内当差，他是位古董收藏家。家中祖辈保存下来的家具陈设和古董的熏陶在我幼小心灵中留下了深刻记忆。这也许就是我与古陶瓷结缘的唯一解释。

　　20世纪80年代的中国，正值"文化大革命"结束以后，改革开放，百废待兴的时代。在这以后的三十余年里，中国国内大举基本建设，市场空前繁荣，古董市场方兴未艾。其间，我有缘结识了共同雅好的朋友，一边学习以藏交友，一边购买些自己喜欢的物件。开始了对古董文玩的研究与收藏。记得80年代后期，在香港逗留期间，有幸参观了罗桂祥博士捐助的"茶具文物馆"后感触颇深，自此将研究与收藏的重心放在茶具这一专题领域。

　　回想起来，自己出于业余爱好，几十年矢志不移，不知不觉把个人所有业余时间都放在收藏和研究古陶瓷上了，期间的赏心乐事及充实难以言表，但其中的辛酸苦衷唯有自己知道。

　　1975年，我进入政府部门从事外事工作，大部分时间忙于工作并被派往国外常驻，很少有时间顾及家庭。非常感激夫人闫淑萍，她非常理解我，替我承担了照顾父母和孩子的责任。她对我的收藏寄予信任和宽容，使我有充裕的时间收集和整理个人的专题收藏。女儿李楠协助我整理和编辑藏品也做了大量工作。

　　特别感谢我的恩师张浦生老师，感谢多年来他给予我的支持和帮助，他的学识和通脱令人敬佩，他的渊雅和谦逊令人难忘。记得90年代初，我去南京出差，他几次把我请到他家里，观摩他多年来收集的瓷器和标本，言传身教，孜孜不倦。

　　特别感谢孙会元老先生在世时对我个人收藏的指教。

　　特别感谢李毅华老师对本书内容的赐教。李毅华老师曾是冯先铭先生的学生与助手，后任紫禁城出版社社长。李老师学养深厚，著述甚丰，待人真诚。他作为中国著名古陶瓷研究专家，对本图录中的藏品进行了认真严谨的鉴定和评论。他对中国古陶瓷精深的认知水平和严谨的治学态度给我留下了深刻印象。在此表示深深的敬意。

　　对宋宝财先生、黄鹏先生，对所有为本书的编写、摄影和出版给予支持、贡献的友人，表示诚挚的、衷心的感谢。

尽管本书的编写历时四年多，虽经多次修改，但由于书中所陈藏品跨越年代久远，对器物及问题的看法难免有不同观点甚至错误，诚恳欢迎批评指正。

编辑此书时，本人已年过花甲，算是对三十余年收藏的一个小结，也是对"收而无鉴为陋，藏而不赏是庸"的理解。书中汇集的某些藏品完整度欠佳，却体现了"有疵为真"的残缺之美。虽有残缺，依然自珍。

进入 21 世纪，生存环境的恶化使人们更关注内在。然而贴近自然、富有灵性的古物能为收藏者带来平和、自然和亲切的鉴赏感受。这本书的出版不仅是为了感恩和还愿，更重要的是希望那些日理万机忙碌的人们，在为了事业和生活而承担巨大压力的时候，能够稍作休息，在品茗之余，欣赏和回味古人留给我们的文化遗产，使我们的精神和心灵上更加充实，让生活更加丰富。

愿那些贴近自然、富有灵性的古物能为收藏者带来平和、自然和亲切的鉴赏感受。

李文年

2015 年 12 月于北京缘珍山房

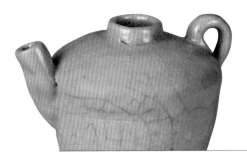

POSTSCRIPT

Brought up in Beijing when I was young. In youth having heard senior said that that my great-grandfather worked inside the imperial palace and he was an antique collector. The furnishings and antiques handed down generations after generations have left a deep memory in my young heart, which may be the only reason to explain why I was so attached to ancient ceramics.

As the Great Cultural Revolution ended in 1980s, China entered a new era for reform and openness as well as rebuilding. Over the next 30 years, infrastructure construction was carried out on a large scale in China, and antique market became flourishing and plentiful. In the meantime, I have come across some like-minded friends and started to make friends and buy my favorite collections at the same time. It was at that time that I started to collect antiques and curios. When I stayed in Hong Kong in late 1980s, I got the chance to visit "Museum of Tea Ware" donated by Dr. Lo Kwee-seong, which impressed me a lot. Since then, I put my focus on studying and collecting tea sets.

When I look back, I have devoted all my spare time to collecting and studying ancient ceramics due to my unshaken love for them for decades. All the joys and sense of accomplishment during those days are beyond words. However, the bitterness and anguish are also beyond the understanding of others.

I entered government sector and started to be involved in foreign affairs work in 1975. Most of the time I was busy with work and I would often be sent abroad for permanent residence. During which time I barely had any time to look after my family. I am very much obliged to my wife Yan Shuping, who has shown tremendous understanding and taken up the responsibility of taking care of our parents and children. She trusted and tolerated my hobby for collection, which gave me plenty of time to collect and tidy up my personal special collections. My daughter Li Nan has also done a lot of work to help me tidy up and arrange my collections.

I'd like to give my special thanks to Mr.Zhang Pusheng for his long-term support and help. His knowledge and open mind is admirable, while his elegance and modesty are impressive. When I traveled to Nanjing for business in early 1990s, he invited me to his home for researching porcelains and specimens he had collected over the years, instructing and influencing me by his word, deed and perseverance.

I'd like to give my special thanks to Mr. Sun Hui-Yuan for his instruction.

I have to specially thank Li Yihua for his instructions on the content of this book. MR. Li Yihua was the asistant and student of MR. Feng Xianming before he took up the post of the president of the Forbidden City Press. Teacher Li has profound knowledge and produces numerous books. He is also very sincere and honest. As a famous ancient ceramics specialist, he has carried out careful and strict appraisal and evaluation about the collections contained in this catalog. His know-how in Chinese ancient ceramics and rigorous academic attitude have deeply impressed me. I would like to take this opportunity to show my deepest respect for him.

I would like to sincerely thank to Mr·Song Baocai, Mr·Huang Peng and all friends who have helped with the writing, photographing, and publication of this book.

It has taken over four years for me to compose this book. Although it has been amended several times, due to the long time span of the collections, my view and attitude about some articles and issues may have varied or even might have been wrong. I sincerely welcome all comments and corrections.

When this book was composed, I was already in my sixties. This book could be deemed as a conclusion for my thirty years' of collection experience, and also a better understanding of "It's humber to collect without distinguish,and merely vulgar to store up without appreciate." Some of the collections contained in this book may be incomplete. Even so, they could have revealed the art of defective beauty. "Flaw is the Real" In spite of their incompleteness, I still cherish them a lot.

As living environment starts to deteriorate in 21st century, people pay more attention to inner world. While collectors can feel inner peace, nature and affability when they get close to antiques. This book is published not only for gratitude and fulfilling my promise, but also for spiritual replenishment and rich life. When the harried people are busy in dealing with numerous affairs and suffer from pressure, I hope they can take a short break to taste tea as well as appreciate ancient culture heritage.

However, natural and spiritual antiques may bring peaceful, natural and genial appreciation experience to collectors.

Li Wennian
Written in Yuanzhen Study Room, Beijing,
December 2015

1. 美的历程
　李泽厚主编　文物出版社　北京　1981

2. 冯先铭中国古陶瓷论文集
　紫禁城出版社　两木出版社　北京　香港　1987

3. 中国陶瓷史
　中国硅酸盐学会主编　文物出版社　北京　1982

4. 中国古代窑址调查发掘报告集
　文物编辑委员会编　文物出版社　北京　1984

5. 龙与中国文化
　刘志雄、杨静荣著　人民出版社　北京　1992

6. 龙泉窑青瓷
　朱伯谦主编　艺术家出版社　台北　1998

7. 故宫博物院藏文物珍品全集·两宋瓷器（上）
　李辉柄主编　商务印书馆（香港）有限公司　香港　1996

8. 故宫博物院藏文物珍品全集·两宋瓷器（下）
　李辉柄主编 商务印书馆（香港）有限公司　香港　1996

9. 河南出土陶瓷
　（香港大学美术馆与河南省文物考古研究所合办展览图录）
　香港大学美术博物馆　香港　1997

10. 河北省出土文物选集
　河北省博物馆编　文物出版社　北京　1999

11. 杭州老虎洞窑址瓷器精选
　杭州市文物考古所编　杜正贤主编
　文物出版社　北京　2002

12. 汝窑新发现
　河南省文物研究所　汝州市汝瓷博物馆　宝丰县文化局编
　紫禁城出版社　北京　1991

13. 唐代黄堡窑址
　陕西省考古研究所编　文物出版社　北京　1992

14. 越窑、秘色瓷
　汪庆正主编　上海古籍出版社　上海　1996

15. 1998 中国重要考古发现
　国家文物局主编　文物出版社　北京　2000

16. 中国陶瓷茶具·茶具文物馆罗桂祥珍藏
　香港市政局出版　1991

17. 瓷壶藏珍
　叶佩兰主编　上海辞书出版社　上海　2008

18. 壶中日月
　赵月汀主编　上海世华艺术馆开馆暨百壶珍藏特展集　2009

19. 茶器　茶事　茶画
　台北故宫博物院　2002

20. 中国古代茶文化研究
　董仲生　主编　科学出版社　北京　2001

21. 试析故宫旧藏宫廷紫砂器
　王健华　主编　故宫博物院院刊　2001

22. 茶禅论
　蔡镇楚　主编　社会科学报　2002

23. 龙泉青瓷赏析
　石少华　著　学苑出版社　北京　2005

24. 道教与中国茶文化
    胡长春　农业考古　2006

25. 佛教十五题
    季羡林 主编　中华书局　北京　2007

26. 青花瓷收藏与鉴赏
    张浦生　主编 南京出版社　南京　2009

27. 青花瓷鉴定
    张浦生　主编　印刷工业出版社　北京　2012

28. 青花瓷鉴赏与收藏
    张浦生 霍华主编　印刷工业出版社　北京　2013

29. 宋辽金纪年瓷器
    刘涛　著　文物出版社　北京　2004

30. 中国文物精华大辞典·瓷器卷
    上海辞书出版社、商务印书馆（香港）　1995

31. 明清瓷器鉴定
    耿宝昌　主编　紫禁城出版社　北京　1993

32. 中国陶瓷全集
    中国陶瓷全集编辑委员会
    上海人民美术出版社　上海　2000

33. 中国古磁窑大系·中国邢窑　北京　2012
    北京艺术博物馆编著　中国华侨出版社